In the
Fullness
of Time

In the
Fullness
of Time

32 WOMEN ON LIFE AFTER 50

Edited by
EMILY W. UPHAM
and
LINDA GRAVENSON

ATRIA PAPERBACK
New York   London   Toronto   Sydney

ATRIA PAPERBACK
A Division of Simon & Schuster, Inc.
1230 Avenue of the Americas
New York, NY 10020

First Atria Paperback edition April 2010

ATRIA PAPERBACK and colophon are trademarks of
Simon & Schuster, Inc.

"i thank you God for most this amazing." Copyright © 1950, 1978, 1991 by
the Trustees for the E. E. Cummings Trust. Copyright © 1979 by George James
Firmage, from *Selected Poems* by E. E. Cummings, Introduction and Commentary
by Richard S. Kennedy. Used by permission of Liveright Publishing Corporation.

For information about special discounts for bulk purchases,
please contact Simon & Schuster Special Sales at
1-866-506-1949 or business@simonandschuster.com.

The Simon & Schuster Speakers Bureau can bring authors
to your live event. For more information or to book an event,
contact the Simon & Schuster Speakers Bureau at
1-866-248-3049 or visit our website at www.simonspeakers.com.

Designed by Kyoko Watanabe

Manufactured in the United States of America

10 9 8 7 6 5 4 3 2 1

Library of Congress Cataloging-in-Publication Data

In the fullness of time : 32 women on life after 50 / editors, Emily W. Upham
and Linda Gravenson.
   p.   cm.
  1. Older women. 2. Aging. I. Upham, Emily W. II. Gravenson, Linda.
HQ1061.L67   2010
305.26'2—dc22   20099026967

ISBN 978-1-4391-0923-6
ISBN 978-1-4391-6915-5 (ebook)

For Emily's mother, Rebecca Calechman Weiss

✦

For Linda's son, Nick Guthe

Not knowing when the dawn will come
I open every door; . . .

—EMILY DICKINSON

Contents

Preface

Emily W. Upham

Once upon a time, when I was a young and beautiful princess of twenty and living in the land of Paris, France, I fell in love with a man of fifty-nine whom I shall call S. He was renowned throughout the entire kingdom of the moving image. Even then there were telephones, and he would call me in my turret and say, "Rapunzel, Rapunzel, let down your long hair" and sweep me away. Our story grabbed me by the jugular, gave me no choice, and shaped my entire life. For forty years we have been crucial to each other; for forty years we have told each other everything. As I write this S. will soon be ninety-seven. I do not know how I will live without him.

Recently, on the heels of my fifth spinal surgery, my performance career as a classical pianist was laid to rest. The journey away from my chosen but unforgiving instrument, its white teeth bared permanently in a glaring challenge, has been marked by a broken vertebra, degenerating disks, semisuccessful surgeries, denial, and finally a snarling quasi acceptance.

It came to me suddenly that my generation, the baby boomers, had arrived at the second half of life and that this half would be laden with loss. The generation of women forged by the 1960s, the "youth" generation, is now facing the death of parents, friends, and spouses, the loss of health, of sexual power, of power in the workplace, of dreams, of time remaining.

Ours is the mapless generation. We came of age at a fleeting moment in history when all traditional expectations were tossed aside and torn up like confetti. Our womanhood was forged at a time when birth control was easy, abortion was easy, pursuing a career was easy, when there were no rules, no boundaries, no directions other than our own inner ones if we were lucky enough to have them. Many of us never married, many of us never had children, many of our lives were skewed by this upheaval, even as it paved the way for the many positive changes for women who came after us.

As we age and begin to suffer the losses common to us all, our landscape is a very different one from that of the women who came both before and after us. When I asked Doris Lessing to write for this book she answered:

Dear Emily Upham

You wrote to me and I wrote back - here is the evidence. But not long ago I found a little cache of several unposted letters, and yours was one. They glid under a book.

The trouble is, I've written more than one pieces about growing old and the thought of doing another makes me yawn.

One has to wonder: do these younger women have no grandmothers?

Women live so much longer now, it is hard to imagine that there are no "role models" to ask.

Good wishes

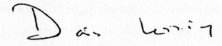

I had to respond that our grandmothers—even our mothers—would not do.

✦

Loss is, of course, visited upon us at all ages. Loss in early life, while bringing with it wounds specific to that time, also brings years of living in which to heal. But in later life our whole lives are not ahead of us. The next love affair is not around the corner, the next job opportunity not so evident. Many dreams have been realized or laid to rest, and our aspirations are tempered by what we suddenly understand to be a finite future. Our children are off and running, and the deaths of loved ones will be with us for the rest of our lives.

My startled awakening to these truths was the impetus for this project. I turned for guidance to Linda Gravenson, a gifted editor and writer a few steps ahead of me, who had suffered and come through a number of losses. She became my collaborator, and together we explored how these storms of change could bring unexpected rewards.

My urgent quest for maps to chart the terrain of later life led us to gather a number of unusual women, world-renowned authors and artists. Ranging in age from 55 to 101, they are immersed in, or have emerged from, maelstroms of change. From Edna O'Brien on one continent to Gail Godwin on another, they have all responded to the universality of our theme and have participated generously in this project. Their essays have been written for this book.

There is hardly one of us who has not been touched by personal tragedy or the erosions of time and who is not aware of the fact that we live in a world that is filled with horror. We know that living on, never mind living well, is often life's reward. One of the great gifts of experience, however, is the ability to choose—not our circumstances but how we interpret them. I have come to focus the lens of my inner camera and to see things differently, thanks in large part to the words of the admirable women gathered here.

Introduction

Linda Gravenson

When this collaboration began, around a coffee table in the Hudson Valley, I was drawn to it from a somewhat different perspective than Emily's. I had grown up in the 1940s and '50s, before the maps of tradition were shredded, and had come through some of the losses she was anticipating but also knew of the rewards that can follow in their wake. I'd moved to the country alone with four animals as family, lived without my city neighbors for the first time, learned to drive at fifty-three, and, most important, resumed writing and editing.

I've always loved the richness of anthologies, particularly essay collections created to explore a complex, even mysterious landscape. We decided to seek out writers and performers willing to go wherever our theme took them. The choices were theirs. Some of the most accomplished prizewinning writers in America, Canada, and Great Britain responded. Many of them admitted that the assignment was more challenging than they'd imagined it would be. They reported on both the fear and the exhilaration of going deep enough to tell the truth. Their bravery is palpable. Some have made discoveries that may lead to new work, even a few new books.

Two playwrights, a biographer, poets, novelists, memoirists, essayists, a physician, a musician, and two actresses are among the thirty-two women who have created this book. They have addressed the unexpected pleasures of living alone, new places as new chapters in life, giving cancer the slip, fear and boldness later in life, the luck of having role models, the solace of literature in a foreign hospital, reliance on faith, both acceptance and despair at being older, raging at the death of friends, new relationships with dead parents, swimming the Bosporus one last time and other urgent yearnings yet to be fulfilled, an adult child's addiction, the painful disappointment of adopting a damaged child in later life. And more.

✦

The journalist, essayist, and memoirist Vivian Gornick manages to turn the inevitable invisibility of older women into something positive in "Even Smart Women Hate Losing Their Youthful Looks":

> For a woman, existential terror is the aging face. . . . When she looks in the mirror and sees herself lined and hollow-cheeked, she thinks, "Tomorrow is here. Now I'm accountable. Now I must do it. Can I? More important, will I?"

✦

The novelist, memoirist, nonfiction writer, and Friday book reviewer for *The Washington Post* Carolyn See writes in "Moving":

> You go crazy when you move (unless you live in a yurt and get used to it). . . . I could say I was in a colossally bad mood. I'd been without John for seven years; that was bad enough. Now, soon enough, I'd be without the better part of my sight and without a car. On top of that, over the years I had cultivated a public persona that I (privately until now) referred to as "Jolly Grandma," a kind of sexless answer to Henry Miller's mantra "Always merry and bright!"

✦

In "It Figures," Katherine B. Weissman, a contributing editor to *O, The Oprah Magazine,* reveals:

> I've always been at war with my body. Encountering it naked in my sixties is like meeting an old enemy who has, unaccountably and regrettably, acquired new weapons since we last crossed paths. . . . I am a seventies feminist who bought *Vogue* secretly every month and whose consciousness-raising group once planned to have a meeting in the nude (I starved myself for days, only to learn that my coconspirators had chickened out). Over the years I have learned to assert my rights, own my successes, get angry, and not apologize so damned much.

◆

In "Songs for Cricket," the novelist Beth Powning says:

> Something is beginning. Last week, I saw the spruce trees sharp and light-sparked as sun broke from scudding black clouds, the fields soft and taupe as deer hide. I might, at that moment, have been a blind person granted sight. Other moments shock me into stillness, out of time. Seven fox cubs sitting in a row, red fur blowing in spring wind. Or the fat silkiness of a granddaughter's braid.

◆

Gail Godwin, the author of novels, short story collections, non-fiction, and ten librettos, reveals, in "Losing Ground":

> After I was turned down for the home care policy and had the losing-ground moment, I went into a depression. All I desired to do was sleep. I couldn't find anything I wanted to read, until I remembered my mother's diaries. . . . Now, as I devoured them addictively during the three weeks of

deepening winter, my curiosity about my future, whatever it turns out to be, revived. Her voice coaxed back to life a fascination for the "fatal tissue" into which I happened to be born. Surely I can do no less with my materials than has been done for me.

◆

In the playwright Tina Howe's essay "Bubble, Bubble, Toil and Trouble," she observes:

> When we're young, we tend to think old people were born that way. That it's somehow a choice. Then suddenly we hit sixty-five, seventy-three, or eighty-two and wonder what's going on. That isn't us in there! It's someone else! Construction workers suddenly don't whistle at us anymore, and waiters call us "Ma'am" instead of "Legs" or "Sweet thing."
>
> . . . WASPy women tend to be tall and uncomfortable in their bodies, so why try to hide it? Make an asset of your flaws. Wear feathered hats and high-heeled shoes. Affect an English accent. Carry a falcon on your wrist.

◆

Laura Furman, a novelist, short story writer, and editor of the *The PEN/O. Henry Prize Stories*, tells us in "Swim Swam Swum":

> Now that I am in my early sixties, swimming is my default, my pleasure, and the place I most often feel love. . . . If each swim is different, the body in which I swim has its differences also. What's smooth and easy one day is out of reach the next. No amount of knowing one's idiosyncrasies can stop the changes. All I can hope for is to keep swimming in the body of the day. I take this with me as I age. The water will support me. All I have to do is get into it.

✦

The biographer and novelist Elizabeth Frank's essay "Woman with a Pink" takes its title from a Rembrandt painting in which a middle-aged woman offers a carnation.

> The woman looks at the pink and sees in it what she once was and will never be again. She will never be a bride or pregnant, and, if she is lucky enough to fall in love, it won't be the way love was when she was younger, because when she was younger she had time. Simple, beautiful, abundant time.

✦

The novelist and poet Erica Jong writes of her father's death in "Loving Mr. Bones":

> What can you wish for as you watch a beloved parent struggling in Ivan Ilyich's black sack? Should you wish for death or life? And how much do your wishes matter?
> The lucky ones die in restaurants after a good dinner. Or die in their sleep in bed during an erotic dream about a lover long since passed to the other side. I hope to merit such a death.

✦

The playwright and novelist Ntozake Shange writes of the changes a major stroke has brought to her life in her essay "what i thought i'd never lose & did/what i discovered when i didn't know i cd":

> See, I will let you encounter the world as I do now.
> "You fuckin' handicapped bitch, get on out the way!"
> a young Chicano screamed at me. . . . I used to run for the

bus in Philadelphia, knees high, flying through crowds &
up to the driver, "Good afternoon!" I'd pant; but not anymore. I can't run. I can't complete a chassé or bench-press
135 lbs. I fall asleep in the middle of intriguing conversations. . . . I just need directions home sometimes . . . & I
talk like I had fifteen shoes in my mouth . . . but I miss
working. . . . I know how to work an audience. . . . I can
attract people to my shows. . . . I am not dead, I am older.
But I can still memorize a stanza or two.

◆

Jane Alexander, award-winning Hollywood and Broadway actress, describes how content and fulfilled she's been in later
life, thanks to a happy family, a refusal to tamper with her
natural aging process, and an appreciation of nature and good
health.

I used to be very, very anxious myself about dying . . . [but]
if one looks at one's own death as something that's perfectly
okay at any time. . . . I just gave up the anxiety. I used to be
so anxious about everything, flying, driving in a car . . . I
just kind of gave it up.

◆

In "My Narrow Escape," the novelist and memoirist Abigail
Thomas tells us:

Sometimes I feel sorry for my friends who are looking
around for a mate. I don't want one, and I don't want to
want one. It has taken me the better part of sixty years to
enjoy the inside of my own head, and I do that best when
I'm by myself.

I am smug. I am probably insufferable.

And then the telephone rings.

✦

Jane O'Reilly, a journalist and essayist, in "Not Yet" adds this advice to her observations on being older:

THE VOICE OF EXPERIENCE (offstage):

Meanwhile, don't forget to brush and floss. It is no fun to outlive your teeth. I would also suggest cutting back sharply on the use of bodily ailments as conversational topics. Let me also point out the importance of striving to be a glass-half-full instead of a glass-half-empty person. You know who you are.

✦

Claire Bloom, celebrated stage and film actress, was asked how she'd reached some resolution of the past.

I was also very much helped by [a little book of] the sayings of Buddha. . . . [W]hen I was very unhappy . . . it always calmed me and centered me. It's sensible and practical, particularly about age and moving forward and moving on, and if you can't find a companion who suits you and is not a fool, he says, then go on alone. . . . [Life has] treated me well. I've been independent. . . . I've been free to work, to travel, to be with my daughter, to be with my friends, in a way that I wasn't when I was in a relationship. I've found it a very wonderful period of my life.

✦

Our later years often bear a striking resemblance to adolescence: we are simultaneously tremulous, opinionated, bold, surprisingly shy, and nonchalant or self-conscious about our appearance, to name just a few of the possible contradictions.

What is not adolescent is our capacity for self-irony, which seems to increase in later life. Finally, we're able to step back, breathe in and out, and poke some fun at ourselves.

Our contributors speak to the events, the inevitabilities that confront us all in a world bearing less resemblance to anything we've ever known. Here, then, are their daring pieces, engaging interplays of darkness and light, offering what is often the most comfort: the company of others.

These are the women I'd want in my lifeboat.

In the
Fullness
of Time

Sedat Pakay

My Narrow Escape

Abigail Thomas

I like living alone. I like not having to make conversation. I like that I can take as many naps as I feel like taking and nobody knows. I like that if I'm painting trees and the telephone receiver gets sticky with hunter green and there's a long drool of blue sky running down the front of the dishwasher, nobody complains. I'm seldom lonely. I have three dogs, twelve grandchildren, and four grown kids. I have a good friend who now and then drives down with his dog. We've known each other so long that we don't have to talk, and when we do we don't have to say anything. When he asks me if I'd like to take a trip around the world, I can say yes, knowing I'll never have to go. Inertia is a driving force in both our lives. Sometimes I feel sorry for those of my friends who are looking around for a mate. I don't want one, and I don't want to want one. It has taken me the better part of sixty years to enjoy the inside of my own head, and I do that best when I'm by myself.

I am smug. I am probably insufferable.

And then the telephone rings. The last time I saw this person was 1955, when he was twelve and I was thirteen. He has called out of the blue, having just finished reading a book I wrote. He loves my writing, and he has a nice voice. He reminds me that he was so smitten and so shy back in seventh grade that all he could do to show his affection was ride past on his bicycle and throw candy bars at me. He is calling from his sister's house, and when we hang up, his sister says, "Next time, let *her* talk." And he calls me back to tell me that.

A week later he sends some old photographs: our combined seventh and eighth grades; our junior choir; his birthday party—a table full of kids whose names I've mostly forgotten. I am sitting to his left. "I was a boy and you were a woman," he writes on a sticky note attached to the photo. We played spin the bottle at that party, and when we were supposed to kiss, I refused. "I don't have to kiss you, I'm not going to marry you" is what he remembers my saying, and he was crushed, having secretly hoped we would get married. I don't remember any of this; it's like being a character in someone else's story. I stare at my thirteen-year-old face, but nothing is revealed. I am a stranger. I remember mostly anxiety, punctuated by bouts of self-righteousness. I decide not to tell him that in those days I was afraid I would murder my parents in their sleep with the barbecue fork. None of this seems important now. After spin the bottle we had a fight, and a day later he called to apologize. "I meant to say it was all my fault," he tells me, "but what came out was 'It was all my fart.' I didn't know what to do, so I hung up."

"You only experience puppy love once," he tells me, trying to describe the sensation. "It's like being tickled," he decides. Do I remember Miss Lee's dancing class? Vaguely. He does. He remembers I was a foot and a half taller than he was. He remembers looking up at me wanting to say, "You are beautiful, you are gorgeous," but all that came out of his mouth was

"You're tall." I look at his picture again. He is darling, he is innocent, but he is twelve and I am sixty-seven.

And then he sends me a mix tape, all rock 'n' roll, and I play it in my car on the way to the city. With the volume as high as it goes, I am listening to the Chambers Brothers singing "In the Midnight Hour"; I have one arm out the window, banging the beat on the side of my car. "I'm gonna take you girl and hold you/And do all the things I told you" could be coming from the mouth of a twelve-year-old boy who has no idea what he's talking about, but I do, and I'm doing eighty on the Palisades Parkway. I imagine myself in a ditch, car overturned, wheels spinning, and when the cops find me the only sign of life is coming from my CD player, "In the Midnight Hour" still cranked. *What was she thinking?* I imagine them scratching their young heads, wondering.

He wants to come for a visit. Is there a hotel nearby? I tell him I have two extra bedrooms, if he doesn't mind the company of ill-behaved dogs. We make a plan. I call my friend. I'm nervous. "He's in love with a thirteen-year-old girl," I wail, "and I'm sixty-seven. How can I lose fifty pounds in two weeks?" What if after all these years since 1955 it turns out we have been making ourselves into two people made for each other? I'm a writer, I'm curious: I want to know how the story turns out, but without living through it. I don't want to fall in love, but I want to see what happens if I do. I want the possibility of change, not change itself. I don't want to be filled with love, or longing, or desire, those emotional states I once pursued, but now think of as distractions from life rather than life itself. I hate this feeling, I love this feeling, and that's why I'm painting.

The last time I painted was in 1966. I had audited a course in *Sir Gawain and the Green Knight* and fallen in love with the line "She brought him to the very verge." I was smitten with words, too, and decided that *very* and *verge* must have had at their roots the French word for green, *vert.* I found an old mirror, a bucket of house paint, and a screwdriver, which I dipped in the green and then dribbled and swooped what I thought of as a bunch of forest fronds surrounding a reflecting pool. When I ran out of mirrors, I moved on to glass. I painted for two years; people brought me odds and ends of glass, storm windows, windshields, and I painted until I ran away from my husband and took my three little kids to New York City, where instead of painting, instead of poems, I concentrated on finding another man.

These days I am painting apple trees, one after another—red apples, yellow apples, blue apples, silver. I have four paintings going at once, waiting for leaves and fruit to dry, and I am covered in paint up to my elbows. To see what progress I am making, I have to turn the painting over. This is tricky, especially if I am impatient and flip it while the paint is still wet enough to slide around, but it's also how I have the lucky accidents, how I discover that merging colors make something better than what I'd had in mind. I can do this kind of work only by myself. I need to work myself into, then out of, a mess. I need paint dripping and papers drifting and sliding; I need to make notes, lose things, I need to stay up late and go to bed early. I need to run out of milk, coffee, cigarettes. I need to burn with my nice hard gemlike flame, the one that gives off no warmth. Just as I'm on the verge of calling the boy from 1955 to tell him not to come, he calls to cancel. He has a complicated life. We discuss a rain check, but I am crushed. I am crushed and relieved in equal measure.

◆

In the way back of my backyard are three real apple trees. Two of them are upright; one, after a long period of rain followed by a windstorm, has fallen on its side, but the branches still make leaves and blossoms and apples that the deer eat right away. The biggest tree is back in the wild grass. High in its upper branches are scores of red apples, fat and glossy. I stand near where the tall grasses are often flattened by what I assume to be a family of sleeping deer, and this morning, for a moment, I wish I had the nerve to wade through, climb the tree, pick the fruit, but the moment passes. I know better. I've taken too many bites out of too many apples already.

Instead I drag storm windows out of the garage. I go to Houst and buy more cans of paint. Today I look closely at the shape of branches. I study the pattern of twigs against the sky. I try to figure out how to invent the shade of green the leaves are turning—kind of a burnished olive when all I have are primary colors. I'm out of danger. I can do what I want, my hair a wild tangle and my face unwashed. I'm free to fling myself out of bed in the middle of the night and run downstairs to put on another layer of apples, another layer of sky.

ABOUT ABIGAIL THOMAS

Abigail Thomas was for a time a book editor and for another time a book agent. Then she herself started writing. She has written three works of fiction: *Getting Over Tom, An Actual Life,* and *Herb's Pajamas.* Her memoirs include *Safekeeping* and *A Three Dog Life. A Three Dog Life* was chosen as one of the best books of 2006 by *The Washington Post* and the *Los Angeles Times* and has been translated into nine languages. She has published in many magazines and newspapers, including *The Washington Post; The New York Times;* and *O, The Oprah Magazine.* She has also written a handbook for writing memoir, called *Thinking About Memoir.* She has four children and twelve grandchildren. She has taught writing for the past twenty years both privately and in universities.

Sedat Pakay

Even Smart Women Hate Losing Their Youthful Looks

Vivian Gornick

People have been looking at me since I was fourteen years old.
All my life, I walked into a room and heads turned. I never knew
what it was they were looking at, certainly I never had a good
time with it, but there it was, a given in my life, that the way
would be smoothed for me because of the way I looked. I knew
that, all right. What I didn't know was how much I depended on
it. I never dreamed that around fifty it would all just stop. When it
did it was like a mallet coming down on my head.
—ANDREA, A CORPORATE LAWYER

The British art critic John Berger, in an influential book called
Ways of Seeing, observed that in our culture, men watch and

women are watched. Think about that for a moment. That means that men grow up thinking it is their right and obligation to look appraisingly at women and women grow up feeling it their necessity to be appraised favorably. This twin activity is lodged deep in the psyche of every man and every woman. No matter who you are—whatever your upbringing, whatever your personal values or actual experience—there's no escaping this particular influence of the culture. If you are a man, it increases your sense of potential to gaze at women, and if you are a woman, it decreases yours when you are no longer being gazed at.

Such a state of affairs is mind-altering. An educated woman in an Arabic country where polygamy is lawful once said to me, "I know that my husband will not take two wives, but the fact that under the law he can affects his emotions and it affects mine." By the same token, a culture that includes men forever watching, and women forever being watched, cannot help but affect, in some important sense, the way we experience ourselves as people out in the world.

The sentence I just wrote was easy enough to write, but its content has been difficult to digest. It is taking me years, in fact, to absorb its full meaning.

When I was thirty-five years old, I belonged to a consciousness-raising group. We were fifteen professional women in that group: writers, lawyers, academics, and one industrial chemist. Everyone in the room was attractive, some were remarkably pretty, and a few drop-dead gorgeous. The sessions were about work, relationships, politics, competition. One evening we devoted ourselves to the question of looks.

In the course of that conversation it became clear that everyone in the room hated the fact that women who were not beautiful spent their lives feeling secretly deprived and discounted, no matter how accomplished they might otherwise be; and that those who were beautiful spent their lives—

secretly or otherwise—feeling superior, whether or not they did anything of value. The whole situation was outrageous, we declared hotly, and we refused to buy into it. We would not lend ourselves to a system of exchanges that daily rewarded us for looking "great" and punished us for not looking "great."

This meeting took place thirty years ago. The women in the room that night are now all in their sixties. One way or another, I stayed in touch with everyone: some are good friends, some acquaintances, some people I run into from time to time. In the years between we have lived our lives, each of us according to her own lights. We have fallen into and out of love countless times, we have married and divorced countless times. We've written, we've taught, we've made scientific discoveries and handed down legal decisions. Our work has been recognized, even applauded. In short, like everyone else, we have thrived and we have suffered. And we have—each and every one of us—lost our youthful looks.

The change in appearance has been an education. Every woman in the group has felt the consequences of her altered looks acutely, and every woman has been embarrassed into feelings of shock and surprise at how much she hates seeing herself grow older.

None of us could have predicted in advance that we'd react this way to the aging process because none of us could have foreseen the hundred little instances—from small perks to large considerations—that, in the course of an ordinary day, provide an ease and a pleasure for a pretty young woman that disappears dramatically in middle age. A young woman needs to do nothing to gain attention and consideration. She need only be. Her unadorned existence provides interest and animation, in return for which she receives unearned privilege. For a middle-aged woman it is otherwise, as she watches low-level attention (and that same unearned privilege) evaporate from her life as a result of no longer looking young. It works like this:

Two women, one young and pretty, the other handsome and middle-aged, are standing together on the street hailing a cab; or in a store or a restaurant waiting for service; or at a corporate business reception. The cab rolls to the feet—of the younger; the man behind the counter turns automatically—to the younger; opinion in the reception hall is solicited—of the younger. These may seem like instances of triviality, minor occurrences if you will, almost non-occurrences, not worth remarking on or even recalling. And a younger woman doesn't. But the older one does. Because the occurrences are cumulative: they mount up, and finally add up, to what's called social invisibility—the kind of public dismissal or discounting that makes one feel an outsider, encourages self-doubt, gives the impression that life is narrowing down.

Dianne, the industrial chemist, was one of the drop-dead-gorgeous women in our group. As a girl and a young woman she bore a striking resemblance to Katharine Hepburn, but her beauty, if anything, had made her uneasy. "My whole life I refused to be impressed by my own looks," she said recently. "I was far more interested in being taken seriously as a scientist. But—and this is what's been surprising—privilege, it seems, came to me *anyway* because people thought I was good-looking. And I, apparently, made use of it (how could I not?), but I didn't know I was making use of it—until it was removed. Now that it's gone, well, it's not that I feel devastated, it's just that—" She stopped speaking, looked vague for a moment, then said quietly, "In some way the world feels smaller."

For Carol, a journalist, the loss of youthful prettiness has brought on revelations of a similar but more severe order. "All my life I was a girl," she says now. "I thought I was a journalist, but it turns out I was a girl. When I was young, there always seemed to be a crowd of people (mostly men) waiting around to hear what I had to say. Today, when I'm out among people, I find myself either ignored or patronized. Men talk to me as if I'm an idiot. It's as though I've committed a transgression by getting older, and I'm being isolated for it."

Last year I, too, was given a startling demonstration—I'm still absorbing the information it gave me—of what it means to be on the other side of the great divide.

I took a trip to Italy alone. It was a time of stress and exhaustion, and I remembered that once, years before, when I was in my twenties, I'd taken a trip alone to Europe when I needed some R & R and had a marvelous time, returning home refreshed and renewed. Just what I needed now. This time, however, the trip was a failure. I came home disappointed and dispirited, more tired than when I'd gone.

It took me a while to figure out what had gone wrong. I realized that when I had traveled years before in my twenties, everywhere I'd gone I had met with a widespread eagerness to engage. People hung around to help me with my lousy French or Italian, to lift my suitcases onto overhead racks or haul them down station staircases, call a cab, hold a train, pass me on through without a ticket, buy me a coffee, fall into conversation at the drop of a hat. A myriad of tiny human adventures had befallen me as a young girl traveling alone that were now apparently unavailable to me as a middle-aged woman traveling alone.

It wasn't that this discrepancy made my recent trip a disaster; it didn't. There were no disasters, but there were no unexpected adventures, either, not of the sort I had been depending on. It was that I had been expecting—intending—to wing it: to sit back and let Europe unfold before my eyes in a panorama of events that everyone around was going to provide for me. All I'd have to do was show up and respond. Vividness and excitement would then wash over me. And why not? I'd gotten myself there, hadn't I? Wasn't that enough? It always had been in the past.

Well, it wasn't anymore.

The trip made me see that life for a young woman is a free ride, and for me the free part of the ride was over. From here on in, I'd have to pay my way. That is, I myself would have to provide the pleasure, the interest, and the energy. I myself would have to stand on line for the ticket, sling the suitcase onto the overhead rack, read the guidebook, start the conversation—and generate the enjoyment. Whatever came my way after that would be gravy.

Now, back home, looking at the situation with greater clarity, I saw that the trip had been useful. It had made me think about the meaning of youthful looks—and all those years of the free ride—as I'd never thought about it before. Suddenly, middle age didn't seem a terrible thing at all. On the contrary, it began to seem interesting. The important thing, I say now, is to have the wherewithal to pay your own way. And by wherewithal I didn't mean money. I mean the self-possession that comes with understanding that a life—anyone's life—has to be made from inside out. So that when the free ride is over, one receives one's new circumstances neither as a surprise nor even a disappointment; certainly not a devastation.

Men fear aging as much as women do, but their anxieties are bound up with the loss of status and position, not looks and appearance. An aging face can never mean to a man what it means to a woman, as youthful beauty has never been a provider of the goods of life for men as it has been for women. It is loss of position that makes a man melancholy and self-doubting (the statistics on men dying soon after retirement are staggering). Yet a man's status and a woman's youthful looks are equivalent. In either case—lose position or beauty—people find themselves startled, drawn up short, suddenly asking vital and fundamental questions (Who am I? Where am I going? What am I doing with my life?). In short: existential terror looms large. It is not, I believe, the fear of death that threatens but the fear that our lives are not being lived; or rather, that we are not living them.

For a woman, existential terror is the aging face. When a woman looks in the mirror and sees herself smooth and young, she thinks, "I'm not yet accountable. I don't yet have to explain or justify my existence. It doesn't matter yet that I'm not taking responsibility for my life. I still have tomorrow. I'll do it tomorrow." When she looks in the mirror and sees herself lined and hollow-cheeked, she thinks, "Tomorrow is here. Now I'm accountable. Now I must do it. Can I? More important, will I?"

Such questions are either a downer or a source of stimulation. I prefer to take them as stimulation. That way, loss is transformed into wisdom and life continues to provide adventure.

But I'm here to tell you: it still takes a lot of stamina and a lot of self-control to welcome the aging face.

ABOUT VIVIAN GORNICK

Vivian Gornick is a literary journalist whose many books include essays, memoirs, criticism, and biography. She lives in New York City.

Moving

Carolyn See

It's past midnight on a hot, hot night in 1965 far up the scratchy reaches of Topanga Canyon. We're in a 23- by 23-foot cabin at the top of a cliff so steep no road can attempt it, so for forty-eight hours almost nonstop, about six of us have hauled furniture and books, our beloved books, up a tortuous switchback path, sweating like horses, yelling "Out of the way, snakes!" and stomping down the dirt path, because we know the acreage is snake-infested. It's our first house. We bought it for $12,000. In the daytime you can see bright sunshine streaming in between some of the slats. The hot water tank works on kerosene; you take your life in your hands when you light it. We don't care! We don't care about the snakes. We love the view, the acrid, healthy smell of eucalyptus.

This place used to belong to an eighty-seven-year-old German Jewish refugee who had made dresses for Theda Bara and Mrs. Igor Stravinsky on her dining room table. Thousands of straight pins glitter on the old rugs she left. (She wept when she left, deprived of her "little shack," as she called it, and was dead less than a month later. Before that she'd scrambled around that cliff like a limber chimp.) We're exhausted, panting, heaving, sweating.

Everything's finally up here. At last! One of our friends—thank God for their loyalty, their crazy generosity on this crack-brained project!—opens a can of beer and sits down on an ancient dining room chair left up here by the eighty-seven-year-old, which explodes out from under him. "This is a stunt house!" he cries, and we reach over to help him up, weak from laughing, from working so hard; weak, period.

It's our first owned house for each of us, my second husband and me, and we are absurdly proud of the place—its tram line, its perilous switchback path, its outdoor shower, its couch that has, for some reason, been cut in half horizontally. The poet Robert Sward will write about that couch. The novelist Irving Shulman will stand at the bottom of the cliff and pronounce disdainfully, "Only for goyim." A naturalist will bury whale vertebrae on the property so that worms will eat the flesh, and the bones will become shiny and bright. Snakes will be killed by the boatload. After my husband leaves, we'll share owner-ship, and he'll wake me up sometimes at seven in the morning pacing the narrow patio (because we have another cliff on that side of the cabin; the whole thing perches on about fifty feet of flat land stuck out there in the sky). "Half of this house is mine!" he yells. "Half of it is *mine*. Nothing can take that away!" "The other half is *mine*!" I'd scream. "Get off my half of the property!"

But the day came a few years after the divorce when I found John Espey, a wonderful man in his sixties who couldn't be expected to walk up and down that grueling switchback path, and so I sold my half of the old Topanga house back to my ex-husband, and we spent another exciting forty-eight hours hauling worldly possessions up and down that path, only thank God, I was moving my stuff *down*, and we did use the tram line, though it was notoriously tricky, tipping over and then off its tracks halfway down the cliff, and you'd have to thrash through the underbrush to right it again, shouting "Out of the way, snakes!" because they were ubiquitous.

◆

I moved further into the canyon, into a three-bedroom house with a double garage and yellow shag carpeting. My teenage daughter was scornful, my younger daughter wept. There was nothing *wrong* with the new house; it was pretty, it didn't give us any trouble; it had tarantulas and snakes and, if possible, even more snakes and an even better view. But, put in marital terms, you'd have to say we loved it; we were never *in* love with it.

We merged households, John Espey and I, and we bought some new and normal things: couches that hadn't been sawed in half. John had scrolls and tea trays from China and a beautiful rolltop desk; he had an enormous collection of gold-embossed books from the 1890s. I had books upon books and all the kitchen stuff and a lot of Mexican folklore gear.

It's elementary math, our life. We're born with nothing and someone gives us a silver baby spoon or a cardboard box and we go collecting stuff until the day or week or year we begin giving away stuff, until we're in the nursing home with a few faded photographs on the wall. It's addition and subtraction, and unless you're a monk by nature, that subtraction feels like a loss. There doesn't seem to be much to be done about it.

In 1998, it was evident that John's health was failing. He slept, sitting up, for hours at a time. He haughtily denied that anything was wrong, and then I came down with macular degeneration. It stabilized eventually, but for about two years I couldn't drive—I'd see two or three white lines dividing Topanga Canyon Boulevard, and that was a dangerous mountain road. We would have to move out of the canyon. John didn't want to go. He wouldn't, couldn't help in any way. It was a question of books again and a double garage full of weird shit that had built up over about twenty-five years.

Besides being a lot like math, moving is a lot like death, that is, people come up out of nowhere to help or they stay away, and in any and every case they leave their superegos in their other suit. A dear friend came by to help me sort some of John's things, and we were like two plastic ducks; I'd throw out yellowed photographs of Presbyterian missionaries in Shanghai from the early twentieth century—people John either disliked or couldn't remember—and she'd bend down into the trash to retrieve them: "You can't throw *this* away!" I'd take them from her and throw them away. And so on. She left that day with a couple of the dining room chairs and a raft of heavy brush-clearing tools including a broken Pulanski plow. It goes without saying that my daughters disapproved. I was throwing away their (tacky) inheritance. John, even with all his sweetness, wasn't speaking to me. Was he furious? Or just trying to maintain? There were cartons and cartons of books down in the garage. I know there were some days that we'd stop by the Salvation Army and I'd unload four unopened cartons of my newly published memoir, so I'm not claiming sanity in all of this. I had to throw everything out!

Then came a day when two Mormon lady friends of mine, a writer and an artist, came to help me pack up John's office. Now, John and I had never been married. He'd been happily married once and I'd been a pretty bad wife twice, so we'd decided to play it safe. It had worked pretty well for about twenty-five years. How, then, was I to explain the close to

1,500 dirty socks we found in his office? I had never snooped in his things. I had never given a thought to his socks. But this day I would open a desk drawer and find an ashtray, a pocket New Testament, five filthy socks, and an old letter. On the top shelves in his closet, neatly folded cashmere sweaters. Behind them, a couple of hundred dirty socks. Behind the couch in his study, a mountain of socks. I couldn't confront him and ask, "What's with the *socks,* honey?" Because he was sitting up in the living room in dignity, almost dead from undiag- nosed heart failure. He wasn't talking, and what about me? Why had I, in our twenty-five years, not thought to address the sock question?

I washed out about a dozen pair. And threw the rest out. And thanked God that my friends, as sophisticated and worldly as they were, had been raised religiously and taught to judge not, lest they be judged. And now that John's been dead for almost nine years, I can say that down in that double garage, I also found get-rich-quick schemes and muscle-building elixirs, evidence of inner yearnings I had never dreamed existed in him. I threw them out, too.

We moved to a beautiful, even luxurious condominium in the Pacific Palisades. John had gone to the hospital the day after moving day and almost died, but he didn't. He would live two more years. Our furniture had been refined down: we still had the dining room table (without the exploding chairs!) that remained from the Stunt House. It was still gnarled and gouged by scissors. But instead of looking like junk, it had taken on the patina of a true antique. The dresser with the beveled-edge mirror that we'd bought at the Salvation Army for fifteen bucks had cloaked itself in somber elegance. The elegance came with the place. It too had that view of mountains, but over here in civilization they were dotted with Spanish-style mansions. And the walls of the dining room were lined with John's beautiful collection of books.

✦

After two years, John died. I loved the place enough, but it was vast—and lonely. Then, seven years later, my macular degeneration worsened again. I wouldn't be able to drive after my license ran out, and I was scheduled to take a driving test on my next birthday. After years of living in various kinds of rural isolation, with eye-ravishing views (I'd read E. M. Forster's *A Room with a View* when I was eighteen, and you could say, without exaggeration, that it had had an undue influence on me), I would have to move down to the flats, to a place with city blocks and apartment houses and stores; I'd have to walk everywhere and hire the occasional driver. The prospects for a view were dim.

You go crazy when you move (unless you live in a yurt and get used to it). I think I could say I was in a colossally bad mood. I'd been without John for seven years; that was bad enough. Now, soon enough, I'd be without the better part of my sight and without a car. On top of that, over the years I had cultivated a public persona that I (privately until now) referred to as "Jolly Grandma," a kind of sexless answer to Henry Miller's mantra "Always merry and bright!" I can hear my daughters snorting as they read this and remember myself in the old days walking three times around the Stunt House backward, putting a spell on it so no one would be happy there after I left, but for almost twenty-eight years I had lived with the civilizing influence of John Espey, I had been a cheerful professor of English; I didn't feel now that shrieking at the top of my voice until my vocal chords melted down to jam would be appropriate. I was losing my vision; well, then, fuck it. I was losing my car; well, then, fuck it. I was losing my nine-year swipe at tentative luxury, well, then. You know. They wouldn't hear me shriek.

The place I bought was small, with a pleasing view of a white stucco wall fifteen feet away and a balcony too tiny to sit on. I told myself the wall looked like an Edward Biber-man painting. The hall to the apartment was long, gloomy, and dim, with holes in the floor under a dark blue rug. I told myself it was a Raymond Chandler hall (and the wall does have a niche used in the old days for a communal telephone). The two bedrooms (one would be an office) looked directly into the rather messy dwellings of people in the condos next door. I would hear them cough, sneeze, fart, and experience depressingly infrequent orgasms. And if you're thinking, Why didn't she get a better place?, there wasn't a better place. I was working on a timeline. I wanted to be close to my friends and my daughters. And Santa Monica, a Southern California resort beach town, is notoriously expensive. And if I wasn't going to have the mountains, I could at least console myself with the Twinkling Pacific—something I could walk three blocks to see.

But I'd have to throw some stuff out! And I'd have only three months to do it. (I forgot—I was moving out of my office too—no more teaching. I felt about as morose as Poe's raven—Nevermore!)

I'm a writer; I live a life of books. I had a terrific collection of Australian novels. I called up the Australian embassy and asked if it would like to have them in its library. Of course not! It did agree, reluctantly, to take them to give to Australian felons who got lonely in American jails. I began looking through my other books, finding stuff I'd never read, or stuff I'd hated, or stuff I knew I'd never look at again, and every day I made a Goodwill run with about three cartons. I kept only the books that meant something to me—the books I'd been rich enough to buy when I was a Van de Kamp's waitress; gifts from my first boyfriend; *The Jungle Book,* because I loved it.

◆

I tried to give away two enormous red couches; the Salvation Army was indignant: "They're too *big*! We can't move those!"

I had to hire a mover to take them to the Salvation Army, and even then the people there were grumpy about it. There were some good pieces, John's pieces, his grandfather's rolltop desk. By the terms of his will I could have kept his possessions until I died; then they were to go to John's grandson. But I wanted to be shut of all of it. I phoned his grandson. And wouldn't he like to take the wall full of John's very valuable "Decorative Design" books? Sure. He'd just gotten married; he'd drive a truck down from Sacramento. John's Ezra Pound scholarship had to go to Special Collections at UCLA. There was one dusty weekend when my brother and stepmother and I packed up those gold-embossed books (keeping a few of the finest for ourselves). Packing books is very hard after a while, when you're up in your seventies. And there were thousands of books, Decorative Design books, volumes collected not for their content but for their beautifully embossed cover art, each book a flurry of gold. My brother sweated, unfolding flattened cardboard boxes, taping up box after box.

A woman from Special Collections came that day to pick up the Ezra Pound books and burst into tears. John had been such a wonderful man! I wanted to smack her. John's grandson came down, and because he's such a bad liar he revealed that his mother, who had managed to ruin her share of John's Chinese antiques, would be getting the beautiful rolltop desk. "I'm keeping the Chinese mirror, then!" I snarled, and his wife said, over my head, "I knew she'd say that."

I was losing everything; I was being squeezed in; I was dying. My daughter and I bought little yellow dwarf couches for my dwarf apartment. Four little red dwarf floor lamps. A sideboard half the size of my old sideboard. I like to think of myself as a fairly nice person, but I felt myself melting, like the Wicked Witch of the West, melting, wailing "What a world, what a world!"

So what's my problem? I've lived here a year now, and it's a very pretty little place. A two-bedroom apartment three blocks from the ocean. No snakes—although I hear tell of a gang of rambunctious raccoons on the other side of this (very small) building. The new furniture is bright and light, even the view of the white plaster wall has something to recommend it when the sun shines on it and my living room bathes in its reflected glow. The artwork is great, I have to admit. But my society now is the society of old ladies—what else would it be? I'm an old lady! We "keep busy." We have lunch with each other.

I'm writing this at the table from Topanga Canyon, the table that once held patterns for Theda Bara's dresses. I want to say: I miss the Stunt House! I deplore the fact that my past is not only lost but gone! Gone, the skeleton of the dead rat I once found in a carton of my daughter's baby clothes. Gone, the raised voices in pointless arguments about whether it was hotter at noon or two in the afternoon (my second husband and I disagreed very strongly about that subject). Gone, the whale vertebrae. I can't find the poem Robert Sward wrote about that couch—rather ham-handedly called "Cut in Half." I do have a wonderful little watercolor by the Chicano artist Frank Romero, a little patchwork of pastels. At the bottom of the picture is one of his signature cars, then two parallel lines—which, if you knew what it was, would be a tram line—and way up in something like a sky a little brown patch the size of a postage stamp, our Stunt House. And one other thing. Back in that old house the dressmaker's dead husband had pinned up a postcard in his downstairs study, really just a hole in the earth. A friend of ours took it and copied it, enlarged it into an exquisitely stitched sampler: *"Arbeiten und nicht verzweifeln"* (or so I read it with my dimming eyes), "Work hard and don't get depressed."

The thing is, I know where all this moving is going to end up, and I can't say I'm terribly happy about it. Sometimes the Jolly Grandma wants to let out an unladylike shriek. A shrill scream at my second husband would be nice, but he has Alzheimer's now and probably would mistake me for a passing police siren. My life is peaceful now, and that's not necessarily a good sign. I don't like to think about my next move. The only thing for it is to . . . work hard and don't get depressed.

ABOUT CAROLYN SEE

Carolyn See is the author of nine novels (including *The Handy Man* and *Golden Days*) and four works of nonfiction. She is a professor emerita at UCLA and the Friday book reviewer for *The Washington Post*. She has been the recipient of a Guggenheim grant and the prestigious Robert Kirsch Award. She has lived in Topanga Canyon and the Pacific Palisades and now resides in Santa Monica, California.

Hugo Glendening

Interview with Claire Bloom

EMILY UPHAM: *I have read your memoir,* Leaving a Doll's House, *which ended in 1993, at the time of your very difficult separation from Philip Roth. I'm wondering if life has been kind to you since that time.*

CLAIRE BLOOM: Oh, goodness, it's treated me well. I've been independent, I've been free, I've been free to work, to travel, to be with my daughter, to be with my friends, in a way that I wasn't when I was in a relationship. I've found it a very wonderful period of my life.

E: *So you haven't felt the lack of an intimate relationship with a man?*

CB: Oh, no. Of course, if you have an ideal relationship, which very few people do, it's wonderful to have a companion, but if you don't, you get on with it and you can make your life very rich when you have no ties, no real ties. I mean, everyone has ties, to their daughter or whomever, but I mean no, nothing that binds you to one place or one thing.

E: *And have you reached a certain kind of resolution about the past?*

CB: Oh, yes, absolutely. If you don't go forward, you go backward, you don't go anywhere. You have to leave things behind, and also if I were to keep chewing over what happened, now fifteen years ago, that would mean I've been stuck in one place. And of course I was lucky enough to have a career, many do, but I had a career that took me, lifted me out of myself in many ways. It's a wonderful thing to have. It also made me travel, made me move. And I had great help from a psychotherapist in New York. But I've always been able to move forward and out. I have neither looked for nor found any other relationships because I feel that that part of my life is over. I think at my age, most women are alone, for one reason or another. I think that this is the time of one's life that one is alone. I mean, I'm not alone in that I have my brothers and sister and daughter and some wonderful friends.

E: *I think as we get older, the important dialogue that we have to have is with ourselves.*

CB: Yes, it is. But I was also very much helped by the sayings of Buddha. At one time, when I was very unhappy, I had a little book of the sayings of Buddha, and I used to take it out and it always calmed me and centered me. It's sensible and practical, particularly about age and moving forward and moving on, and if you can't find a companion who suits you and is not a fool, he says, then go on alone. There's nothing worse than being tied down by something that is not for you.

E: *Yes. And in the losses to death that we all must go through, I assume that the loss of your mother must have been enormous for you.*

CB: Yes, of course it was, but even that, you know, was 1983.

E: *Did you find that besides the passage of time, mostly the investment in your work life was what carried you along?*

CB: I don't know about that. The terrible bereavement one feels when you lose someone whom you loved as much as I loved my mother . . . it takes a long time to . . . There were years when I used to get to the airport and think, "Oh, I have got to buy cigarettes for my mother." And also I didn't want to fail her, you know. And I feel that if I had let myself go down in 1993 [the year of her separation from Roth], which I could have done, I would have failed in all the things she tried to do for me and tried to tell me.

E: *I so admire you for not having gone down.*

CB: Oh, no, but I'm tough. Actresses have to be, because it's a tough life. There are moments when you're coddled and spoiled, and then you're completely let go, you drop right out of favor, into a kind of loneliness and feeling nobody wants you, and then you get picked up again. It's a very hard life. And then being over . . . overly adored. If you don't keep a balance in that, you're in real trouble. I do think it makes you strong. Well, no, it doesn't make you strong, you have to be strong to do it. Strong-natured, in some way. Resilient. I guess that's the word.

E: *I understand that because I too am in the performing arts. But it's also true that a lot of even great artists do go down.*

CB: They do. I was thinking the other night about the past as one does, at this point in one's life anyway. I think a lot about the past. And there were four actresses of my generation who have committed suicide. Very gifted, very wonderful women. My God, that's an awful lot out of a small group of successful actresses of a certain age.

E: *It's also probably true that the arts, for obvious reasons, attract people of tremendous feeling and—*

CB: And sometimes need.

E: *And instability, perhaps. I think one of the reasons we need to do our art is to make up for something that's not quite right in the rest of life.*

CB: Oh, absolutely. First of all, it's quite amazing when you read the biographies of actresses, not actors, how many have no fathers.

E: *Yes, as you did not, essentially.*

CB: I'm one, but many, many. I mean, Bette Davis wrote a wonderful book called *My Lonely Life.* And she said, "I'm a self-made man, my father made me one." I would have liked to have had a male figure that I relied on, I suppose, and adored, and I didn't have it.

E: *You had no habit of it to begin with.*

CB: I had no habit of it to begin with, which is maybe why I chose not badly, but strangely.

E: *Yes, but so many of us have chosen strangely.*

CB: Most people, quite honestly, and yet— It must be, I mean, I've had it briefly, a wonderful relationship. It's really terrific.

E: *Terrific, but it's very rare.*

CB: Very rare. And I see marriages and people who are together who are very unhappy. And that's weird, because we know . . . that's *really* dreadful.

E: *Terrible. But as we've been saying, relationships are not everything. God only knows you've been one of the icons of the stage. Has knowing that about yourself, knowing what an extraordinary amount you've brought to theater and how admired you are, helped you through difficult times?*

CB: Yes, it does. Of course, there are times when I feel less than nothing, as everybody does, and then I do say, "Wait a minute, whatever it was, you have accomplished something." And also not only that, but I did what I wanted, and how many people can say that? I was in a profession that I dreamt of when I was a child. I made—well, my mother and I made my dreams come true.

E: *And the fact of time running out that we all must face—how does that affect you, does it force you to prioritize your time?*

CB: Yes, I think it does. Mind you, of necessity, actors have to wait about, but I don't want to waste *any* time. It's so infantilizing for actors to wait to be called, and it's a waste of life. I do feel now, of course, I don't have time, and I don't.

E: *Do you do a lot of teaching and passing on—*

CB: I don't, I don't at all. I did a little while in New York. But no, I don't, I try to do things that interest me. Go to classes or read and go to the museum and travel. My interests are very much alive still. But I don't, yes, there's very little time to waste now, and I'm very conscious of that.

E: *Is it a fearful time in some ways?*

CB: No, it isn't. I don't think, "Well, my God, in ten years, I won't be here." Everybody faces it, and I'm not any different.

E: *People face it very differently. It's interesting, I was speaking yesterday with Marta Casals Istomin, and she herself has had a very amazing career. She's a practicing Catholic, and she believes very strongly in an afterlife, and she believes that the good that she has done in this life will have an impact for her in the afterlife.*

CB: Lucky woman. I'm afraid I don't believe anything. But I do think people who do are very fortunate.

E: *Yes, I envy them.*

CB: I do, too. But it's not anything I ever, ever needed or wanted or had. I also would prefer not to be deluded, as I see it. I know that the end comes and that's the end of it. And memories . . . like my mother, she's alive as long as I'm alive, up to a point, and my daughter, too, remembers and loved my mother, and when we're gone, that's it. I've no illusions.

E: *Many of us started out as very attractive and talented young women, and that fact gave us all a kind of free ride up to a certain point. And then we lose the power of our youthful beauty, and in*

*our professional lives we are replaced by younger talented artists. I
assume that your unique stature in the theater world has protected
you from this.*

CB: Well, it is true for me in a way. One can't be completely
replaced in the theater because roles are so much a matter of
age. But it's really interesting that now parts that should be
suitable for me are played by younger and younger people.
Instead of it being a woman of my age playing a woman my
age [seventy-seven], it will be a woman of fifty-five. It's not as
it used to be. Now ageism has reached as far as my generation.

E: *I understand. But it seems that you've made the transition
from young stardom to being an older, venerated actress quite
gracefully. So many have not, as we said earlier on. Do you find
that these later years, besides that we're simply forced to adapt
to them, offer something positive that our younger years couldn't
provide? Something to look forward to?*

CB: I don't know, I think old age is not so much fun. So really into one's old age, I have my doubt about what pleasures
there could be.

E: *But let's just talk about your sixties and seventies. It sounds
like there's been a certain kind of peace.*

CB: Absolutely. The worst for me, quite honestly, was after
my divorce. Terrible financial fear. I think that I'm pretty okay
now, though you never know what could happen, of course. So
I don't have that worry. I'm ambitious in a way that I still want
to do something good, but I don't expect it to be on a grand
scale. I mean, the main thing is, really, to be healthy. So far
I've been incredibly healthy, and then the last two years I had
a knee operation and then I had sinus problems. It is nothing
compared to the stuff many people have had. All I mean is that
you gradually think, "Oh. I'm not quite where I was a few years
ago in terms of strength." I get very tired. Very. And yet, if I had
something to do professionally—

E: *You would rally.*

CB: Oh, yes. And then you pay for it after, but still.

E: *But it's worth the price.*

CB: Absolutely. Now, I'm not saying that it's wonderful to get older, it isn't, but as there's no alternative, I have to say that these years, so far, have been . . . I'm rather happy in that . . . ambition was such an enormous part of my life. I would be crazy to have that now.

E: *Yes, I've had an injury, so I've put aside my performing career, but I also found some relief in the putting aside of some of that ambition.*

CB: Oh, God, yes.

E: *And not being driven that way anymore.*

CB: And not being guilty if you're not doing this or that or someone else is doing it and you're not doing it.

E: *Exactly. So you've removed yourself from the maelstrom.*

CB: Up to a point. There are certain things that can still upset you, but they're so rare. And it is wonderful, isn't it, to let go?

E: *As long as one has something to go to or hold on to. It doesn't matter what it is, but that something has to be there.*

CB: Something has to be there, even if you just make it up for yourself. I always wish I had talent to paint or to— I have none, absolutely none. The only thing I really know how to do is to act.

E: *You certainly did that superbly well.*

CB: I did that okay. But it's unfortunately not a hobby, it's not something you do by yourself.

E: *Also, don't you find that because of the demands of being, in my case a classical musician, in your case a superb actress, that we're so used to maintaining a level of excellence, which has demanded so much training, that it is difficult to do things in an amateurish kind of way?*

CB: Oh, yes.

E: *Yes, that's why we're kind of stuck.*

CB: Absolutely. Either it's got to be good and the real thing or not at all. Or, sometimes in my case, to make money, I've done some pretty horrible television. I don't care, as my friends aren't going to see it. It's unpleasant, you know, you play some old dodderer.

E: *Yes, but the reality is we all have to do things for money. Sometimes that's just the way it is.*

On a different subject, I was a child when I learned about World War II and what happened to the European Jews. I was born in 1949. It had an enormous impact on my psyche. You lived through that war as a child, and I was wondering about its impact on you. Perhaps because you were a child you didn't really understand what was going on.

CB: No, luckily. Well, as you know, I was born in 1931, so I'm eighteen years older than you. I've just been reading an interesting book about Winifred Wagner and a lot about the rise of Hitler that I really didn't know. But I do remember, as a child, my mother and father listening to this ranting lunatic on the radio, and I knew it was something to fear. You know how you feel that animal fear and revulsion. But we didn't know, of course we didn't, nobody knew. I remember my grandmother buying her sister out of Germany, and she had been in a concentration camp, but this is long before extermination. And I remember going to hospital to see her when she came to England and knowing something horrible was going on and certainly knew that because I was Jewish, it could well affect me. But I didn't know it, I wasn't old enough to understand. The only thing I will say, and this sounds awfully self-righteous or something, but I do feel, especially as a European Jew who by some miracle was spared, when so many millions were not, that I do have a duty to live my life decently. I've always felt that. Yes, a duty to live your life. And really to live it as best you can and not to complain, because Anne Frank was almost the same age as I am, and her life was over at fifteen. It is consciously with us all, if we have half a brain, to know that in many ways we are living life for other people. They weren't able to live.

E: *It strengthened your will to be.*

CB: Enormously, and I think this probably had a lot to do with my tremendous ambition to succeed, but then that is a Jewish thing. You want your children to lift themselves up and out and away, as my mother did.

E: *There must have been great satisfaction in having fulfilled so many of your mother's dreams for you.*

CB: Yes, yes, there was. Whenever I go into an interesting church—not in Germany, I never lit a candle for my mother in Germany because I knew she wouldn't like it—but when I go into a beautiful church, particularly in Greece, where I lived for years, I light a candle for her and I just thank her for giving me this wonderful life.

ABOUT CLAIRE BLOOM

Claire Bloom, a venerated film and stage actress, was born in London on February 15, 1931. She made her stage debut at fifteen, with the Oxford Repertory Theatre. Two years later, she received great acclaim for her portrayal of Ophelia in *Hamlet,* the first of her many Shakespearean performances. She has appeared in numerous plays and theatrical works in both London and New York.

Bloom's first film role was in 1948, in *Blind Goddess.* She was chosen by Charlie Chaplin in 1952 to appear in his film *Limelight,* which catapulted her to stardom.

Bloom has appeared in several films, series, and serials for television, perhaps the most memorable of which was her portrayal of Lady Marchmain in *Brideshead Revisited* (1981). She costarred with Sean Connery in *Anna Karenina* (1961) and played Cathy in *Wuthering Heights* with Keith Michell as Heathcliff (1962).

She has appeared on the American television series *Law & Order* and *As the World Turns.* She continues to be active on the stage.

Bloom's memoir, *Leaving a Doll's House,* was published in 1996. She had a daughter, the opera singer Anna Steiger, with her husband Rod Steiger. She subsequently married the producer Hillard Elkins and the writer Philip Roth.

Nick Guthe

My Mother and Me and Betty Grable

Linda Gravenson

"Mashed potatoes!" My mother sits straight up in bed in the intensive care unit in New York Hospital on yet another of her emergency admissions for heart disease. Her head is wrapped in a printed scarf, her lipstick is a fuchsia slash, her eyes are as wild and roving as all the other times she's been in this manic state.

"I am dying here, and they bring me mashed potatoes!" She stabs at the air with her index finger and gestures for me to take my seat. She is in the middle of her aria.

How this Mad Hatter in a Carmen Miranda turban can be holding court in the intensive care unit speaks for her sheer force. She's got the staff jumping. Nurses adjust her tubes, shaking their heads in disbelief, muttering objections to being ordered around. Diabetes and heart disease have joined with manic depression to complete the circle of illness that has held her hostage from my earliest memories.

None of the doctors can figure out what keeps her alive. As her caretaker for thirty years, I know her better and know she still has the will to jump into action, if only with her voice, which rasps and growls, as words are swallowed and spit out again. The antipsychotic drug Thorazine has destroyed her once lovely singing voice.

Her thoughts leap, dipping and diving as the familiar manic soliloquy takes over: "Middle of the movie . . . mad money . . . that salesman your father . . . Teddy's daughter!" She sneers at the thought of my father and goes on to me. "You, you Sarah Lawrence girl, you! . . . the doorman, the doorman . . . sailing on the *Liberté* . . . those twerps . . . wrapped in wildflowers . . . I was."

Settled back against the pillows, she glares at me, "They gave me the wrong baby!" she bellows, her eyes narrowing, aiming for the bull's-eye, instinctively knowing what will hurt me the most. But probably not knowing she's identified the pain of our long, entangled story; of my attachment and revulsion. My obstinate wish for reunion that keeps me in her thrall.

When she summons one of the nurses, I slip out of the room. She and I know I will be back. I will be in the grip of her seductive power until the end, until that moment when I am finally off duty, when there is nothing more I can fix for her, when I can ask myself, how did this woman get so many chances with me?

◆

A few months later, we gathered at my friend Gail's apartment on the Upper West Side to remember my mother with a gentle, thoughtful party that would not have been possible when she was alive. She'd have disrupted our efforts, been inappropriate, made a scene, canceling the very impulse that had created this evening.

My mother had died on my father's birthday, an irony not lost on anyone in the room. After thirty-five years of separation she had once again gotten his attention and divided mine. My father had traveled to Rhinebeck, in upstate New York, where I was living, to spend his birthday with me. This had become a tradition since my divorce and his admission that his second marriage was not what he'd hoped for. I had been worried that his visit would conflict with my mother's current hospitalization and the trips to New York I had to make. We hadn't imagined I'd be at her bedside on his birthday.

Her death just on his day deepened the Daddy's-girl guilt I'd felt since my teens when she'd become crazier and crazier. In the late 1950s, when I was eighteen, her life was a full-blown emergency, with midnight ambulance rides to psychiatric wards, with shock treatments crudely given and medication management years away. Because my father asked for my help, I went on those rides with him. When he left, I became her unofficial guardian, at twenty-two, and went on those rides alone.

Not until I was way past the agoraphobia that hit me in my thirties could I link the condition to those dramas with my mother, to the sanatoriums I dutifully visited, unable to admit to the terror and guilt they provoked; of being like her—or the survivor guilt of being *not* like her.

◆

When my husband and I moved out of Manhattan, the phone, which had always been her weapon, became even more powerful. Several times a day she could reach across the river to Brooklyn and invade our brownstone, in which I was somehow raising our little boy. Over the wires came pleas and demands peppered with attacks. I never drew the line, because I didn't know where the line was. My mother had entangled me, drawing me close and banishing me with the speed of light. I kept coming back, ever hopeful for reunion. I didn't suffer in silence. All my long-listening friends knew the score and knew I swung between longing and fury.

Whenever I was tempted to walk away, as my father had, I was drawn back by the binding question: What was illness, what was my mother? Not all manic-depressives are as mean as my mother could be, just as not all alcoholics are mean drunks. For fifty years I've been haunted by the debate. I'm told that in the psychiatric community, the vote is still out on illness and character.

◆

In lieu of a funeral, we were a tiny group, remembering her in an informal way. My son, Nicholas, a new college graduate, had flown in from L.A.; there were a few friends and two male cousins. My mother's friends had fled years before. The lamplight glowed against yellow walls, and the ficus tree twinkled with its year-round Christmas tree lights. By this first week of November, dusty autumn leaves were curled between parked cars, afternoons were shorter.

My friend Gail's living room was a safe place in which to remember such an unsafe person. This woman, who had signed her letters to me at summer camp "Bea" and then, in parentheses, "Mother," had finally died as a result of a botched procedure at New York Hospital, where "accidental" death was becoming less of a surprise. Andy Warhol had led the way, and most recently, the young daughter of a famous television producer had died unnecessarily.

My mother, an inveterate snob, would have been gratified to be in such illustrious company. Identifying with the finer things had been a lifelong preoccupation: embossing cloverleafs on butter pats no matter how disheveled or unsanitary her kitchen, holding one white glove when the other had gone missing. Despite her helter-skelter presentation, she was undeniably a pretty woman. In their early days, my father would boast that Bea had been a dead ringer for Mary Astor, Humphrey Bogart's costar in *The Maltese Falcon*. I didn't know who Mary Astor was then, but from his bright tone I could tell that was really something. I got the idea that they'd had a madcap 1930s romance, like the ones I saw in movies at the Museum of Modern Art.

✦

My mother never lost her will to make sure you knew her worth, although that very impulse was the giveaway to her bottomless insecurity. When she was introduced to my fiancé, in the director's office of the mental institution to which she'd been committed, she made sure he knew that in better days she'd sailed to France on the *Liberté*. It would take ten more years for her to tell him, in hushed tones, that she wished he'd known her before all this had happened to her. She never did acknowledge to me that there had been a *before* and an *after,* never once admitted to the manic-depressive diagnosis her doctors had made in a vain attempt to treat the illness that entrapped her. And never asked why I had stopped coming into the city alone, had stopped working, was staying so close to home.

✦

That evening, *recalling* Bea was what we were doing because *celebrating* her would have been hypocritical. She'd been too much trouble, and my friends knew it and were there for me, not because of their affection for her. Still, my childhood friend Wendy spoke as one painter to another: "Bea couldn't organize a linen closet, we know that. But she could organize a painting."

Wendy's recognition of my mother's talent hit hard. I'd never been able to hang much of her work in any of our houses, the ones with my husband and son and now the one I lived in alone.

In this inviting room, where color and shape felt deliberate, her violent, accidental death seemed impossible. We passed the smoked salmon and poured the wine. Another friend from our Greenwich Village years spoke up. Toni smiled her shy, gorgeous smile and said quietly, "I always envied Linda. I loved going over to her house on Sunday afternoons. Her father would be making spaghetti sauce, and her mother would have everything out on the table for decorating white mugs. She showed us how to paint the mugs, to make birds and flowers . . . the dog was there, there was a lot going on. I was happy to be in the middle of all that life."

For an instant, Toni's rendition of our household took my breath away. How had I not seen all that, even years later? Why couldn't I have said that, given my mother that?

Nicholas raised his glass and looked at each of us. He began evenly, "It seemed as if my grandmother drew a magic circle"—until his voice broke—"around me. She never went after me the way she treated my mom. She seemed interested in me, always wanted to read to me when I was little. She even remembered odd details, like what position I was playing in Little League."

A few days later, after my son and my father had left, I went to empty her studio apartment, the command post of my terrorizing, terrified mother. She had lived alone on Seventy-second Street and First Avenue for thirty years. Long before ADD entered the language, my mother had a knack for layering her rooms, her dresser drawers, the refrigerator. As her one-room apartment became more and more alarming, the floor-to-ceiling paintings, in amazing colors, spoke of her real priorities.

Without being asked, Gail came to help clear the apartment. With kindness and firmness she pressed on, not allowing me the frozen reverie I was courting each time I picked up an object and held it to the light. She reminded me that I needed to get back to my new life in the country, to the house where I'd hoped to resume writing the book that hadn't been born but also hadn't died, and to my dogs who anchored me with their promise to be forever kids.

At the end of the day, with all the blue trash bags piled in the corridor, Gail stopped short, held the door ajar, and surveyed the empty room.

"We need a ceremony. We need ritual to make an ending."

I was light-headed and silent. No good words came from me. She put her hand on my arm and said quietly, "Good-bye, apartment. Good-bye, Bea. You are remembered."

◆

That last afternoon in the hospital, I had been torn between staying with her and returning to my father, who was waiting in Rhinebeck. It had become clear that my mother would not make another of her miraculous comebacks; the chief resident admitted that keeping her on the ventilator was a futile exercise. With my agreement, it would be removed in the morning, when I could be with her. Her wrists would be untied. There was a chance she might speak before her breath ran out, that I would be able to get close to her without all the tubes between us.

As the train carried me back along the Hudson, the sun was sinking. She's dying, I thought, right now as the sun goes down. I entertained the idea for a few minutes and then dismissed the image as too melodramatic. In the morning I planned to be on the train again, heading back to her. A few weeks before, she'd stretched out a bony arm and whispered, "You are my lifeline." I'd nodded but had not taken her hand or moved one inch closer to the sofa where she was encamped, awaiting the next shift of home health aids, women she tormented, women who tormented her.

When the hospital called, just a few hours later, to report the details of her death, it turned out I *had* been on the train at that time. The wallop of the news, the wash of nausea, and the weakness in my legs made me feel childlike (at fifty-three) and had me asking my father if I should return to see her body, to say good-bye. "What's the point?" he asked. "You've just been there today." When you ask the wrong person for advice, the consequences are etched. Instead of being relieved by her death, I compulsively re-created images of that last week. I didn't let myself forget the grotesque apparatus filling her mouth, breathing for her but silencing the woman for whom words were projectiles. Her wrists had been tethered; I imagined the intern unknowingly piercing her jugular as he changed the catheter in her throat, filling her lungs with blood. When the mistake was discovered, a surgeon was summoned to insert a needle to clear the blood, but instead he induced the shock that killed her.

Unable to have helped her, to change anything, it seemed I still needed to pay. Although she was dead, I was compelled to keep the events indelible. I knew the hospital body bags were bright blue, like the bags we'd used to empty her apartment. Seized with regret at not having gone to see her one more time, I focused on the color she was carried away in.

Without ritual, I was on the loose, making things up to *do* something. When I had turned my back on my mother, blood had filled her lungs. That's how I imagined her, that's what I was memorizing. Unable to use the time and space her death brought, I still jumped at the sound of the phone. We weren't done, after all. When she'd become lost to me, I'd made sure I was lost to her. Ever since my freshman year of college, when her hospitalizations had begun, I'd gravitated to two new friends whose mothers had died of cancer. Secretly, I began describing myself as *motherless*, as well.

Now that she was gone, my mother was manageable. Without her endless drama, in the raw stillness of an upstate winter, I could go back.

✦

When we walk home from school, with my mother's arms filled with packages and my jaws aching from the Dubble Bubble gum I've been given, as a treat and a lure, for the artistic detour she wanted to make into the Whitney Museum, I chatter my way up Eighth Street. Telling about dodgeball, about not getting Out until the end of the game, about how the art teacher sent me out of the room for talking, for talking!

"Pearl pinched my arm when she took me out of Art. [All our teachers at the Little Red School House were called by their first names.] She's a boss, a real meany."

I wait to see if she's listening. Her eyes don't meet mine, even for a flash. I keep going as if *more* will get her attention. "What's wrong with talking and painting? Lunch was yucky anyway."

She's still not looking down at me as we climb the marble staircase of the old Whitney mansion. I prattle more softly, becoming quiet under the gauzy haze streaming from the skylights. We are often the only two people in the gallery. It is as if I am there without a grown-up.

The silence, the soft light, and not having her attention make me feel lonely, but because she is so peaceful, I am also relieved. Her usual sharp, sudden movements are slowed, and she seems calm as we glide from one painting to another. I hear the rain beating on the skylight; everything is so muted I could be dreaming there with my mother, who could disappear into the paintings. She stares at the pictures in the same way she will, years later, stare into a mirror when she is depressed, nearly catatonic. Deep in and far away.

✦

When a squall approaches, when this same person can turn the blouse department at Lord & Taylor into scorched earth or shame me on the Fifth Avenue bus when she barks to a crescendo, I am not her girl, her *daughter*. I couldn't know I long for her, want to fix her, as much as I want to run from her. And so I console myself with my magical ability to disappear. If she raves on, the locomotive on the loose, I have the power to detach from the tumult. As the bus heads toward our stop on Tenth Street, I can pretend to be gone, to become invisible.

✦

Although I am four, my mother and I sometimes pretend I am still a baby so she can sing her rendition of Brahms's Lullaby. I lie on my stomach in the dark and feel her hand lightly patting my back as she sings in her perfectly pitched voice. This is not the crazy voice that can snarl or rise in gasps of rage, this is the soft tone of another woman, another mother. As she pats my back in tentative irregular beats, she also touches my hair, so lightly that I can't be sure it's happening, but when I am grown and even middle-aged, a light touch on the back of my head, ruffling my hair, can bring me to tears.

When she leaves the door ajar, so I can see the hall light, I pretend to be asleep so that she will know she has taken me there with her singing. I don't expect the snarling mother to reappear because I still believe the scary woman is accidental and the real one, the soft mother, will be there in the morning.

✦

The winter I am seven, my best friend is Janey Brodman, whose parents care about being Jewish. My parents have ironed themselves out of their Jewish immigrant origins and have Christmas

trees. Except this year, when my father announces, without explanation, that there will be no tree. My mother takes my side
and argues for a tree all through supper.

The next day, as we come down Eighth Street at dusk, with
shop lights casting color on the hard-packed snow, she impul-
sively buys a small fat spruce from the Italian with the truck.
This time my father isn't with us, to carry it home across his
shoulder. My mother pays quickly, as if she is buying on the
black market, and tells me to pick up the top as she lifts the
trunk. Suddenly Janey's mother appears, greeting us, beaming.
My mother smiles back, grasping the tree with a gloved hand,
blithely behaving as if there are no branches bobbing behind
her and no small girl holding tight with mittens sticky with
sap. I don't say a word. I am in awe of my mother's pluck, to
have stood up to my father, who was the boss in those days, to
get the tree, and now to face Mrs. Brodman red-handed.

✦

The Loews movie theater is our Egyptian palace of burnished
brass, right there on Sheridan Square. When my mother lets
me play hooky on a school day and we sit together on red velvet in the darkness, we are in perfect collaboration: conspira-
tors against the regular world of homework and housework.
Every time we are at the movies together, there is the exquisite
pleasure of the lights dimming, the crackle of cellophane as I
open the box of chewy jelly Dots. This moment of transport,
out of this world, into the movie. Me and my mom. And Betty
Grable.

✦

The long-lost rays of stillness, of early morning or western
light. Edward Hopper's light, in which I see early times with
my parents. The three of us digging into sandwiches on plaid
picnic blankets, our dachshund, Cokey, excited to be on grass.

I want to believe I am revisiting contentment. This is an un-verifiable premise, tantalizing, possible.

◆

In the years that followed my mother's death, I was left in a void. She had been my life's work. This woman I'd allowed to be the interrupter was gone. There was all that time and space I'd wanted but now couldn't use. I was light-headed and dizzy, having balance problems and hints of the old agoraphobia. But because my nature wants to come to the party, I could also let go of my gloom. Slowly I discovered that concentrating on what interested me rather than on what worried me was a reliable way to change the channels. I was relieved to be writing again, to find I could be seduced by work instead of tumult.

Most days, I am able to admit to my old addiction to drama and chaos *and* remain committed to giving it up. Forgo it completely? Not a chance. But the prospect of doing these last years differently continues to be intriguing. My relationship with my mother keeps getting better and better. I can approach her now and take from the family album what I need. I can even return to the mischievous little girl who runs wildly around the garden as her mother holds out a sweater, insisting on protection from the evening chill. I am shrieking with glee as I skip just ahead of her, proud of my speed, and happy to be fooling around with my mom.

ABOUT LINDA GRAVENSON

Linda Gravenson was raised in New York's Greenwich Village. After graduating from Sarah Lawrence College, she was a researcher, editor, and freelance writer for *Esquire,* Fawcett Publications, and other magazines, writing pieces on Philip Roth, Lotte Lenya, Günter Grass, and Anthony Quinn, among others. She was the American correspondent for the German monthly *Twen* and spent several years in West Berlin. When Linda returned to New York, she continued freelance editing and writing. Her son, Nick, introduced her to Ojai, California, where she lives part of the year. The rest is spent in New York's Hudson Valley. In both places, she is a freelance editor and conducts writing workshops. She is working on a memoir.

E-mail: lsguethe@aol.com

Jessie Curtis

My 1968

Susan Schneider

When I heard that an event marking the fortieth anniversary of the 1968 Columbia student strike was going to take place on the campus, I knew I had to go. A dropout from a women's college in Westchester with a boyfriend at Columbia and an acquaintanceship with one of the strike leaders, I'd missed the strike itself. But at that time I'd been poised to begin my own political odyssey into a sect of left-wing politics that took me to some strange places.

Why revisit that time? My life since then has not followed that path. I'm a women's magazine editor, not a community organizer or a teacher or someone who attempts to do the world some good. Lately I've been trying to put the pieces of my life together. How did I get from my particular 1968 to this particular 2008? I want to understand myself—I always did, but now more than ever.

This evening, as I enter the university auditorium for the "multimedia event," the Buffalo Springfield song "For What It's Worth" is playing full blast: "It's time we stop, hey, what's that sound, everybody look what's going down." The scene, the mood, are set.

On large screens at the front of the room, grainy black-and-white footage shows students sitting with their legs dangling from the windows of Columbia's mausoleum-like buildings; kids facing cops and hordes of angry, clean-shaven athletes; black students standing side by side; kids with bullhorns, guitars, signs. It was a huge, unprecedented protest against the university's ties to the Department of Defense as well as its plans to build a gym in Harlem's Morningside Park.

The "children"—now gray-haired, ordinary-looking people— have returned to the scene, welcomed back by the university. (How times have changed!) The mood is not exactly festive, certainly not fierce, but in the hugs and greetings there is an unspoken understanding: we were there.

For me, my boyfriend's roommate, Sam, remains the face of the strike. I watch him flickering hugely on the screen, slender and boyish, forever speaking into the bullhorn with unambiguous passion, certitude—I want to see what's become of him.

We're all sixty—or older. We've had lives, jobs, marriages, families, divorces, accountants, hairstylists, dentists, and so forth. After the 1960s were over, I stumbled on, shocked by the end of life as I knew it, getting a job at a women's magazine, becoming a rising star for about two minutes in the 1980s, by the 1990s a single mother ricocheting from magazine to magazine, watching in dismay as the models and my colleagues got younger and younger, and now wondering if I'm shortly to have the honor of becoming the world's oldest living women's magazine editor.

In spite of the blurriness of the old footage, or maybe because of it, everyone looks so beautiful! Faces fresh and soft, sweet as flower petals, newly born, they look to me. In 1968, Sam was ruddy and bearded, with a lock of hair that brushed his forehead, his eyes a burning blue. He was so brilliant. So intense. I remember him spending a lot of time at his desk, reading in a little circle of lamplight. I was in awe.

The campus had separated into warring male tribes, the Jocks and the Pukes. The Puke, a scraggly-bearded guy in a flannel shirt and ill-fitting blue jeans, had a love of competitive debate and an awe-inspiring grip on all kinds of philosophical and social theories. The Jock, a showered, clean-cut athlete slash thug, liked to beat up Pukes just because. Needless to say, Pukes were anti-war; Jocks were pro-war. Also, needless to say, only Pukes will be here tonight. I remember the day that Sam, a consummate Puke, shaved off his beard; seeing me gaping at him, he explained that he was off to debate the war in the enemy camp—a frat house—and he wanted the focus to be on the issues, not the animosities. My awe threatened to explode into hero worship.

The evening begins. "It was a circus, a spectacle," one man recounts, "everybody yelling, milling around, but if you looked closely you saw the anger and the hurt—our university was contributing to the war and apartheid and the gym. Our university was in the center of a world gone wrong." As I listen, I am freshly outraged at venal Columbia contracting with the government to do research on napalm. An African-American man opens up about what happened once the black students heard the cops were on the way: "I knew that whatever was coming, I could do it because we stood together." Another man in this cohort describes how he felt upon learning that after Columbia built its gym in Harlem's Morningside Park, it intended to allow the black community to enter—through the back door. He says he had a sickening feeling in the pit of his stomach, and he can still feel it today. Someone else speaks about his participation in the strike as a result of being from a family killed in the Holocaust: "Our university was building a segregated gym in a public park—in our names. I couldn't be silent. I was haunted by the thought of being a good German." This was who we were.

◆

In the snow-white suburbs of the 1950s, where my family had landed when my father was hired to teach at a blue-blood women's college, I was a true oddball. My father was an intellectual leftist, my parents were nonreligious Jews, and I was one of two Jewish children in the local elementary school. Somehow the kids suspected. "Are you Jewish?" I was asked numerous times. No, I said. I didn't have the slightest idea what it meant to be Jewish or why, apparently, it was bad. Then one day, in an episode of Stockholm syndrome, I said, "I'm Presbyterian." (I knew they were Presbyterians, whatever that was.) But my tormentors were no fools; they interrogated my sister, a kindergartner, because they knew she was too little not to tell the truth. "We're Jewish," piped little Nancy. I was cornered for the kill.

Cornered was the operative word for all of us who didn't fit in. Our school had three black children, who lived in the servant neighborhood. I remember one shy little girl named Bernice. In music class when we sang "Ole Black Joe," the kids would change it to "Ole Black Bernice." I remember that she sat stoically bearing the abuse.

The black children tried to fade out of sight. I tried to pass. But when my parents heard I was claiming to be a Presbyterian, my father came to my room, made a fist, and pointed at me. "You're not good enough to be a Jew!" he shouted. I was nine years old.

Eventually I came to ally myself with everyone who suffered. As the civil rights movement began, I watched it play out on TV, sobbing as little girls were blown up in church or spat on and screamed at as they tried to go to school.

Selma, Alabama, happened when I was fifteen. Students from my father's college were planning a march along the road between two suburban towns. I begged to go, and somehow my parents allowed me to. As we held up our handmade signs calling for an end to segregation, cars passed, slowed, people stared, and I felt a sense of being exposed—the real me—that was both liberating and ominous. My parents, citing the possibility of violence, wouldn't let me attend the March on Washington. I didn't understand why they were afraid.

◆

Now an African-American man explains why his cohort insisted that the white students leave Hamilton Hall to them—they knew they had more to lose and couldn't risk the possible undisciplined behavior of white students, who didn't know how deadly serious this whole thing could turn out. The black kids—kids only chronologically—did not want to draw attention for the wrong reasons.

A former Barnard student recalls that the all-male SDS leadership had been arrogant toward women. Another recalls how the college had locked its iron gates to "protect," or perhaps imprison, its female students against what was happening across the street at Columbia. "At Barnard, we still had tea in the afternoon," she adds. Another woman describes her anxieties about joining the building takeover. Should she take her Italian book? Off she went and by the end of the night had cut up her yellow Villager cable-knit sweater into eye shields for tear gas.

In 1968, many were swept along with events—these were the accidental activists, as someone puts it—"My friends and I were majoring in sex, drugs, and rock 'n' roll," one man says— but somehow they became embroiled with the crowd heading over to the gym construction site in Morningside Park. There one boy lost his glasses, turned to go back, and got arrested. The photo, now projected on the screen overhead, was iconic: long-haired rebel student fights with cops. But I can see that beneath his floppy bangs the boy was squinting and panicking, as any nearsighted person does when he can't find his glasses. The boy left Columbia, joined a commune for a while, and a couple years later shot himself in a cornfield. As this tale is told, a collective sigh wafts through the auditorium.

✦

I was never an accidental activist—my choices were so clear that they didn't even feel like choices. I was seething with pain and rage at cruelty and injustice. My conscience was fully awake and throbbing with energy. I could not understand how people could go about their daily lives when the cops were shooting black people in the ghettos and soldiers were killing and dying in Vietnam.

"You can't fight against oppression part of the time, you have to do it all of the time." At some point Sam said this to me, and in the fall of 1967 it became my mantra. That and "Less talk, more action." Going to class in an unjust world was obscene. I had to *live* my politics; I needed to be wherever things were happening. By March 1968 I had dropped out, found I really had nowhere to go, and ended up back home with my parents, thereby missing the April strike.

I picked up my father's *New York Times* on the day that Sam's photo appeared on the front page. Something incredible had happened at Columbia—without me. I sat there with a sinking heart, but it sent me out of the house for good.

After the strike, Sam was thrown out of Columbia, and in 1970 he helped found the Weathermen. By then I was living in upstate New York and had joined the rival Progressive Labor Party. The Weather people, so tough and sexy in their leather clothes and combat boots, with their martial arts and gut checks, terrified me. PL was far less cool. We dressed like "the people," in cheap shift dresses or polyester pants and shirts, had working-class jobs, and considered ourselves "serious" revolutionaries, unlike youth-culture revolutionaries.

One day, driving my car to a meeting, I pulled over, laid my head on the wheel, and sobbed, knowing I'd never be a good enough revolutionary. I *knew* I'd never do anything important enough to make any difference.

I went on to become a factory organizer, the favorite of the leader of our cell, Cora, a pale, blind redheaded woman married to a man who worked the night shift in a meatpacking plant. In her house we ate huge potluck meals at a dining room table presided over by an iconic portrait of Chairman Mao wearing a long tunic and holding up *The Little Red Book*. I had my own *Little Red Book*. Cora ruled us children with an iron hand. She presided over criticism/self-criticism meetings in which we all were made very aware of our weaknesses. Why had I not invited anyone from work to the PL picnic the week before? How many PL newspapers had we, as a collective, sold this month, and who was falling down on the job? At her urging, some people in the collective married each other and started families.

I loved Cora, her gruffness, her generosity—she was a woman who took in children, whether college dropouts or the children of needy neighborhood women. One day people from Boston PL showed up and called an emergency meeting. While Cora sat in her rocking chair, listening with the special, absolute stillness of the blind, they accused her of revisionism and purged her from the party. Why did this happen? How did Boston PL just happen to show up to kick Cora's ass? I never knew.

Now my attention is drawn to a white-bearded, round-shouldered man whose stomach schlumps over his belt. Several men quickly cluster around him. It's Sam! Above him, projected on the screen, stands the young man with the light in his eyes, while the new old Sam shares hugs, with much back patting that resembles condolences.

Condolences. Is this all that's left? The evening has become depressing. That time was like a flame that burned violently for a few moments and whooshed out. I crash-landed, returned to New York City, and finished college. Reality settled in, and I got a job, becoming an accidental editor.

What followed were twists and turns on the career path, a marriage, a baby, a divorce, and single motherhood. When the Iraq War began, my daughter, India, was fifteen, and we went to the huge demonstration at the United Nations. It was thrilling in that old, sweet way, when you felt, through the magic of the laughing, shouting, singing crowd, that the forces of good would overcome everything. India cried, "Mom, we *can* make a difference!" At that moment my heart broke, because I realized I still so much want that to be true, and now I wanted it to be true for her as well. But I just didn't believe it anymore.

One day I got a call from the police while I was at work. I was told to come pick India up at the precinct station. She and some other people had lain down on Fifth Avenue to protest the war.

"You're one of the mothers?" sneered the cop at the desk. Invoking the name of Dr. Martin Luther King, Jr., I told him that civil disobedience had a long and distinguished history in our country. He shut his trap, knowing he couldn't say anything bad about Dr. King. (Some things have changed!) But I was actually furious at India for cutting school and endangering herself. Recently she told me she'd been more scared of me than the cops.

◆

Things have become more complicated; I'm not the person I once was, who'd think nothing of getting arrested at a demonstration. I've changed, but so has the world. I felt that the demonstrations and lie-downs on Fifth Avenue were hollow imitations—that there was no fire, no real substance behind the style. I wasn't surprised when it all petered out.

Then, during the presidential campaign, something happens to change my feelings. I find myself volunteering, along with God only knows how many other people, to spend Saturdays calling voters in Ohio, Pennsylvania, and North Carolina. We sit in an Upper West Side apartment, huddling over our cell phones and lists. We make forty or fifty calls a day, reaching answering machines and disconnected numbers and maybe four or five actual living people each. I feel exhilarated and energized about being political again—the first time in forty years!

One day I have a bad moment. How disappointing that each of us as individuals can do so little. Talking to four or five people in a distant state on a Saturday afternoon seems so paltry when you look at everything that needs to change.

But finally comes election night—and the world suddenly seems fresh and alive. My friends are dancing around the TV; outside, people are screaming and blowing their horns with wild abandon. The pieces fall into place: my cell phone calls were part of something so much bigger than I was that I couldn't even see it. Now I see where my 1968 fits in—our generation, for all our mistakes and youthful egoism, was on track. I think about my own child, and I'm thrilled to know she has the capacity to feel injustice and a desire to right the wrongs—and to know that she got it from somewhere (meaning me!). On election night I feel that, from my anti-war days to this moment, I've done what I could to make a better world. My contributions don't have to be glorious, they just have to be good. And whether it's making forty phone calls or raising a child who has goodness in her, I've done my bit.

ABOUT SUSAN SCHNEIDER

Susan Schneider has written for and edited women's magazines for longer than she cares to remember. Once upon a time she was *Mademoiselle*'s fiction editor, as well as a fiction editor for *Redbook*. Her work as a fiction editor was twice nominated for a National Magazine Award in Fiction. She also used to write the monthly column "The Intelligent Woman's Guide to Sex" for *Mademoiselle*. Her articles and essays have appeared in *McCall's*, *Lear's*, *Child*, and *Sesame Street Parents*, among many other periodicals both extant and defunct. Her essays for *Victoria* magazine were collected in a recently reissued volume entitled *The Quiet Center*, an anthology of women's writing. She cowrote two nonfiction books on relationships between women and men. All she really wants to do now is garden, write fiction, and hang out with her beloved daughter, India, and their two cats.

Sedat Pakay

Woman with a Pink

Elizabeth Frank

When I think about aging and loss, three old women I know come to mind. Let me start with K. She is in her late seventies. An American, she has lived for nearly fifty years in a large city in Europe. For a long time she had what she once described to me without regret as a "second-tier" career as a pianist. It was second-tier because she chose, very consciously, to devote herself to her husband, a composer, and her two children, who are now grown up and living in the United States. On their twentieth anniversary, her husband informed her that he had made a great mistake in marrying her, that as a man of genius he deserved to have love affairs with more interesting women, and that he thenceforth required her to vacate the marital premises on Thursday evenings so that he could entertain a lady friend undisturbed. For a couple of bizarre weeks, K. actually complied with this barbaric arrangement and then, coming to her senses, told her husband to move out and get an apartment of his own, which he did. They thus separated, though not legally, and never divorced. K. remained a valuable asset to her husband's career and often played his music when she gave concerts. Although arthritis eventually stopped her from playing in public, she continued to set up performances for his music and to negotiate his publishing deals.

Several years went by, and then he had a stroke. By this time her children were on their own and she had sold the house and moved to an apartment. Nevertheless, she supervised her husband's medical care and made daily visits to the hospital. Often his lady friends both past and present would show up at the hospital; as they stood weeping by his bedside, she was very good about not laughing in their faces.

He had another stroke and died, and she has continued to invest time and energy in furthering his posthumous reputation.

She now shares her apartment and her life with a friend who provides her with steadfast devotion. But for K. there has been no getting around the late failure and loss of her marriage. For the greater part of her adult life she loved her husband and gave herself wholly to their life together, only to be told that he had never loved her, never wanted to marry her or to have children. Perhaps hardest of all, those revelations came at a time when she would never again possess that bookended eternity, the thirty or so years between twenty and fifty, when life can flower the way you think it's supposed to and you have energy and looks and a body that obeys your commands.

During the early years of the marriage they had been too poor to travel, and so she decided, after he fled into the arms of his various mistresses, that she would see the world. The question was: How to pay for it? The money she earned giving piano lessons didn't go very far, and far was where she wanted to go. Then she had a brainstorm and got the first of what became a succession of jobs as a pianist on board the luxury cruises she yearned to take. Thus off she went, year after year. "Where did

I go on all my voyages?" she wrote me recently, in reply to my query. "Well, everywhere, with the exception of Japan, Vietnam, and Antarctica. Otherwise, every port a ship stops in, which is why I stopped doing that when I figured out that five times in Papua New Guinea was enough. . . . All the little Indonesian islands, Pitcairn, East Africa, West Africa, Australia from A to Z, meaning Sydney to Darwin, Sydney to Perth, New Zealand, Rarotonga, various Tonga islands, Fiji, India, Pakistan, Aden (ick), Egypt, Israel, Greece—well, the whole Mediterranean including North Africa, the Canary Islands, Madeira, Spain, Portugal, France, Jersey, all around England and Ireland and Scotland, the Orkneys, the Shetlands, all those little islands like Man and the Hebrides, the Azores, St. Helena, all ports in the Baltic Sea from Oslo to Danzig and St. Petersburg, back up the Norwegian coast to Spitzbergen, of course San Francisco and Hong Kong and Canton and then there's South America—all the way around—and Mexico and Costa Rica and everything— everything—in the Caribbean, and have I mentioned Iceland? Or Sumatra, the Celebes, Nias, Bali, Java (well, that's all Indonesia), Kuala Lumpur, Singapore, Sri Lanka when it was still Ceylon, Mauritius, Madagascar, etc. etc. etc. And to think that they actually *paid* me to go to all these places! What a life."

But she is getting old now. An avid sightseer who loves paintings and old churches and Italian landscapes, she has developed macular degeneration. She has aches and pains and is *not* uncomplaining, I'm happy to say. Kvetching, grousing, moaning, and groaning are as second nature to her as enjoying a piece of music or a new book or a particularly good schnitzel. There are days when she will speak about her husband's perfidy with forlorn bafflement and an arsenal of quips, although she has "moved on" as much as any human being can without denying the old attachment in the first place. She realizes that there are some things she's never going to do. I've always wanted her to write her memoirs. But she was a disciplined musical artist and won't write unless she does it in a disciplined way, and she's had it with discipline.

Her voice, lilting and funny, is exactly the same as it was when I first knew her at the age of nine, when she would come to our house in Los Angeles to give me piano lessons. I want her just to go on and on and on, forever. But we both know she won't.

✦

Let's consider someone a little older. B. is now in her mid-eighties. A couple of years ago she broke her hip, but it mended, and she drives and walks and remains vertical and energetic. All her life she played tennis, and I remember as a child coming into the den on a late afternoon and seeing her in a short white skirt and a white shirt and white tennis shoes, her face alive with a luminous freckled suntan, her thick blond shoulder-length hair wavy and glamorous as she sat in the love seat with my mother, each of them with a dry martini. She had an unforgettable laugh, this golden girl, a high-spirited rapid-fire owl's hoot. She was resplendent then with gaiety and health, qualities that cling to her even in old age.

"My memory keeps getting better and better," she says, "but I've outlived all my friends." B.'s husband, a movie director, died about twelve years ago. She lives alone in a house over-looking the Long Island Sound, where she can watch the birds and the change of seasons. Gregarious, elegant, interested in everything, she has lunched for years with a group of women friends she knows from earlier times and places, but many of the women have now died and the circle keeps getting smaller and smaller, a phenomenon she observes, along with every-thing else, with a certain dispassion. She often says, matter-of-factly, "I've had a life of unearned felicity," acknowledging with that present perfect verb that she has more past than future.

She and her husband lived in Europe after World War II,

when it was still a big adventure to do so, and knew lots of interesting and attractive people. She misses her husband very much. They had exquisite marital manners in that they were careful not to inquire too closely into what each understood to be the other's dalliances. Some years after my father died in 1988, I asked B. on a hunch if she had ever "fooled around" with him; my father, who was very fond of her, was a philanderer. She answered straightaway that she had, though I neither inquired about, nor was offered, details. Somehow I had guessed it, and since my mother never found out, and since B. liked and appreciated my mother, and since I learned about it long after both my parents were dead, I simply saw it as an instance of my father's being my father and B.'s being B.

Now, B. was well brought up in an old and wealthy family. She is very well spoken, doesn't use vulgar language, and acts, as we used to say, like a lady. Some years ago, on a dark, cold February day, my cousin and I were sitting with B. in her living room, sipping a glass of wine and talking with her about the old days. Having been friends with our parents, B. had known both of us from early childhood, and even though both my cousin and I are well into middle age, we continue to think of her with that quasi-filial love you can have toward friends of your parents, who, you can't help feeling, still see you, warmly and fondly, as a child.

As the logs crackled in the fireplace and we summoned up gossipy remembrances of characters past, B. suddenly blurted out that she had had "a little encounter" in the fifties with the notorious playboy Aly Khan in the Swiss ski resort we'd just been discussing. With the still thick waves of her blondish white hair framing her radiant face and her blue eyes open very wide with barely suppressed hilarity, she then told us that since neither she nor the prince had thought to bring along a contraceptive at the time, he had decided to practice the gentlemanly art of withdrawal. When he had done so and was contemplating the seed he had just spilled on her belly, he sighed, "Just think: all those millions and millions of little Aly Khans going to waste."

For an instant I couldn't quite believe what I had just heard out of the mouth of eighty-five-year-old B. Then all of us—my cousin and I and B. too—let out a howl. I saw that she was blushing slightly, almost as if she thought she might have offended our delicate ears. But what I felt most powerfully was gratitude, really—gratitude that she had lived so richly and wildly, and how in the midst of making mischief she nevertheless hadn't failed to take note of the prince's self-regard. Moreover, this was not a story you tell to children, particularly the children of your friends. She was letting us know that nostalgia is all very well, but that my cousin and I were grown-ups now and had been so for a long time, and that she was treating us as if we were our parents and not their offspring. The pleasure of both telling and hearing the story depended on the recognition by all three of us of just how far in the past the incident had taken place—and what a rollicking past it had been.

B. remains the proverbial person on whom nothing is lost. It would be neat and tidy if I could also say that she is someone from whom loss itself has taken nothing, but that simply isn't true. Her husband and friends are gone, and there will no doubt be other cruel raids to come. But my wish for her, as for K., is that she just keep going.

✦

My oldest old friend is H. Like B., she was a lifelong friend of my mother's. A great beauty, she was a famous actress in the thirties who willingly gave up her career to devote herself to her husband, a screenwriter who adored her, and to become a domestic genius. By that I mean that she cooked and gardened with passion and skill, gave wonderful parties, and was famous for her warmth and hospitality. She had always painted seriously, but in her seventies she took up the printing of "artists' books"—fine editions of original drawings done by herself to accompany writings by noted authors. She mastered that art as she had all the others. When I was a child, I visited her from time to time with my mother in a plant-filled apartment in West Los Angeles and later in a house in Brentwood whose garden overflowed with exotic flowers as well as row upon row of carefully tended bonsai trees, including a tiny orange tree with real, minuscule oranges. Her bed had carousel horses at the head and the foot, and she often said that a husband and wife should have separate bedrooms.

Now in her nineties, she has cancer and is in pain a good deal of the time. It's hard for her to cook and garden and print, but she does them nevertheless. Her daughter, a widow in her seventies with grown children and a writer, moved in with her, but they soon discovered that they got on each other's nerves and agreed that the daughter should move out again to somewhere nearby. It may be that with age certain illusions die before we do. A mother and daughter who are devoted to each other discover that they can't live together. We get on our parents' nerves, and they get on ours. The recognitions and reversals so necessary in drama don't perhaps happen when we think or hope that they might. Or they bring with them rather stark and unlovely truths. Love can be real and lasting, but it isn't necessarily or infinitely "unconditional." I know someone whose parents lived to their late nineties, and the longer they were together, the more they couldn't stand each other, even though for most of their long years together they had been quite happy. When the wife died at the age of ninety-seven, the husband's final year was a paradise for him of relief and tranquillity.

It seems to me good that H. and her daughter recognized their differences and did something about them. I remember learning in high school biology that irritability is a sign of life. Yeats tells us that it's good to be irritable in old age, to cling tenaciously to one's intractable self. Let's resist, by all means, mute or bitter resignation, having one's daughter move in to wait out the end, arriving at the point where everything is understood and nothing can prick up the needles of one's inner porcupine. Retaining one's vanity and selfishness and crankiness for as long as possible, even being something of a pain in the ass, slams the door in the face of loss when that particular postman keeps ringing the bell.

After a long and mostly happy marriage, H.'s husband died, and for a long time she lived a widow's celibate life, but then she took up with a man with whom she had briefly been in love in her very early twenties, when she was an art student and before she became an actress. He was a widower with grandchildren and kept his own place so that he could remain close to his family but otherwise began spending the better part of the week with H. at her place. I remember hearing from my mother how H., after years of celibate widowhood, had gone out and bought one of those books that tell you how to have sex and was relearning things about positions and interesting variations—things she had assumed were long gone from her life.

For a time she gloried in her love affair. She and the boyfriend had many common interests. But eventually he turned out to be a jerk—self-absorbed, mean, insensitive to the point of callousness. This was a tremendous blow. All her life, H. had been treated by her husband and those who loved her as a star—someone gifted and beautiful and deserving of every extra effort and consideration. But after the first few years of rediscovered romance, the love offered by this man turned out to be such inferior stuff that she was, by the time of his death, reeling from repeated instances of his boorishness. And so, in her early eighties, she had to get over the kind of bad breakup you go through in adolescence or in your twenties or after your first couple of marriages. Still, there was not just something heroic in her fury but also something that spoke of inextinguishable vigor and raging appetite, so much, in fact, that I was reminded of a cartoon I had seen once, perhaps in *The New Yorker,* showing a woman of about ninety-nine hobbling out of a divorce court and swearing "Never again."

Luckily, just about the time of this debacle, H. was approached by a big-shot producer to play a role in a movie that had a major part for an old woman. Other actresses who wanted the part had balked when they were asked to read. Not H. "I'll even audition for you naked!" she said to the producer. She got the part, and millions of people all over the world have seen her beautiful face and been moved by her performance. After my daughter saw the movie, I asked H. to send her a photograph of herself and she did, inscribing it and adding, "Work and dream."

◆

K., B., and H. have been, for me, exemplary. I love them and learn from them and honor their courage and resourcefulness. But are they so rare? When I stop and think about other old women I know, I can't think of a single one who isn't active and energetic. My partner, a Bulgarian with whom I spend the summers in Sofia, told me recently that he had listened to a program on Bulgarian National Radio about old women who go to places where they can dance—both folk dances and dances to old-timey *gradski pesni,* or town songs—sentimental love songs popular in Bulgarian towns, especially Sofia, some fifty and sixty years ago. "These old women are fantastic, really," he told me. "They were interviewing them, and do you know, they all like to dance and sing songs. They are all full of life and"—he searched for a word—"libido!"

That libido isn't necessarily directed at anything or anyone, except life itself. My friends who are old women have taught me something very important: that after a certain point it doesn't matter what's on the report card. Their marriages were good or bad, or good *and* bad. Their kids have grown up, and their lives are working out—or not. Their careers have been successes or failures, or successes some of the time and failures some of the time. Or they haven't had careers. Ambition remains a habit or a joy or a relentless torturer—or just goes away. You do what you can with whatever you have left. A friend's uncle had a devastating stroke that left him almost completely paralyzed. His well-meaning daughter, who had absorbed all the contemporary pieties about letting go and quality of life and health proxies and living wills, decided that it was time to pull the plug and kept asking him to indicate by blinking his eyes if he wanted to be taken off life support. One blink meant yes; two blinks meant no.

He was a two-blink guy and hung on for many more months until his heart gave out.

The earlobe of a woman of ninety I know tore just the other day. "Being ninety is such a nuisance," she said to me over the phone. "In fact, it's a mistake." But she is going to have the earlobe sewn up so that she can continue to wear the little pearl studs she has worn her whole adult life.

✦

Sometime in the late 1940s or early '50s, a group of women whose husbands were all in the movie industry were spending a pleasant afternoon beside a swimming pool. Then a woman they all knew showed up and announced the death of a premature baby who had recently been born to a woman in their circle.

"Oh, God, how awful," said one.

"How terrible," said another.

"That's the worst," said a third.

Then, after a pause, a voice piped up with "Well, you gotta go sometime."

The voice belonged to my mother, Anne Ray Frank. At the home of the American ambassador to Great Britain in London some twenty years later, my mother's dinner partner recognized her name and said, "So you're the author of that infamous remark!" And some fifty years after that poolside afternoon, I was introduced to a movie producer who, learning my parents' names, instantly remembered my mother's line and said it was "the best worst-taste joke I've ever heard."

Anne died of lung cancer in April 1986, at the age of seventy-three. Her story is not like that of my other old women friends. Though she had often said that she wanted to live until the turn of the century, when she would have been eighty-eight, she never stopped smoking. Unlike K., who fought back against her husband's rejection and worked and traveled, Anne never got over the pain of learning about a long-term affair of my father's. For the last twenty-three years of her life, she took to her bed, where, with the help of booze and barbiturates, she managed to be out cold almost every day for perhaps twenty out of the twenty-four hours. My father finally divorced her and married a woman my age. By that time Anne already had emphysema and heart disease. The discovery of the lung cancer was a year or two away; probably those "small cells" of small-cell carcinoma were already budding in her tortured lungs. When it was finally diagnosed, it had already reached her liver. She went through two rounds of chemo, and then a year later the cancer migrated to her bones and her brain and killed her in just a few weeks. She never saw my daughter, who is named for her.

I don't believe—or rather, I am not persuaded—that my mother wanted literally to die, though no doubt her long decline has to be seen at least in part as a form of self-destruction, if not outright suicide. What matters is that she had staked her entire life on romantic love and faithful marriage. When both failed her, she couldn't believe in anything else.

Having had only a high school education, she tried going to college, but as a former radio writer who was very well read, she found freshman comp classes absurd. Going into and out of rehab, she would come back sober and would start thinking again in full unanesthetized consciousness about my father's affair, so sobriety, for her, simply meant endless anguish. She took a cruise to Alaska after my father divorced her and was lonely and bored, though she had nice things to say about seals and walruses. She tried to write her autobiography, which she called "An Old Wife's Tale," and it was full of good things, but she was unable to finish or revise it. Her life narrowed down to a circle of three loyal friends, one of them H. She would leave her bed only when invited to dinner at the homes of these three friends. There she made them laugh, calling my father, who had rejected her sexually many years before, "No-Nookie of the North." Referring once to both his overhanging belly and his prowess with his new young wife, she quipped, "If she can find it, she can have it."

She stopped drinking after she had a heart attack, which occurred on the day she was scheduled to move out of the house and into an apartment (where she would live alone for the first time in her seventy years), and to a very large extent she became once again the person my brothers and I remembered from our childhood—someone all there, still willing to scratch our now grown-up backs, and as free of bullshit as anyone on this earth. During her last year my father visited her all the time. He clearly enjoyed her company much more than his new wife's. But one evening, when she was too tired to keep him amused and wanted simply to watch a little TV and go to sleep, she asked him to leave. He didn't want to go; he was enjoying her company and, even more than her company, his own guilt-assuaging visit. "Look, Mel," she said, "I hate to ruin this death for you, but for now would you please go home!"

To my bafflement and anger, my mother seemed to lack all

of the "inner resources" that my other older women friends possess in such abundance. She had knitted and crocheted and done needlepoint; she had made elaborate mosaics; she read and stayed informed and in the past had worked for the Democratic Party. But one by one, consumed by hurt, she abandoned all of these. She once said to me, "Don't think my life has been a failure. I've had pleasures you've never had and never will have." But to this day I wonder what they were. I know she liked California sunsets and Wil Wright's ice cream and British comedy on TV. A woman of enormous gifts and natural curiosity, she didn't become an artist, take trips, discuss books with a reading group, or do anything consistently except grieve. She was into and out of AA, put off by its insistence on a higher power. "God is an underachiever," she always said.

Our culture loves emergency room drama and despises chronic illness and chronic grief and chronic anything that can't be fixed. She couldn't be fixed. "I'm all out of endorphins," she would say. "I'm running on empty." She could never be made over or reborn. Knowing how impatient most of us are with intractable pain, she withdrew from others and suffered alone in her room because she was incapable of faking what she felt, and what she felt was incurable hurt.

◆

There is a painting in the Metropolitan Museum of Art, *Woman with a Pink*. Painted by Rembrandt in the early 1660s, it is a portrait of a woman well into middle age. The skin of her face is plump but fleshy, faintly mottled, and loosening with incipient decay. "The unidentified woman in this warm but somber portrait," says the museum's online commentary, "offers a pink (or carnation), symbolic of marriage, to her husband in *Man with a Magnifying Glass*," the companion portrait. You can see the crow's-feet around her eyes, but she doesn't yet have double chins, though there's more than a touch of sag to the way the skin hangs on her neck. Why does she hold the pink? Of course we don't know. But if it is "symbolic of marriage," I can't help feeling that she's thinking that she's been married a long, long time and that she's no longer the girl she was as a young bride. As I myself have gotten older, I've begun to suspect that she's looking at the pink with what I know is the secret knowledge all aging women eventually have: that your vagina dries out unless you fill it with estrogen tablets and great goopy shots of Replens; that your pubic hair migrates from your balding pudendum to your face in the form of coarse black wires that require constant plucking if you are not to develop the mustache and eyebrows of a Civil War general; that although there are women who remain sexually active with living partners, for many others in our fifties and sixties who are single, widowed, or divorced, sex with a partner happens rarely or not at all; that still loving male partners may suffer from compromised potency or simple loss of interest, with sexual ambitions that don't go further than a foot rub or a cuddle; and that all too often Viagra and Cialis are one-shot deals that work the first or second time but cannot revive diminished desire. The woman with the pink knows that she may soon have to nurse a husband through a heart attack or a stroke or cancer, diseases to which she too is susceptible, and that one or both of them could develop Alzheimer's disease or some other form of senile dementia; that incontinence and adult diapers and the old age home loom in the diminishing future; that, in short, loss, pain, and extinction are out there, lurking, like the menacing phantom Ginzburg in Bernard Malamud's "Idiots First." The woman looks at the pink and sees that she will never again be a bride or pregnant, and, if she is lucky enough to fall in love, it won't be the way love was when she was younger, because when she was younger she had time. Simple, beautiful, abundant time.

The night before my father's first open-heart surgery, my mother, who was still married to him at the time though she was eleven years into her endless mourning, suddenly started screaming, terrified that he would die the next day on the operating table. Yet it was from her, from that quip about the dead premature baby, from the way she took my brothers and me to her father's funeral and allowed us to see him lying dead in his coffin in a pair of blue pajamas, that I learned of the inevitability and the *reality* of death and loss. She once remarked about my ninety-six-year-old grandmother, "She's too dumb to die. She doesn't know you're supposed to."

My daughter is almost nineteen. I hope that when I am an old woman I can be to her what my old women friends have been to me: vital, energetic, connected to life in every way. But I also want her to know what my mother taught me about the dignity of inconsolable grief, as well as the certainty of death. My mother, with her dry wit and her endless sadness, loved me enough to teach me not to lie to myself about the human heart. And not to think that life lasts forever. She was smart and knew she would have to die one day. And me too: I've gotta go, sometime.

ABOUT ELIZABETH FRANK

Born in Los Angeles, Elizabeth Frank is the author of *Cheat and Charmer,* a novel about Hollywood in the McCarthy era, and *Louise Bogan: A Portrait,* which won the 1986 Pulitzer Prize in Biography. She is the cotranslator of two contemporary Bulgarian novels, *Farewell, Shanghai,* and *Isaac's Torah,* both by Angel Wagenstein, and the author of a monograph on the painter Esteban Vicente as well as a short introduction to Jackson Pollock. Since 1982, she has been a member of the literature faculty at Bard College. She currently lives in New York and spends summers in Sofia, Bulgaria.

Sedat Pakay

Taken Aback

Jenny Allen

I had my health, and then I lost it. Overnight, I turned from a person who took her health entirely for granted, like air, into a person with a terrible disease. This was the kind of disease it was: if I'd heard the same news about someone else, I would have winced and then not asked too many details about it. I wouldn't have wanted to think about it too much. By not too much I mean not at all.

It was shocking to be told I had this terrible disease. It shocked me. I had spent forty-nine years blithely—smugly, even—checking off the No box in the questionnaires you fill out when you see a new doctor: Allergies? Asthma? Heart palpitations? Heart disease? Hepatitis? High blood pressure? Shingles? Shortness of breath? Venereal disease? No, no, no, no, no, no, no, no, and certainly not.

Always sometimes never? Never and never and never.

Could the doctor please just see me now? I don't even need this checkup. I'm just here because I'm conscientious. I'm a responsible adult, I have two children and a husband who need me. Also, I have medical insurance that pays for this visit, so it's no skin off my back anyway. Let's just move this along, shall we?

For no reason at all, being able to check off all those Nos made me feel like a winner. It was my only taste in life of what it felt like to be a very smart student, one of those people who breezes through tests and spends the rest of the exam hour slouching showily at her desk while the other students toil away, one eye on the enemy, the ever-ticking clock. Healthwise, I was in the Gifted and Talented Program. I loved sitting in waiting rooms, check check check check check. Done!

And then I was a person who had to check off Yes in the little box next to Cancer. Below that, next to "If so, what kind?" I had to write "Ovarian." I couldn't believe I had to write that. It seemed unreal. Corny, almost. It felt like a movie. Not a very good movie, maybe something you'd see on the Oxygen Channel, but a fiction, a story. The movie was about someone else, someone very like me, only sick. I could picture the sad ending—the woman would die, leaving her lovely children and the memory of her laughter. (*Flashback:* Jenny, head thrown back, laughing. She looks really fantastic, even with a scarf covering her bald head.) Sometimes picturing the sad ending made me cry real tears, but I felt as if I were crying at a story.

At first, anyway.

I even felt a little sorry for the unsuspecting doctors I was filling out the forms for, at least the ones who were seeing me for something that had nothing remotely to do with cancer— my broken toe, a teeth cleaning. I felt sorry for tossing this bad news at them out of left field, for how they were going to have to arrange their faces to convey sympathy but not alarm (one doctor forgot: "Oh, that's awful!" she said when she looked at the questionnaire), for being the downer of their day.

I both knew I had cancer and thought, if you could call it

thinking, that I somehow didn't have real cancer. I was just cancerish, and it would pass, like the flu. Even as my hair fell out in clumps in the shower, even as other women I met in the waiting room died in the months we were all in treatment. I felt bad for them, but I identified with them as little as if I'd been told they'd been shredded by piranhas. *Poor woman, what a way to go.*

You may have had a similar experience—that sense of ir-reality and of focusing on the unimportant detail in the face of something hideous. *That bone sticking out of my leg—I guess I've taken a tumble skiing out here. I'll just stick it back inside my leg and schuss on down to the bottom. I sure hope they have Band-Aids in the lodge.*

It's called denial, and it's a necessary thing. It keeps us from going berserk. "You never get more than you can handle" goes some phrase I keep hearing around, a phrase I particularly dis-like. People get more than they can handle all the time. That is why they check themselves into mental hospitals or throw themselves off the forty-seventh floor of the Time-Life Build-ing. Denial saw me through chemotherapy, it let me turn away from the scary statistics of my disease, it allowed me not to dwell on the looks I was getting from people I knew. People I knew well looked at me as if they were about to cry; people I knew less well, people I ran into on the street, looked at me as if they'd seen a ghost or a freak. "You look great," they'd say, surprised and relieved, as if they'd expected that the disease, or the chemo, would have turned me a glowing green or covered me with boils. Denial let me take care of my children. It let me lead a life.

But denial gets you only so far. Sooner or later the realness of the horrible facts whacks you in the face, and you're thrown back on your own resources.

It turned out that the realness of the horrible facts whacked me in the face after my two surgeries, after my months of chemotherapy, after all my treatments were done and I was sent home with no discernible cancer.

All I could think about was the microscopic cancer cells lurking in what I now knew to call my abdominal cavity and the discouraging prospects for recurrence. Every time I opened the paper, I opened it to an obituary of some woman who had died of ovarian cancer. Every time I looked at my children, it stopped my breath. I was in anguish about dying and leaving them.

This kind of upset, too, is not uncommon among cancer patients. It's called post-traumatic stress disorder, and the fact that the phrase seems to be used in every sentence in every article in every newspaper every day doesn't mean it doesn't exist. I might have known that ovarian cancer patients suffer from it if I'd Googled "PTSD in ovarian cancer patients." But I didn't. I was too busy having it to do that, I guess. I just thought I was overreacting.

I was in mourning for my life.

I pitied myself.

If you had asked me before I got sick whether I thought life was fair, I would have said, Well, of course not. Of course bad things happen to good people all the time and for no reason. "It's so unfair," people would say about a friend who had been diagnosed with an awful disease, and I would think, What's fair? What would the fair portion of health calamity be for this person? What would I consider a fair health disaster for, say, me and my loved ones? A little arthritis in the knees? Psoriasis? Bad skin? I think I'll take . . . weak nails. Your turn.

"She doesn't deserve this," they would say of a lovely person with a catastrophic illness. As if her disease had been aimed at a bad person but had taken a wrong turn and run her down instead. This outlook seemed childish to me and unbelievably limited. Hadn't these people heard of genocide or tsunamis or plagues? What were they talking about?

I knew bad things happened to good people, many millions of good people. I just didn't think those people would be me. I thought that life would make an exception in my case.

The truth is this: I assumed that, as far as I was concerned, there were doses of misfortune, and I'd already had mine. I'd had a hair-raising childhood, years and years of having the wits scared out of me by an angry mother, and all I wanted—I deserved it! Was it too much to ask?—was the opportunity to pursue happiness. Like people who win money in lawsuits against people who have wrecked their lives in some way, I thought that nothing would ever really make up for that old misery, but a trauma-free middle age would be at least some compensation. Sadness would revisit me, but not for a while. My husband and I would get old and sick and lose friends and experience sorrows we couldn't anticipate. But I'd have this nice safe middle time. My own little window of happiness. My share.

And now I was mired in self-pity.

I wasn't alone, but I felt that way.

I wasn't abandoned, but I acted that way.

I was comfortless.

I quit therapy. I didn't want to Talk About It. I went to one support group and never went back. I told my friends how all the women did at the meeting was talk about two women in the group who were in the hospital "not doing that well." I made the meeting sound funny in a morbid way, a way that I knew would make them agree that support groups would be very bad for me. I drew back when people touched my arm and asked how I was feeling. I declined any invitation to any event at Gilda's Club. I made fun of the woman comic who opened the new-hope-for-ovarian-cancer evening at my local community center by bringing up Gilda Radner and Madeline Kahn. *Who needs this? Give me a break!*

Meanwhile, I cried all the time. I would be standing on the

104 bus and blink, and tears would run down my face, tears that had formed little pools on my lower eyelids. I cried sitting at my computer, I cried on line at the market. I cried walking down Amsterdam Avenue. I got used to pressing the knuckle of each thumb into my eyes to wipe off the tears. I got used to looking down when I walked, so people couldn't see I'd been crying.

I cried standing at my kitchen window, my mouth open and my hands pressed to my cheeks, like the person in the Edvard Munch painting. I tried to cry alone, but once, having had too many glasses of wine already, I cried while having a postdinner glass of wine at a dinner party.

I cried for my sad childhood; I cried for my father leaving when I was seven; I cried for how I had needed my brother and sister, who had gone away to boarding school, leaving me alone with my mother. I cried for how my mother had told me she'd never loved me and how, as a child, I didn't think that other mothers did that. I wanted to think that other mothers did that, I kept hoping that other people's families were like mine, with mothers who looked normal enough on the street but who told you inside your house that they wished you'd never been born, but I doubted it.

I cried because I was going to die just as I was beginning to feel I could be happy.

I thought I would never stop crying. This bloody crying is going to go on forever, I thought. I am going to be anguished and sad until the day I die. Which would be any day now. I even sometimes thought that dying would be better than this kind of sad gray life.

The sadness went on for a good year and a half, two years.

I'm not sure what brought me out of it. I would like to say that I had an epiphany on a Martha's Vineyard beach at sunrise, but I didn't. Drugs helped, I'm sure—I went on something called Celexa, and it brightened my outlook. My body settled down; the deep aches and pinching pains, the side effects of chemo, finally ebbed. A mysterious two-year-long siege of pain that seemed to roam around my abdominal cavity, the very place I was terrified of getting cancer again, went away. The hormones shaken up by my hysterectomy settled down, meaning that I didn't want to kill everyone all the time and that I didn't cry quite as much.

But the cure was probably just that old standby, the passage of time. I wasn't dead yet, and if this trend continued, I was not going to be able to cry over my imminent death. If this trend continued, I might have to consider life after cancer. A life that would upstage what had gone on a long time—a very long time—in the past. I had cried a river over my old life, and maybe I was done.

Lost and Found

Jenny Allen

Tempus fugit, baby. And how. Oh, the cruelty of passport renewal.

The last time they took your passport picture, back in the day, you were okay-looking, even in that ghoulish post office fluorescence. You didn't think you looked okay at the time, but it turns out you were incorrect.

You should have appreciated what you had, the medium-attractive looks you had. Standard rather than "interesting," but, you know, so what. You could have taken pleasure in them! You could have used them to get people to sleep with you and buy you things!

Particularly in light of recent events. Recent events being that your looks seem to have gone away. Just straight down the toity.

This time when they took your passport picture—oy. This time when they took your passport picture and you playfully placed it next to your old passport picture, it was like . . . like what? Like something you're reminded of but can't quite remember.

Oh no, oh God, you've got it now. You know those before-and-after pictures of crystal meth addicts in magazines? How they have the pictures of the addicts before they started snorting crystal meth (attractive) and after (ruined)? And you think, Lord in Heaven, don't these poor people see what they look like? They are so far gone on crystal meth they don't see what's happened to them! That is so sad!

But now that is what your two passport pictures look like

side by side. Before and After. Of course, the After is not precisely as bad as the crystal meth people, but it is more like than not, and just . . . horrifying. All you need to do is not wash your hair for two weeks, and you would look exactly like.

You just didn't see that things had gotten to quite this point. You knew, but you didn't know. You didn't see the extent of the situation. You weren't thinking enough about why Hispanic people now call you Mommy and why the only men who flirt with you are very drunken men who live in subway tunnels.

You used to have gums between your teeth, but now your gums are retreating—like the tide, only never to return. Now you have gums above your upper teeth and below your lower teeth, but not in between your teeth. And there are less and less of the gums that remain. You are literally long in the tooth now, like Mister Ed.

In between your teeth is empty space. That's why you are so often getting a sesame seed or something stuck between your teeth. In order to dislodge the seed you have to shoot some air through that space, directing the air with your tongue. And then it's out, but it's usually on someone's sport coat lapel or fresh white blouse, and you have to flick it off while you both pretend not to be dismayed.

You have so many flossing regrets.

Also, the front of your hair is missing. Like your gums, your hairline is ebbing. It starts further back on your head now. If this trend continues, you are going to look like George Washington or Queen Victoria by next Tuesday. If this trend continues after that, you will be an old lady whose remaining wisps of hair can be rolled onto one roller, and the girl at the beauty parlor will have to spend an hour fluffing out the wisps to fashion a hairdo and then spraying it to death to stay that way. You will look like a dandelion going to seed.

Absent too, now, is your chin line. Your chin used to join your neck via a line that ran horizontally back from tip of chin to throat. Now, instead, that line goes not back but straight down from your chin to the two little bony knobs at the base of your throat. You have the profile of a bullfrog.

When did your lips turn the same color as your face? When did it happen that you had to paint your lips with lipstick so it looked as if you had any?

All the contours of your face are getting blurrier, out of focus. You had sort of counted on getting into sharper focus as you got older, so that you would be all lines, in a good way— cheekbone line, jawline. A Myrna Loy type. Now you see you are going to be more of a Shirley Booth type. A doughy type. A puffy type. A type that looks like she drinks too much, even if you gave it up. Why give it up if you're going to look like this anyway?

For that matter, if you're going to look like this anyway, you could have been taking drugs all these years and walking around in a total, fantastic, irresponsible stupor. You could have not filed your taxes, slept until three, ordered in. You could have just tossed the dirty cat food cans right into the regular trash instead of rinsing them out, instead of having to touch those stubborn pieces of disgusting cat food that cling to the side of the can and placing them in the recycling bin. You could have not signed up for trick-or-treaters at your apartment door on Halloween.

My God, you could have skipped Curriculum Night!

No, no, mustn't dwell on the might-have-beens. That way lies self-pity.

You're just never going to get your passport renewed again. You will travel only to places that you don't need a passport to go to. You can visit Chicago. Chicago is a lot of fun. Also, if you stay stateside, think how great it will be not having to learn the money. You won't have to try to remember how many francs or yen or blutties make a dollar; or whether those wee coins, the ones that look like dimes, equal twenty dollars or one; or why the gilded, most important-looking paper bills of the country's currency are worth merely a ha'penny; or why 332,000 of them make a dollar. No need to know that, due to a money misunderstanding on your part, you just paid fifty-seven dollars for a banana.

Meanwhile, you can hope. You can make a wish. Your wish is that if the looks you lose find somebody else—some yet-to-be-born baby, still a glint in her mother's eye—those looks should go to someone who truly needs them. You do not want your looks going to a person who already has a lot of other things going for her. You do not want them going to a princess, for example. Princesses are out. You also do not want them going to anyone who is a "legacy" anywhere. No legacies.

You want them going to someone for whom they will make a difference, whose life they will change for the better. Who will use them to get people to sleep with her and buy her things, and who will maybe even let them give her a moment's pleasure.

ABOUT JENNY ALLEN

Jenny Allen's articles and essays have appeared in *The New Yorker, Esquire, Vogue,* and many other publications. She has performed her one-woman show, *I Got Sick Then I Got Better,* directed by James Lapine and Darren Katz, at many theaters. She is also the author of *The Long Chalkboard,* a collection of fables for grown-ups, illustrated by her husband, Jules Feiffer. She has two children and lives in New York.

Ave Bonar

Swim Swam Swum

Laura Furman

1. SWIM

Two gifts from my childhood serve me well to this day: I was never told to get my nose out of a book and go outside to play, and I was never taught that swimming was good for me.

The background to our summer mornings was my mother's work in the house and the vegetables and flower beds, and her constant improvement of the old brown-shingled farmhouse where we spent all our free time.

Our afternoons were given over to swimming. The ponds we swam in were bulldozed out of spring-filled fields, and some had islands we could reach, though the islands always looked better from far way. Often, my sister and I swam with another pair of sisters; I was the youngest and felt flattered and flustered when they concentrated their attention on me. My goal in swimming was never to touch the bottom, which, I believed, was covered with a thin shell of duck poop. My parents had attempted such a pond, but it had resulted in a foot of clear, cold spring water covering two feet of silt.

When we swam with the sisters, I was happy to stay in the water and, like them, had to be called out of the water many times before I'd relent, teeth chattering and lips blue, to the sun and the tickle of the lawn under my towel. My swimming, I now see, wasn't really swimming; there were no strokes, no breathing, only existence and kicking to stay afloat, or floating on my back looking at the clouds until one older girl or another tickled me from beneath or pounced from above.

My father tried to teach me to swim, in a pantomime of opposing movement of arms and the turn of the head to air and water. He held his hands in a beautiful point, which is now old-fashioned for swimmers. But somehow in the sunshine, the noise of the other girls, the water, I never got the simplest and basic principles he offered: take air in, push water out. I turned my head, but meaninglessly, and often sputtered my way across the pond, hoping I looked right even if I didn't.

Eventually, my parents built a concrete pool and painted it aqua. The pool was filled with cold spring water that never heated up, no matter how warm the sun. Unfortunately, the pool leaked and on weekends my father drained it to patch the cracks.

My father spent weekdays in New York and took the train to the country every Friday night. His Monday-morning exit announced the five wonderfully purposeless days ahead. But before my mother drove him to the train station in Gladstone on Mondays, my father would take an early-morning dip. He would stand at one end of the pool, measuring his distance and his will, raise his arms in an elegant streamline, and dive in, staying underwater until he reached the opposite end. Then he would emerge, dry himself with a rough, line-dried towel, and walk back into the house, loins girded for work.

2. SWAM

When my mother died, I lost my body and at fourteen no longer ice-skated, took ballet lessons, or ventured into water. When I tried to swim as an adult, I choked up, couldn't put my face into the water, and generally failed to move. Until my early forties, I did no more than dip.

We lived in a small town south of Austin. My husband worked in Austin, and he began taking swim lessons in a pool in North Austin. After a while, I tired of waiting for him to come home and tell me how great swimming was, so I met him there in the evenings. Our teacher nodded when I said I hadn't swum in years. He told me to get into the water so he could observe me, and I felt as though I were walking the plank. My swimming was just as it had been when I was a child; I faked my way halfway down a lane, then began gasping for air. In adulthood there was the addition of panic; when the pool sloped and deepened, I saw blackness and death and had to force myself to keep going past that point. Our teacher was younger than we were, a sturdy, patient person who said we'd work on breathing, and we did. Several nights a week I drove into the city, passing rush hour on the way. By the time the lesson was over, dusk was beginning and the pool lights were turned on. When the summer was over, I could make it from one end of the pool to the other, and my husband and I joined a masters swim team. "Masters" referred to age, and in my case had nothing to do with mastery. He swam in the middle of the pool and I in the far-left lane, the traditional spot for beginners. The team met early, five mornings a week, and slowly and surely my swimming improved. I adored the swimmers who did a smooth butterfly and discovered that the breaststroke felt good.

The next summer my husband and I were waiting to see if we would be allowed to adopt a baby. We were a little too old for most adoption agencies; I was Jewish and he had been born Catholic, another strike against us. Then I wished to stay underwater and had to force myself to rise for air. My desire wasn't for death but to feel safe, contained, and thoughtless, the last being the most important.

3. SWUM

A few summers ago, my son and I spent a month in Ashland, Oregon, and I swam at the Y. The pool was heated to at least 85 degrees, 17 degrees warmer than the water I was used to at home in Austin. Most mornings while I swam back and forth, an aerobics class for elders was taught across the pool. In the next lane an elderly man swam. He was scrawny out of the water but pretty sleek in it, though he didn't kick and neither did any of the other octo- and septuagenarians who swam around me. Their arms worked just fine, but they pulled their legs behind them like baggage. I vowed to keep kicking for as long as I could, as probably they had in their time.

✦

For one reason and then another, I hadn't seen my stepsister and her husband for years, but last June I got to see them. Their house is a block from Lake Champlain. Though it seemed awfully early in the season to swim, my stepbrother-in-law joined me in the water. We stepped onto sand rippled by the movement of the 125-mile-long lake. I hesitated and then immersed myself, moving over a band of sticks and junk washed in toward the shore. The water was clear enough to see through and frigid beneath the surface. My arms didn't linger in the cold. Sunlight penetrated the water. Darkness and cold are a frightening combination, but when you can see into the water, the temperature matters less. Two boats were anchored offshore. If I could get to them, then maybe I'd go beyond them, and maybe farther to a peninsula jutting out into the lake. When I was almost at the first boat, though, I turned onto my back and realized that I didn't know the water or how far out I could swim safely. The hesitation was fatal, and I returned to where Karl stood, waist-deep in the water.

He complimented me on my swimming, and I told him I'd been attending a class all winter, Swim 101, and what I'd been learning, how my left shoulder didn't hurt any longer, how my stroke was improving.

He nodded and said, "Isn't it great to learn?," freeing me from a feeling of not having gone far enough. I'd ventured out, I was learning.

◆

My Swim 101 coach is twenty years younger than I, and from her I've learned a lot about finesse. It turns out that if you have technique, you can do pretty well without other things like strength and youth. The right body position, the correct way of using the hands and arms, of holding the head, and of recognizing when you're tired and how to adjust accordingly, all these can keep you moving. Once when I was dawdling down the lane, the coach said, "Put some integrity in your workout," and this reminder, as much as anything else she's taught me, earned my gratitude.

Even in times of equanimity, the concentration that swimming demands can be its greatest reward for me. To focus on the torso pivoting through water, on the finish when the hand passes the hip, on turning for breath without lifting the head, on counting strokes—all this is to seek to be present. An errant worry destroys the rhythmic meditation. Though the body remains in the water, I've departed and must work to rejoin it.

Now that I'm in my early sixties, swimming is my default, my pleasure, and the place I most often feel love. During a good swim, I concentrate on the edge between the water and the air, turning for breath without stressing my neck, relaxed enough to trust the water to hold me, returning my face to the water as if it and not the air were my natural place to be.

However old I am, I hope to be able to plunge into a body of cold water, see what's underneath, feel the water as it surrounds me and the air as I rise for breath. Each swim is different, however familiar or strange the water. Chlorinated pools 25 yards in length, a dammed-up Hill Country creek, a pond surrounded by lawn and trees, a lake reaching the distant mountains: each swim is different from the last.

If each swim is different, the body in which I swim has its differences also. What's smooth and easy one day is out of reach the next. No amount of knowing one's idiosyncrasies can stop the changes. All I can hope for is to keep swimming in the body of the day. I take this with me as I age. The water will support me. All I have to do is get into it.

ABOUT LAURA FURMAN

Laura Furman was born in Brooklyn, New York, and educated in the New York City public school system and at Bennington College.

Her first story was published in *The New Yorker* in 1976. Her fiction has since appeared in *Yale Review, Epoch, Redbook, Southwest Review, Ploughshares, Antioch Review, Prairie Schooner, American Scholar, Subtropics*, and other magazines. Her books include three collections of stories (*The Glass House, Watch Time Fly, Drinking with the Cook*), two novels (*The Shadow Line, Tuxedo Park*), and a memoir (*Ordinary Paradise*).

She has received fellowships from the Dobie Paisano Project, the Guggenheim Foundation, and, in 2008, the National Endowment for the Arts.

She was the founding editor of *American Short Fiction*, a journal nominated for the National Magazine Award for Fiction while she was editor. In 2002, Ms. Furman became series editor of *The PEN/ O. Henry Prize Stories* (Anchor Books) and selects the twenty prize stories each year. (See www.ohenryprizestories.com.)

She holds the Susan Taylor McDaniel Professorship in Creative Writing at the University of Texas at Austin, where she teaches graduate and undergraduate students in the English Department and the Michener Center for Writers.

Laura Furman lives in Austin, Texas, with her husband and son.

Losing Ground

Gail Godwin

The nurse who is going to appraise me for a "cutting-edge" home care policy is due at one, but when I return home from errands at twelve thirty, her Explorer is parked in the driveway. "I started early in case I got lost!" she calls brightly, sliding down from the driver's seat to help me with my packages. She is a vigorous woman in her prime with a thick mane of blond hair, dressed in loose, colorful clothes.

She accepts a glass of ice water, and we take adjacent seats at the dining table. She unpacks her briefcase and lays out papers. She takes my blood pressure sitting (127/80) and standing (126/90), writes down all my medications (I have lined them up so she can copy right off the labels), and then asks a long list of questions:

"Do you: have frequent headaches, spells of dizziness, stomach pains? Need help climbing stairs, going to the bathroom, shopping? Of course I can see you don't, I've been watching you move, but I have to ask anyway."

Her name is Theresa ("With an 'h.' Take out the 'h,' you take out the heart.") She's a home care nurse herself, works five cases at a time, and conducts these interviews for the insurance company on a part-time basis.

At her request, I offer up my own list of imperfections: pacemaker since 2003 for skipped heartbeats; mother, maternal grandmother, and grandfather had heart disease.

"What about your father?"

"Oh—ah—suicide." Feeling the need to qualify: "But otherwise he was in excellent health."

"Now, some of these questions will seem silly to you, but bear with me. What is your complete name? Address? What state are we in? What is the date? Repeat this series of numbers after me."

Next come multiplications, additions, and subtractions, done in the head.

"Now I'm going to show you a series of ten flash cards. On each card there's a word. I want you to make a sentence with each word. Then in ten minutes I'm going to ask you to recall as many of those words as you can."

1. CHIMNEY. "The chimney is on the house."
2. TABLE. "The table is in the dining room."
3. HARP. "The harp is in the dining room."
4. SALT. "The salt is on the table."

If I can keep all the words under the same roof—even better, think of them all in the same room, I can remember them as part of a picture/story.

5. FLOWER. "The flower is in a vase on the table."
6. TRAIN. "We hear the train passing outside."

7. RING. "The ring is on my finger."
8. MEADOW. "The meadow is outside the window."
9. CARPET. "The carpet is under the table."
10. BOOK. "The book is on the table."

During the ten-minute waiting period, Theresa and I talk about the gambling aspect of these long-term home care policies. "You want to die at home with your familiar views and no horrible institutional lighting and no one taking away your individuality," I say, "but when you're imagining this future, you can't quite get your mind around the fact that you may be much altered from the you who is now projecting this future. You may be blind and unable to see any views or be disturbed by the institutional lighting. You may be gaga enough not to care where you are—or even to know you are an individual. But now you feel that if you can just qualify for the policy and get to stay at home, you'll go on being yourself and everything will be all right." I tell Theresa how antsy my Robert got each time he was in the hospital. "If he could just get back *home*, he felt, he would be safe." I also tell her about my mother's promise to God: "If he would keep her out of a nursing home, she would do everything she could to help the people in them while she was still able to wield some clout, which she did."

"And did he keep his part of the deal?" Theresa is eager to know.

"Yes."

Theresa tells me a bit about her life. Like me, she was in her early twenties when her father committed suicide. Her mother died at forty-nine from undiagnosed kidney cancer. Her husband divorced her after thirty years of marriage, and it hurt. But she believes that everything that happens to her, no matter how painful, has a reason. Whenever she starts fretting about what *might* happen, she makes an effort to "change her flow of thought." It's possible, she says, but you have to work hard at it. She is fifty-six and has five visits to homes per day. She does what nurse things have to be done and coordinates the whole home care plan for each patient. She loves her work.

It would be nice to have someone like Theresa coming here every day in that vaguely imaginable future in which I am, in some vaguely imaginable way, homebound. ("Now, Gail, you need to stop fretting about that right now and change your flow of thought. It takes work, but you can do it! Meanwhile, how about a cup of tea?")

The ten minutes are up. I visualize the scene I have created. First the CHIMNEY on the house, the TABLE on the CARPET in the dining room. The vase with the FLOWER, and the BOOK and the SALT and the RING on the finger of someone at the table. And the MEADOW and the TRAIN passing by outside.

"How many is that?" I ask.

"That's nine. You're doing really well."

"I can't get the tenth. I give up."

"Well, if you're sure, it's—HARP."

"That damned harp! Who keeps a harp in the dining room?"

"But you did exceptionally well. Believe me, you really did."

It turns out she has left her mother-in-law in the Explorer. "But you should have brought her in," I protest. "She could have been sitting on the terrace all this time." "No," explains Theresa, "we're not supposed to do that during the interview. But I'd like to bring her in now." She returns with a tiny, vibrant lady in an ankle-length black skirt, black stockings, and elegant embroidered jacket. ("Theresa bought this for me. She has such good taste.") She praises the house in what sounds like an Irish accent, but no, she's English, met her American husband in Plymouth on D-day, was married for sixty years. "He was wonderful, and I miss him terribly. I'm brokenhearted that my son isn't married to Theresa anymore, but she will always be my daughter."

"Do you need to go to the bathroom, Mother?" Theresa asks.

"Already taken care of!" the old lady replies, mischievously swiveling her eyes toward the woods outside.

I walk them out to the Explorer. "We're going to come back to Woodstock and take you out to lunch," the old lady tells me. Theresa gives me a hug. "You did really, really well, Gail. You are a great lady. No one would ever guess you were seventy-one."

✦

The insurance agent calls me in November. I have been turned down for the policy. A representative of the famous company has read through my medical records for the last five years and decided I was not a good risk. "You fall into that category of people who take *too* good care of themselves," explains the agent, hoping to comfort me. "And the more you keep track of yourself with your doctor, the thicker the paper trail. I'm really sorry about this. Hey, I wanted you to get that policy. That's how I make my living."

First bubbles up the incredulous outrage. The first examination I have ever failed! If I apply to another company, I will have to check the "yes" box next to "Have you ever been turned down for a long-term home care policy?" My record is ruined, and this faceless representative (probably gets a bonus every time she/he roots out a risky applicant) doesn't even know me, hasn't seen the agile way I bop up my front steps laden with packages. Damn it, I got nine out of ten of the memory words, and Theresa says that's exceptional. I just finished a 550-page novel. I lift weights at my gym. I watch my diet.

And so on, staring out the window, until I pass over into what I recognize as the "losing-ground place" in my psyche. I first found myself in this place at the age of eighteen and have been there many times since. It is a place I have learned to pay close attention to.

It is a still, dreary landscape, open and lonely. You look all around you, feel the dry mouth and the pang in your chest, mark your position. You note that you are not in the slightest moved to cry or get drunk or curl up in a ball and seek oblivion. Alertness is all, and you hold on to it for dear life. Alertness is its key attribute. You sense that if you were to stop paying attention you could lose yourself. Though the place is somber, there is plenty of air here; if anything, it's superastringent. And something else is here with you that you might as well welcome because it's all you have. That something else is your fate, as it stands at the moment, with all the other people in it, and you are fixed in its crosshairs.

Many years after that first time, I would come across this passage in a 1954 letter from Dr. Carl Jung to his good friend Father Victor White:

> A "complete" life does not consist in a theoretical completeness, but in the fact that one accepts, without reservation, the particular fatal tissue in which one finds oneself embedded, and that one tries to make sense of it or to create a cosmos from the chaotic mess into which one is born.

I would note the similarities between Jung's regard for his "fatal tissue" and mine for my losing-ground place. But when I was eighteen, I had never heard of Carl Jung. Currently there was no wise person available to me, though there had been several in the past.

We were living in a tract house in Glen Burnie, Maryland, a suburb of Baltimore. There were about two hundred identical houses in the development, which ran alongside a busy highway. Inside our house were my seven-months-pregnant mother; my stepfather, who had been transferred from chain store jobs six times in four years; my two-year-old half sister; and myself, just graduated as salutatorian from Woodrow Wilson High School in Portsmouth, Virginia. Because of our many moves occasioned by my stepfather's transfers, I had attended six high schools in four years: ninth grade at St. Genevieve's, in Asheville, North Carolina, on the full high school scholarship I had won in eighth grade (and forfeited when we left town at the end of ninth grade); tenth grade in Anderson, South Carolina, where my little sister was born; eleventh grade split between Norview High in Norfolk, Virginia, and Woodrow Wilson in Portsmouth; twelfth grade divided between a first semester at Woodrow Wilson, three weeks in a high school in Louisville, where our family lived in a hotel while my stepfather and his latest boss quickly discovered they were not compatible, then the last two months at Glen Burnie High—and finally back to Woodrow Wilson for graduation.

And now summer was beginning and everyone but me seemed to have a future. My mother was expecting her next child in August. My stepfather was starting over in another W. T. Grant store with a brand-new boss he had not yet alienated. That morning I had received a letter from Mother Winters, my eighth-grade teacher at St. Genevieve's, one of the wise figures in my past. She congratulated me on being salutatorian of my class in Portsmouth, asked about my plans for college, and brought me news of some of my classmates at St. Genevieve's. "Pat has received a full scholarship to Duke, Carolyn will be going to Radcliffe, Stuart and Lee to St. Mary's in Raleigh, Sandra to . . ."

Here I stopped reading and underwent my first losing-ground experience.

> You look all around you, feel the dry mouth and the pang
> in the chest, mark your position.

My position. At that time I couldn't hold all of it in a steady glimpse. If I had tried, it might have defeated me. I might have despaired and harmed myself or somebody else. Fifty-three years later, I find it hard to focus steadily on that juncture in my life. In many ways it was the worst of all because I had so little experience or means of escape. Over the course of my writing life, I have lifted pieces from that time and doled them out to this or that character to deal with. But never all the pieces. I won't reveal all the pieces now, only give a broad narrative summary of the situation.

I was eighteen, good-looking, and smart. I loved learning and was disciplined in my study habits. I had developed a persona to get me through our family's frequent moves. This persona was more extroverted than I; she pretended to far more security than I felt. I became a pro at embellishing and editing my history. Whenever I entered a new school, I "went out" for things I knew I was good at: the school paper, the drama club, painting posters and scenery, entering extramural speech competitions—and, of course, getting high grades. I dated lots of boys, was cagey and "hard to get" until each got exasperated and moved on—usually just as I had begun to appreciate him.

That was the outside of things. Inside our various rented domiciles other dramas were playing out. We were not free people. Our embattled breadwinner was frustrated and angry most of the time. There was no money for us except what he doled out of his wallet. There was no going anywhere except where he drove us. All too frequently the mother and the older daughter were backhanded or knocked to the floor for challenging him. The breadwinner "loved" his stepdaughter, who was twelve years younger than he. He confided this to her in unctuous undertones during "drop-bys" to her room. She would wake to find him kneeling beside her bed, his hand taking liberties.

The mother had shed her former confident self. I had come to consciousness knowing a woman who arrived home on the 10 P.M. bus after her wartime job on the newspaper, a woman who taught college and in her spare time typed out love stories she made up in her head and sent off to an agent, who sent back checks for $100. This powerless woman seemed more like someone I was visiting in prison. Only I was in prison with her. She suffered because there was no money to send me to college: she who had earned a master's degree in English! She made phone calls to a private college in Baltimore to see if I could go as a day student. The registrar said a partial scholarship might be arranged, given my academic record, but where was the rest of the money to come from? There *was* no "rest of the money," my stepfather reminded us, as though we were dim-witted. He suggested I take a year off and find a job, "maybe in sales work," and save up for the college next year. He added magnanimously that I could continue to live under his roof free of charge.

That's the way the ground lay, that summer morning in Glen Burnie, when the girl sat cross-legged on the bed, the letter from her old teacher clutched in her fist: Pat to Duke, Carolyn to Radcliffe, Stuart and Lee to St. Mary's . . .

> This is your life, but you may not get to do what you want in it.
> I can't see a way out of this.
> Things will not necessarily get better.

That's the kind of language that speaks to you in the losing-ground place, whether it happens to be oppressive living conditions you lack the means to escape from, the crushing realization that someone you love does not love you back, a sudden falling off in health, the loss of prestige in your profession, the death of someone who did love you back—or being turned down for a health insurance policy that would enable you to "die at home"—a code phrase for remaining in control until the end? Or maybe even for cheating death altogether?

◆

> . . . a distinct sense of loss, a flavor in the mouth of the real, abiding danger that lurks in all forms of human existence . . .

That's Joseph Conrad describing the sensations of the commander of a stranded ship in *The Mirror of the Sea*. Marking one's position in the losing-ground place has been richly chronicled in the literature and religions of the world. In Buddhism—of which I also knew nothing in 1955—the practice of "mindfulness," of bringing your mind completely to bear on *whatever confronts it,* is considered a form of prayer.

In the novel I just completed, two old nuns are being driven back to their retirement house from doctor visits, and one says to the other, "There was a sentence this morning in that Prayer for Holy Women: 'In our weakness your power reaches its perfection.' What do you think it means, Sister Paula?" Sister Paula thinks for a minute and then replies, "I think it means you have to admit you can't save yourself before you're fully available to God."

In 1955, God was undergoing some very slippery changes in my psyche. He was no longer the comforting heavenly father who was always aware of me, and he had not yet expanded into the "mystery beyond my ken" that I could finally feel comfortable with. All I could be certain of, that long-ago summer morning, was that I could not save myself.

But something else did, something already in place in the "fatal tissue" in which I was embedded—my earthly father, who had spent most of my life being unaware of me. I had sent him an invitation to my high school graduation, though I hadn't seen him since I was a child. Mother said not to expect him to show up, but he did. He and his new wife and his brother drove from Smithfield, North Carolina, to Portsmouth for the ceremony. After that, we began to correspond. Finally, at the age of fifty, he had achieved a stable, though all-too-brief, respite from his troubled life. He had stopped drinking, had married a widow with a prosperous brother-in-law, and was making good money in the brother-in-law's car dealership. He wrote that he would like to know me better. Could I spend a vacation at the beach with them? The vacation turned into my going to live with them in Smithfield and boarding at Peace College in Raleigh. When I was a junior at UNC–Chapel Hill, he killed himself.

> At every age, in every person, there comes a partial imprisonment, a disabling psychic wound, an unavoidable combination of circumstances, a weakness that we cannot banish but must simply accept.
> —HELEN M. LUKE, "KING LEAR," *OLD AGE*, 1987

When my mother was seventy-five, she divorced her second husband and moved to a condominium. It was her first experience of living alone. She had gone straight from her parents' house to a college dormitory and from there to share her first husband's itinerant life until they parted ways and she set up house with her widowed mother and young daughter until in 1948 she married an ex-GI who was taking her college English class and lived under his various roofs for thirty-nine years, raising their three children.

"How wonderful it is not to have anyone around to tell me what to do," she wrote in her meticulously kept diaries in the new condominium, which she called "The Happy House." She had just begun her forty-eighth notebook at the time of her death. In high school, she had used her diaries to keep secrets from others in a tiny, illegible script. Now she taught herself calligraphy in order to be fully readable. She intended to account for her days and nights in a form meant to be shared. She faithfully caught up if she missed a day. What is remarkable about this record of her two years of independent life is not just the fullness and scope of her activities but how every person on the diary pages comes across as a fully rounded character: each woman and man she regularly visited in nursing homes all over the county; every good-hearted slogger and canny power grabber on the many committees she joined or chaired; the battered women she met and drove to Helpmate shelters. ("Only a year ago, I was where you are now," she told one young woman whose husband had blacked her eyes and dislocated her shoulder. "If I could get out at my age, so can you.")

After I was turned down for the home care policy and had the losing-ground moment, I went into a depression. All I desired to do was sleep. I couldn't find anything I wanted to read, until I remembered my mother's diaries. I fetched them from the file cabinet in the hand-sewn slipcases she had made for them, two at a time, before she mailed them off to me. I had read them while she was alive. I had told her they should be published for their sharp observations and character studies and social history, but she'd said some people might be hurt or offended. Nevertheless, she assented to their being included in my archives at UNC–Chapel Hill, her own alma mater. Now, as I devoured them addictively during three weeks of deepening winter, my curiosity about my future, whatever it turns out to be, revived. Her voice coaxed back to life a fascination for the "fatal tissue" into which I happened to be born. Surely I can do no less with my materials than has been done for me.

On the next-to-last day of 1989, my mother died at the age of seventy-seven, two years into her rich independence, when her car went off the interstate and crashed. Her doctor thought it most likely that her heart had at last given out and that she had never felt the impact.

ABOUT GAIL GODWIN

A three-time finalist for the National Book Award, Gail Godwin is the author of thirteen novels, two short story collections, two works of nonfiction, and ten librettos for the composer Robert Starer. Her new novel, *Unfinished Desires,* was published in January 2010 by Random House. She lives in Woodstock, New York.

It Figures

Katherine B. Weissman

I'm in the bathroom, which is warm and has a large mirror and a lock on the door. I bring a sketchbook and pencils. I take off my robe. I look at myself in the yellow stare of the fluorescent light. My silent commentary loops like the news crawl at the bottom of a TV screen: Fat. Pendulous breasts. Big stomach. Skin that is starting to sag and crinkle. Fat . . . I turn to the side. It is as if I have taken the profile of a sixteen-year-old body from a magazine and pasted it on the mirror, then compared each part. It's cruel, even sadistic, this ritual. This is my sixty-three-year-old body, familiar as a lover but not an object of charity or affection. Nonetheless, I start to draw.

Dressed, I look pretty good. I'm strapped and supported and camouflaged (one thing you can say for growing older, you make fewer fashion mistakes). Clothes are a soft armor. Undressed . . . there are no words in my vocabulary—no neutral words—for what is happening.

I've always been at war with my body. Encountering it naked in my sixties is like meeting an old enemy who has, unaccountably and regrettably, acquired new weapons since we last crossed paths. I know all the proper rhetoric about "embracing" your "curves" and valuing one's body for what it can do rather than what it looks like. I know that my obsession is tyrannical, enforced by the distorted images of pop culture. I am a seventies feminist who bought *Vogue* secretly every month and whose consciousness-raising group once planned to have a meeting in the nude (I starved myself for days, only to learn that my coconspirators had chickened out). Over the years I have learned to assert my rights, own my successes, get angry, and not apologize so damned much. Yet for my whole diet-ridden, disordered-eating-plagued life, I've never really accepted my physical self, much less loved it.

I'm not an artist, but I've always loved to draw, and since my forties I have gone back to many things—dance, music, art—that I gave up in my ignorant youth because amateur didn't "count." (Now I glory in being nonprofessional.) A few years ago I started studying art and in a bold moment signed up for a "life" class—so called because instead of something plucked from nature (a bowl of pears, a bouquet) you are drawing a living, breathing, sometimes shivering nude model.

I was nervous before the first session, but mainly about seeing men naked: inadvertent erections; embarrassment, theirs or mine. Unexpectedly, what got to me were the women. Some of our models were young and thin. A lot of them weren't: older and heavier, they had substantial thighs; big, squishy rear ends; generous breasts to which the word *perky* would never be applied. After my initial automatic response, a mixture of pity and knee-jerk competitiveness—who's thinner, they're fatter, look at that cellulite—I found that I *preferred* those models. They had weight and lusciousness and a certain courage and pride that more conventionally beautiful bodies did not. The longer I drew them, the more I loved them and the more I forgot that the stomach isn't "supposed" to bulge like that and that breasts are "supposed" to stand up by themselves. (Who made those rules?)

Of course, maybe I liked those models because they allowed me to feel superior.

I might have gone on drawing other people's bodies forever, except that the following summer I found myself in a foreign land, the deep countryside, with nothing but my pencils and paints—no art classes, no models. Except me: I was available. I started by doing portraits. I made myself look eighty years old lest I be accused of vanity: every wrinkle, every loose jowl; the hooded eye, the failing chin. I did faces for days and days, and then I thought: I can do my body, too. In the mirror. Without clothes on. I pretended that it was an art exercise, but I knew, really, that it was a dare.

I keep on with it, day after day, writing rough notes in pencil in my sketchbook after I finish the day's drawing. I continue when I get home, in a cold bathroom, in a winter light. It is hard facing myself, like taking bitter medicine first thing in the morning. (Of course I do it before eating anything. Of course!) It is a way of not hiding. The moment of disrobing reminds me of the beginning of a therapy session, that threshold of revelation when you struggle to resist idle chitchat, editing, and posturing and get down to honest work.

Actually, the parallel with therapy is not bad. Drawing my body, I learn myself. But it's hard to put into words, because the process is not an analysis so much as a feeling out; an instinctive, tactile business; autobiography as relief map. I think a lot of us gaze at older age through a scrim of self-deception; by squinting we can imagine that our faces and bodies, made gauzy and approximate, are the age they always have been. Or maybe we barely look at all. We glance hastily to check the teeth for lipstick or the shirt front for dried egg, and then we avert our eyes.

Drawing my body "as is" (as they say in clearance sales) without hating it is a struggle, I admit. By doing it every day I hope to make the sight of my nakedness ordinary, undramatic. I try to regard myself with tender, dispassionate interest. Detached though not unemotional; detached in the Buddhist sense of "having a place to breathe and see from, like a hilltop" (as I wrote in my sketchbook). It is in fact a bit like learning to meditate—your wandering, unruly mind drifts, makes lists, wants to escape. You have to bring it back calmly, relentlessly, quietly.

Patience is crucial. When I first look at an object, whether it's my face or body or a tree or an apple, I see only a few basic lines. As I continue to draw (or look), more details come into focus. Relationships between shapes emerge. Texture seems to bloom. I find myself entering the structure of my own body and becoming absorbed in its intricacies—the way the bones fit and the muscles move beneath the skin; the curves and slopes and angles; the coherence and flexibility of the whole machine. My pencil seems attached to a hundred invisible threads that radiate from each part of me. I am literally drawing myself, pulling my body out of my clothes, into the bathroom, onto the page.

✦

After a Sunday morning making love there I am in the bathroom, scrutinizing myself, pencil in hand. Is it better at this moment? Is it different? While I'm engaged in physical pleasure I can (momentarily) forget the way my body looks because it feels so good. I remember how transformed I felt the first time I had sex, as if I had leaped to some astral plane where goddesses walk clothed only in beauty. It doesn't last, though. Self-consciousness comes roaring back.

Distress at the body's decline certainly has a lot to do with loss of attractiveness, the snatching away of sexual power, the fear of being seen—and felt—naked by another person even with the veiling of sheets and (sometimes) darkness. If you have a partner, you can count on a certain familiar intimacy and indulgence. If you don't, the prospect of a stranger in your bed is daunting. You know that your relevant parts still work and respond, but will anyone want them, now that they are no longer fresh and shiny and new?

After her divorce, in the early 1960s, my mother dated. Lying on her bed, I watched her get ready, sheathed elastically in a longline bra and panty girdle. She liked sex; her face lit up when she explained to me what an orgasm was. She told me men adored her breasts, big and drooping as they were (she had pressed them into submission in the twenties, when flat figures were the cat's pajamas; I did the same years later, trying to be Twiggy). At the same time, she was always down on her body. She was short, not much over five feet; she had ugly scars from childhood infections so serious that the doctors (this was the preantibiotic age) had literally cut them out, and from two cesareans; she had a protruding belly; she had always wanted to be thinner or more boyish-looking.

I realize that when I look at my body, I see my mother's. I don't mean the emaciated, old-child body she had in her final illness (cancer trumps vanity, but until the moment it's obvious that weight loss is no longer a victory but a symptom, we persist in our lifelong preoccupations), I mean her ordinary figure. My mother's conflicts about her body took root in my psyche long before she fell ill. Sick or well, dead or alive, she haunts me. Looking in the mirror, I see not only her wary brown eyes but a dangerously familiar shape.

◆

It makes sense that our mothers are the root of our body image. We come out of them, feed on them, mirror them, and sometimes watch them shrink into almost nothing and vanish. Except for glimpses in the gym locker room, there are few available images of mature American women with no clothes on (compare this to a European beach). It takes no guts at all to draw or photograph a woman—oneself or a model—who is young and bulgeless. But it is still fairly radical to show women over sixty wearing chic clothes in a magazine or to make the old and the naked into art.

Because I am a new art student, I go to museums more frequently now, looking at paintings for inspiration and drawing sculpture for practice. There are, of course, lissome nymphet types from the art nouveau era, the forerunners of fashion models. But there are also nobly proportioned Greek and Roman matrons; hefty and bejeweled Renaissance ladies, usually reclining in a bower or bathing in a glade; a buxom, muscled modern torso in black basalt.

Alice Neel's self-portrait knocks my socks off. Painted at age eighty-four, it shows her well coiffed and wearing her glasses, sitting in a striped chair, completely naked. She has a big belly, and her breasts nearly reach her waist. She holds a brush and a painting rag, and her expression is keen, blunt, penetrating. Only her right foot, turned in, reveals (perhaps) a certain tension.

Old flesh revealed may be the last taboo. It is considered unseemly, distasteful, as if grandmothers should have the wisdom to keep themselves covered up until finally they shrivel up and die. (Throw a pail of water on them, and maybe those witches will dissolve even sooner!)

✦

A teacher of mine once said that drawing a person's arm or leg is not unlike drawing the branch of a tree—the same joints, the same rules of perspective. And we, too, have a trunk, that robust middle section. You have only to look at a still life or landscape to see how the shape and texture of a piece of fruit or mountain or flower parallel the form of the human body. But we accept their existence without placing them into an aesthetic hierarchy.

I think human beings have difficulty seeing themselves as part of the natural world rather than above it. (That would imply, among other things, that we die.) Drawing the body is a way to make the connections, to feel in our very bones that our physical selves are not for judging (no one would disparage a massive, elderly oak or an older lion that had, perhaps, put on a bit of weight now that he had retired from hunting) but for perceiving.

I don't want to suggest that I have suddenly, in my sixties, become all healthy and wise about my body. I am split in two, my pleasure in the ripples and creases, bones and bulges, sturdiness and abundance overlaid by the habit of disgust. It's like a double exposure.

And yet, and yet . . . There's a corny but curiously touching (and astonishingly handsome) black-and-white film about Rembrandt, made in 1936 and starring the great English actor Charles Laughton. In one scene, he speaks to a skittish kitchen maid he has brought into his studio. An artist sees differently, he tells her (I'm paraphrasing): "I look at you not as a man would look—my glance is like the air around you or the light that falls upon you. It is as if no one is there."

In drawing myself without cover or defenses, perhaps I enter a different realm, where bodies are neither good nor bad; where we are at one with the air and the light; and where we grow old like trees, without shame or loathing.

ABOUT KATHERINE B. WEISSMAN

Katherine B. Weissman's work appears regularly in *O, The Oprah Magazine*, where she has been a contributing editor since 2001. She has also had fiction and nonfiction published in *Seventeen*, *Ploughshares*, and *Cosmopolitan*. She was an excellent student (B.A. summa cum laude, Washington University) and sees no reason to stop taking classes (piano, ballet, Pilates, painting) just because she is on the other side of sixty. She lives in New York City with her dear husband, the philosophy professor and writer David Weissman, and is fortunate enough to have three remarkable stepchildren.

Sedat Pakay

Interview with Jane Alexander

EMILY: *The impetus for this project comes directly from my own fears and, curiously, from my coeditor's moving out of a fearsome time in her life. There are a lot of important people in my life who are going to die before I do. There are so many different ways to live events, and sometimes one can adjust one's inner camera slightly and live something differently. I was gathering people's experiences and perspectives on healing and getting through in the hope that it might help me and others.*

JANE ALEXANDER: I think that it's a very worthy thing to do. I'm just feeling in such a good place right now, but there were a lot of losses earlier on in my life, and my parents died . . . my gosh, over twenty-five years ago, so they died fairly young.

E: *I'm particularly interested in the healing process and how one comes out the other end because I can't believe that I'm going to— Did you find that anything unusual helped you other than the passage of time and investment in your work and the various and common ways we all comfort ourselves?*

JA: I think that . . . you don't bury the person forever, you talk about them, you keep them. You know, I sort of feel sometimes in our society we get so down and morose about death even though premature death is a shock and not the order of things. You can just keep that person alive somehow, and talk about them and celebrate their lives and say how lucky you were to be a part of their lives for so long. That sounds really very Pollyannaish, I suppose. You never get over a certain grief—it's just something that you live with, and time, time certainly helps a lot of things.

And I have had a surrogate mother ever since my mother died when I was a little over forty. Within the year my mother died, I did a movie in Greece and I met a perfectly wonderful woman who had been living there with her husband and running a school. She was an American, and she was just two years younger than my mother, and she became like my surrogate mother. She is going to be ninety this year, and I speak to her once a week. I just spoke to her on the phone, and she said, "Do you believe that John (that's her second husband) has been gone now for eleven years? You know, I still think about him every single day, I still want him to hold me every single day."

Isn't that something? Then my friend said, "But then I say to myself, there are many people who never met the love of their life, and I did." That's another blessing, you know.

There were some heavy losses for us during the nineties. In '96 one of our boys died. Geoff was Ed's middle boy. My boy, Jace, and his three had been friends since '65, when they were all very little.

E: *Was it a long, long road back for Ed after his son died?*

JA: Oh, yes, and we talk about it fairly regularly. But the kids do, too. This is another thing, you know, we don't shut out Uncle Geoff from the grandkids' lives. He's very much a part of our lives. He's one of their uncles. We talk about him, it's very nice, everybody talks about Geoff.

In that same year [1996], our accountant of twenty-three years embezzled everything we owned. Everything but the house that we lived in . . . the worst thing was that he had not paid our taxes for five years, and the IRS is not forgiving at all. So we had to literally leave the house. It took close to ten years to get in the black again, and that was at an age when my husband was no longer young. There's ten years between us.

But my feeling is that despite all of this, the last decade has been so great.

You know, there've been clinical ailments for my husband and for me. But I don't at all experience a sense of loss about aging. I think that's a fortunate thing.

I'm sorry to go on, but I'm on a little bit of a roll now.

When I was a girl growing up in Brookline, Massachusetts, I lost one of my best friends. She died of spinal meningitis at the age of ten. And then my college roommate of two years was hit by a car and died, and then my best male friend committed suicide, and so I had three very close people to me die at a young age. . . . Again to look on death in a different kind of way—maybe some people are only on the earth for a certain amount of time and they do all they need to do.

E: *I had similar experiences, which probably played a part in my being very vulnerable to loss, very anxious about it. But I think that what we do with it is everything. . . . As you get older, you have a choice in how to react, you don't have to simply react. You can almost choose a reaction, which is what this book is also about. I'm thinking that I don't have to go down through the rabbit hole of loss. I can perhaps look upon it differently.*

JA: I do think you go through the sadness, you can't avoid it.

E: *At the time that both of your parents died, for instance, you didn't feel that the planet had changed, that the tectonic plates had kind of moved under your feet and it was an unrecognizable place?*

JA: No, I didn't, and I don't. And here's another thing. I used to be very, very anxious myself about dying. I always thought

I was going to die young and all. And then finally, when I was in my forties, I said, "You know, it's okay. If I die, I die." If one looks at one's own death as something that's perfectly okay at any time, at *any* time—

E: *What do you think allowed you to feel that?*

JA: I don't know. I just gave up the anxiety. I used to be so anxious about everything, flying, driving in a car, people going too fast, people doing this-that, and I just kind of gave it up.

I'm not religious at all, either. I don't pray, but I'm a bit of a nature girl, so I'm out birding almost every day, wherever I find myself, I'll just be taking a walk into the city and looking at birds if I can. I found my relationship to the sky was very liberating. If I'm feeling very, very down, I'll just look up and force myself to laugh, and it's very healing for me, it's like a trick.

E: *When you decided in your forties that it was okay to die, did that have to do with feeling fulfilled and that you had accomplished whatever it was you had wanted to?*

JA: Well, what was most important was by that time the kids were grown.

E: *This may be too intimate a question, so forgive me. . . . Having gone through the loss of Ed's son, is it horrific for you to imagine being separated forever, because of your natural death, from your boy, Jace?*

JA: It's not, I don't know. And I don't even believe in Heaven. It's not that I think we're going to be united or—

E: *No, no, that's the point, I don't think we're going to be united either.*

JA: I don't know, I have long flirted with the idea of ghosts because I swear that I have felt them and seen them and heard them, so I don't know what's on the other side. I don't know.

E: *You're not counting on it, I hope.*

JA: Oh, no, no, no!

E: *Neither am I. But it sounds like you've really made peace with it all.*

JA: That's why I'm afraid that I'm not the material for your book.

E: *On the contrary, we don't need to hear how terrible it is to grow older. In Vivian Gornick's essay in this book, she writes about why even intelligent women hate losing their youthful looks. Her piece is about how hard it is for all of us to lose that stage, lose the power of our youthful beauty. I think we all go through a time when we start to feel less powerful in that respect. Was this a hard transition for you as an actress?*

JA: Early on, I realized, as a young actress, that I was never going to be an ingenue; I was always a kind of "young leading lady"; people always talked about the character in my face or how handsome I was or how pretty my hair was. It was never "You're a real beauty." And so I never had that image of myself. I knew as an actress I could make myself into what I needed to do for the character, but for myself, I never thought of myself that way. Now what is interesting . . . as long as my body is healthy and strong so I can do the things I want to do, like go out and walk, or sports or whatever, as long as that is okay, then I have no problem with my looks. I never cared to get involved at all with cosmetic surgery, mainly because I'm a chicken. I'll stay as far away from any knife as possible. I think when you grow up in a doctor's family you learn to stay as far away as you can from hospitals and clinics. So I never concerned myself with that, nor with Botox.

Now, this is the interesting thing that's happened over the past ten years. I have four very, very close friends, and none of us have had anything done, not Botox, not any cosmetic surgery, and we are absolutely *fascinated* with each other's looks, mostly because we've known each other for so long now, fifty years. And I'm also fascinated with what happens with my face. I'm age sixty-seven now. For this series I'm doing for HBO, I had to get my nails done, a pedicure in case my feet show! And the little Korean woman looks up while she's doing my nails, and she says, "You're so beautiful." I was taken aback because she was really, you know, this young, gorgeous Asian woman, and I said, "*You* are beautiful." She said, "No, you're very beautiful." I had no makeup, so there's something. . . . Now, she's an Asian woman, and they have respect for older people. You don't hear it very often from youth in our society, but I was really taken aback by that and delighted.

I'm certainly not opposed to cosmetic surgery for anybody who wants to get into it. I just don't want to limit myself in terms of character roles.

E: *And you've made the transition from the NEA without difficulty?*

JA: You know, that was more difficult than I expected because there was a lot of media attention on the NEA when I was there, mainly because the Republicans were trying to close down the agency. People began to view me as somebody in politics or a woman of authority, and I didn't realize that it would take probably a good seven years for that image to die and for me to get back into being an actress.

Now, here's another thing that might interest you. The series that I'm doing right now is an HBO series where I play a sex therapist, and I also have sex scenes with my husband in the story. So you're seeing an older woman and an older man who are still engaged in sexual activity, which doesn't happen very often on television. In fact, in the HBO series, ours is a very long relationship and a very loving one. It's weathered a lot of storms through the forty-three years that we've been married in the story, but we've come to this lovely, lovely place together. And as a sex therapist, she's very free, you know, she's a free person herself, so I think it will be an interesting depiction for the public.

Back to your subject of loss. . . . When we go through grief, it's probably a scenario many of us share . . . the same dark hole . . . but there is some light somehow there, and the wonderful thing about human beings is that we can forget the actual pain of a lot of events. My husband has been suffering through chronic pain for many years, but he's coming out of it now. I've also had clinical ailments, but right now I'm in a very good place. I do believe if we have our health we have the possibility of real redemption every single day.

It's a very sweet time for my husband and me because the kids are grown and we're very much in our grandchildren's lives. That's another thing that changes the dynamic. When you see the little ones come after you, you just realize it's all part of the order of things. It's a very sweet and very fulfilling time after a long and happy marriage to be moving into this time, too, and really feeling very good about it. We're very appreciative of each other every single moment of every single day.

ABOUT JANE ALEXANDER

Jane Alexander was born in Boston in 1938. A Tony and Emmy Award winner and four-time Oscar nominee, she has starred in dozens of movies, including *The Great White Hope, All the President's Men, Kramer vs. Kramer, Eleanor and Franklin,* and *Testament.* Her stage credits include *The Great White Hope, Shadowlands,* and *The Sisters Rosensweig.*

Ms. Alexander interrupted her busy acting career to become chairman of the National Endowment for the Arts from 1993 to 1997.

Sedat Pakay

what i thought i'd never lose & did/what i discovered when i didn't know i cd

Ntozake Shange

. . . sometimes surrounded by my antique negrophilia orphans, I am overcome with my first experiences of racism. Why, you may ask, am I digging this up now? Smiling like my wooden pickaninny dolls, I answer. I was strolling with my daughter, Savannah, down a broad street off hwy 59 near merrilee lane, between a lovely spot to fetch fresh coffee beans & an upscale businessmen's strip club, when this car took the corner like a bat outta hell. The woman screamed, "Ya'll niggahs get out of my damned way!" Then it had happened again. There was no way out. I couldn't protect my daughter from the word "niggah," any more than I could protect myself from the lil white girl at Sampson Air Force Base who said, "I don't serve niggahs milk." This is to say that losses occur and reoccur, intertwining & ricocheting like electrons or electrolytes. Our state of mind jockeys for peace, anxiety, or despair as these startling new episodes splatter our lives with fewer options, more regrets, and warm recollections, maybe, of the way things used to be.

I was a dancer, rushing thru Bay Area traffic to get to Ed Mock's Dance Works or Halifu Osumare at Everybody's Dance Studio, dancing, a dream I nurtured thru childhood. Later in New York I sped from Thelma Hill, Fred Benjamin, Pepsi Bethel, & Loremil Machado uptown to Dianne McIntyre at Sounds in Motion next to the Lenox Bar on 125th St. I took from four to six classes a week, and if I was in luck I was rehearsing with somebody for a concert somewhere. I'd throw my leg over a parking meter as a mode of courtship. A streetwise battement when my baby was five. I danced in *Love Space Demands,* choreographed by Mickey Davidson, at forty-two. I thought I was physically set for life. I even had my eye on the senior Miss Universe contest. Then in 2004 I was beset by two separate maladies.

◆

I fell prey to water intoxication or low sodium, which is characterized by hallucination, memory loss, and corporal ineptness; a veritable cornucopia of psychoses. I could hear voices, see four different images on the television at one time, read a book in which each word cd separate to fill the page. I'd ask people on the phone who they thought they were talking to cause i certainly didn't know. & I fell constantly.

On top of this phantasmagoric experience, I had a stroke.

The stroke put an end to nanoseconds of images & left a body with diminished vision, no strength, immobile legs, slurred speech, and no recollection of how to read. With the help of physical therapists, hospital visits, weekly trips to the neurologists and psychotherapists, I gradually improved over a five-year period. I am no longer on a walker or cane, but I fully realize the limp in my legs and the crushing pain I now know to be me trying to tackle the stairs. My sister says that at first there were so many spaces between my words she thought I had forgotten what I was saying. So much for "quick-tongued wit." Let alone a world of ideas.

Maya Angelou was wonderful. She sent me children's books of hers so that I cd learn to read again. My sisters, Ifa & Bisa, and my brother, Paul, continued to encourage me with contemplation of the world or girl-time memories. My mother, Eloise Owens Williams, and my daughter, Savannah Thulani-Eloisa, bore with me stammering words and tipping off balance. In this condition I endured three major surgeries, a hematoma, and a series of as yet inexplicable seizures.

With my brain and body literally fallen apart in front of me, my memories of my father's passing & his living among us family, patients, community & music heartened me. I was drawn more to old salsa or 1940s Beny More & Sonora Matancera. On the other hand I retreated to doo-wop music, new black music, and reruns of all versions of *Star Trek*. A poem was beyond me, but I could follow plots with Klingons & Vulcans. In the midst of my brain-body tomfoolery ripping at my soul, my good longtime friend claude e. sloan came to help me when Mama left to go back to her life. The weeks in between felt like repeated repeats of the same task: to take a step; to hold a cup still; to get up & sit down. Instead of living day to day, I lived task to task. Instead of being all about town, I was all around a room. Sleep. Task. No more. Just now again I can ride trains, airplanes, but I cannot be alone.

I was so frustrated; so afraid I'd never write again, I sought out other forms to use what was left of my creative energy. The class that had openings was "foundry" at the Cauldron. I knew nothing about metal sculpture other than I liked it. Now on my cane & backless stools I made clay molds & prepared like my classmates for the 2,100-degree Fahrenheit molten bronze. Yes, I was weak. Yes, I was limping, but I got two rather crude but striking pieces from the process. I slept for two hours afterward, leather gloves, chaps, & the plastic ironworker's shields dancing in my head.

I cd go from Brazil to Paris, & now I am blessed I can cross the street. This but one change in my life so far.

There are still the memories and acute pain associated with those i loved who've their spiritual transition/just up n died. My father, P. T. Williams, M.D., who passed away from a heart attack in North Jersey on his way from a wrestling match where he'd been the ring physician. I was relieved; not that Daddy had died but that he had died doing something he loved. All my life I'd been around gyms, boxers, training camps, and my Papi. The tradition was so intransigent that he even began to take my daughter. Whatta whirl of life my father created around himself & shared with us from Sonny Till, Dizzy Gillespie, Chico Hamilton, Miles Davis, the kids at the PAL Club, the staff of the free clinic, and his friends from the prestigious Boulez, Inc. Once when I was very depressed, Daddy took me for a tennis lesson. Sometimes, he'd listen to my poetry very intently & he cd dance any dance any hyphenated African had ever executed. Batum.

When Pedro Pietri moved from this level to the sphere where to be called negrito is to be called love, I was still hobbling around in Oakland & felt astonishingly close to all those who'd been compadres. At one point Pedro had called his apt. at Manhattan Plaza the Puerto Rican Men's Shelter, and I answered the phone in a very official tone. We shared countless days & nights over a forty-year period (we met when I was nineteen), reading poetry to our respective families, even driving down the westside hwy with no breaks. My times with Pedro & his briefcase, coffin-altar, his black cross & gorgeously curly hair kept my parents up all night fearing for my safety. As time went by Pedro grew to be part of our extended family as he was hailed as an essential of Nueva York.

And there are still dear folks I miss but can still linger with by word, song, or music, who include June Jordan, Veve Clark, Octavia Butler, Lorenzo Thomas, Tally Beatty, Raymond Sawyer, Lester Bowie, Fred Hopkins, Andrea Dworkin, Stanze Peterson, Steve McCall. They disappeared. Then Ana Mendienta & Vicki Miller, my cousins Charles "Petey" Forde, Jeffrey Williams, Luan Williams, & Anthony Wright passed in murky more violent ways. After all we are Black in America and no number of poems can shield me from that grotesque reality. And then there are my artist daddies, Romare Bearden, Joseph Papp, Nicolás Guillén, Guillermo Cabrera Infante, C. L. R. James, and Héctor Lavoe. I am lonely for them.

Yet when I think of my grandmother, Viola Benzena, and my Great-Aunt Effie Owens Josey, I feel as if I am being visited by a slew of roaring twenties bronze beauties cause not only did they teach me how to cook, they taught me how to flirt like a nice southern girl. It is such a hoot since I've got a real urban edge to me. Nevertheless, my true picture of womanhood and strength grows on me more every day since my mother passed away. Eloise Owens Williams, my ebullient, brilliant & highly opinionated mother, finished Hunter College at eighteen. She was a race woman. Her passions about injustice, discrimination, and all those hell-bent on the Negro suffering never wavered during her eighty-four years. My mother was my best friend. We whispered together, drank together, saw art, heard music, met all my friends, bought clothes, read books, and cooked together. I miss her terribly. Every time I hear Ben E. King sing "Stand By Me," my eyes water; I grind my teeth; I'm recognizing & missing my mother, Ellie.

How do I fill up all these empty spaces? I discover my life goes on. Some I can't fill, others I make altars to & pray so long as I can see them & some articles they might have held precious to em; we can commune. & I won't be lost for so long.

See, I will let you encounter the world as I do now.

"You fuckin' handicapped bitch, get on out the way!" a young Chicano screamed at me with my cane outside San Francisco's Yerba Buena Center. I'd been to see my friend and colleague Billy Bang perform his new "Vietnam: The Aftermath Suite"; now I felt I was in a jungle being stalked. I used to run for the bus in Philadelphia, knees high, flying through crowds & up to the driver, "Good afternoon!" I'd pant; but not anymore. I can't run. I can't complete a chassé or bench-press 135 lbs. I fall asleep in the middle of intriguing conversations only to wake in what I thought was the middle of a sentence totally alone. The complications and implications of my brain-body befuddlement leave me quite challenged by a set of stairs or a five-minute wait at the bus stop. Heaven forbid I lose track of where I am or forget my address. Then I seek out the nice neighborhood policeman, not caring that he might believe me to have Alzheimer's or a crack high. I just need directions home sometimes. I can't remember. I just can't remember. & I talk like I had fifteen shoes in my mouth. Clunky, banal, vaguely pedantic words fall from my mouth like dead cats, but I miss working.

I need things to do with my life. I do not want to teach creative writing anymore as I've done that for so many years & find it too emotionally draining. I've been disabled because of my interweaving health battles, but I see myself searching for opportunities to be productive. That's why I decided to perform in a new production, "Dangling Participles & Shady Syllables," a compilation of poems from the last twenty-five years, with Craig Harris (trombone), Mickey Davidson, Diane Harvey, & Shireen Dickson (quintessential improvisational dancers), Billy "Spaceman" Patterson (guitars), Sabor (percussion), and M., an evocative eight-octave vocalist. I decided with Claude E. Sloan, the director, that I shd perform in the piece rather than having a younger actor or performance artist. I know how to work an audience. I can do my own work. I can attract people to my shows. Why shd I let someone else do my work because they are younger, and—, and—, and—. I don't care abt that. I need to work. I need to work. I miss the expectation of being legitimately, authentically, and intrinsically employed & productive. I am not dead, I am older. But I can still memorize a stanza or two.

What I have memorized is my child's face at different points in her life. At least she wasn't with me when I could not recognize those close to me, but she has been there with me throughout my continuing rehabilitation. It's as if we've traded places; she sometimes taking care of me, the mother. And I loved being Mommy. I loved my little girl with her violin, her hockey stick, her dance outfits, her breezy smile. I loved being thrilled, reading my eleven-year-old's college-level papers. Cooking together, a forty-clove garlic chicken or lobster-fried chitterlings, & meditating together at her invitation. I miss the regular schedule of mommydom & the warm hug & kiss after the evening's bath. Now we still kiss & hug; I make the pie crust & she makes the filling; she's going to graduate school, and I'm applying. Gracious. Our lives as mother and daughter are in constant flux but solid, as Ashford & Simpson say, "as a rock." Like all our mothers before us more than we imagine ourselves to be. & who after all can tell what we are missing.

ABOUT NTOZAKE SHANGE

In the Zulu language of Xhosa, *ntozake* means "She who comes with her own things" and *shange* means "She who walks like a lion." Fearless in her quest to affirm the realities of women of color, Ntozake

Shange demonstrates that her name reflects her approach to both her art and her life.

While Ms. Shange is first and foremost a poet, she constantly extends her talents into other realms. Aside from *For Colored Girls Who Have Considered Suicide/When the Rainbow Is Enuf*, she has written three novels—*Sassafrass, Cypress & Indigo; Betsey Brown;* and *Liliane: Resurrection of the Daughter*—six volumes of poetry, numerous essays and screenplays, and a plethora of critically acclaimed plays, including *Spell # 7, A Photograph: Lovers in Motion, Boogie Woogie Landscapes,* and *The Love Space Demands: A Continuing Saga.* Ms. Shange has also inspired the youngest of imaginations by creating five children's books, including *I Live in Music* and *Ellington Was Not a Street,* which was chosen as the 2005 winner of the Simon Wiesenthal Center's Once upon a World Award.

Ever mindful of a responsibility to help inspire and guide the next generation of writers and poets, Ms. Shange has devoted much of her time to teaching as an associate professor of creative writing and drama at the University of Houston, a Melon Professor at Rice University, an associate professor of English literature at Prairie View A&M, and an associate professor of women's and gender studies at the University of Florida.

Through her poems, books, and more, she continues to teach us all to find the strength and courage we have within to "walk like a lion."

Noah Siegel

Lullaby

Laura Siegel

As the plane makes its final approach into Chicago, I think of the word *relinquish*. I draw out the word, savoring the sounds. The syllables are soft, sensual, liquid—a cradle rocking on water with barely a breeze—*l*, as in *love; qui,* like *quiet,* or the shape of lips trying to form a kiss; then the *sh,* evoking the *hush* a mother whispers to blanket a drowsy child. The beauty of the word's sounds belies its meaning. The sounds are so caressing; the meaning is raw, poignant, painful. Relinquish: to release, to let go. I am taking my daughter to begin her freshman year at college.

Memories resurface as I gaze out the window. In the delivery room, Rachel has just been placed on my chest. She peers at me with eyes like "E.T." Softly, with one finger, I make a brushstroke across her forehead, offering an earthling welcome that says, "This is a gentle, safe place." I try to imagine the sensation of her first glimpse of the world beyond the womb.

What must it look like? I, too, am filled with wonder. I cannot believe she is here.

At midnight, a few hours later, after phone calls to family and my husband's departure, I lie awake. Nearby, in the midst of the large maternity ward I share with several other women, a deaf-mute couple from Africa is signing to each other. The father is wildly slapping the fingers of his signing hand into the palm of the other. Preternatural sounds issue from the mother's throat. Then I hear, blended together, the soaring song of their laughter.

At the far end of this immense room is the nursery, curtains drawn closed over the large glass picture windows to shield sleeping mothers from the bright fluorescent lights and active attendants within. Resting, relaxing now, I am almost ready to doze off. Suddenly, over the wailing sounds of the eight or nine other infants born that night, I hear a cry. Instinctively, I know it is hers. In a flash, I'm out of bed, across the vast room, and standing in the nursery doorway. A very young night staff nurse has set a huge fan on high speed and has placed Rachel in front of it, hoping, she tells me, that the noise will calm the baby down. The sleeves of my bathrobe are flapping. I clutch the collar more tightly around my throat. With all the diplomacy I can muster, I suggest that the fan may be too intense for newborns this particular October night and offer to bring in a chair to rock my daughter to sleep. The nurse is relieved to have an extra pair of hands. Rachel and I have become a unit.

When my sister visits at the hospital the next day bearing birds-of-paradise, I imagine that every mother must feel in these early moments that her child, too, is a rare, exotic creature. My urge is to cast away all the preconceived names rationally selected before our child's arrival. I want to find new words, new sounds in the language that have never been uttered, to celebrate her uniqueness, as astronomers do after discovering a new star. Like Galileo entering a new galaxy, I am voyaging beyond the boundaries of my experience.

At the end of the week, following my release, my husband and I go for a long walk slowly, arm in arm, in our neighborhood. On this Saturday night, the air is cool and crisp, requiring only an extra sweater. The sidewalks are crowded with passersby, who seem to be moving at a speed I cannot process. As we pass a small Korean market, pumpkins startle me. Suddenly, I realize, that's right, it's autumn . . . October . . . Halloween is almost here. I understand more fully now the expression "over the moon," which no longer seems hyperbolic. Emotionally, in terms of the distance traveled, I have just returned from a journey light-years away.

In the days that follow, my favorite e. e. cummings poem becomes the birth announcement:

> i thank You God for most this amazing
> day: for the leaping greenly spirit of trees
> and a blue true dream of sky; and for everything
> which is natural which is infinite which is yes
> (i who have died am alive again today
> for this is the sun's birthday; this is the birth
> day of life and love and wings: and of the gay
> great happening illimitably earth)
> how should tasting touching hearing seeing
> breathing—lifted from the no
> of all nothing—human merely being
> doubt unimaginable You?
> (now the ears of my ears awake and
> now the eyes of my eyes are opened.)

The fractured syntax, the frenetic interruptions, the welter of emotions that overrun the logic of the lines and thoughts embody the feelings that I want to convey: wonder, renewal, tumultuous joy, affirmation, and religious gratitude. With a woodblock carving and fresh green ink, I place the image of a new leaf on each card.

◆

As I lean back in the seat against the headrest, my mind flashes forward a few years to Rachel's toddlerhood. She is less than three years old when I begin looking for potential nursery schools. I call, among them, the Barnard Center for Child Development, where I'm told to bring Rachel in for an interview. Upon arrival, I'm asked to place my daughter in a wooden rocking boat, tell her I'll be back soon, and then leave the room. I am ushered into an adjacent viewing booth to observe through one-way glass. Rachel seems to be enjoying herself in this new environment. About ten minutes later, someone instructs me to retrieve her and then dismisses us. The next day, a staff person phones to say that this particular year the research will focus on the issue of separation anxiety. Since Rachel did not exhibit any of the characteristic signs—in fact, in her case separation seemed to be a nonissue—she would not be of interest to the program. I could not foresee that in the ebb and flow of our attachment, at the age of twelve, she would write home from camp nearly every day for eight weeks—and I would answer each letter.

As the plane banks to the right over Lake Michigan, my mind revisits another scene. It's five in the morning. Strewn across our living room floor are a bright magenta cancan dress, boa, and sequined garter; the retro uniform of a gruff, gum-snapping diner waitress; and a white satin wedding dress trailing tulle clouds. The night before, a trunk of costumes arrived, a gift from grandparents to Rachel, age six. Unable to sleep, she dashes into the room. Seizing a floral centerpiece from the coffee table as an impromptu bouquet, she leaps into the bridal gown and then bellows Mendelssohn's "Wedding March" to a bow-tied teddy bear groom.

For the rest of the day, she dresses up in all these costumes, each time concocting new characters, scenarios, and fictions. More than simply a childhood game, the world of fantasy seems to promote the passions that make her feel most alive. In succeeding years, I sense the interweaving of her personality, individual enthusiasms, and talents with the leitmotifs of our home: love of language and music—poetry, great speeches, songs, symphonies—and the joy of performance. She becomes a unique lattice, a synthesis of influences yet separate, when theater becomes the direction of her life—and, at this moment, her intended college major.

The PA system crackles as a flight attendant fumbles for the microphone.

"Ladies and gentlemen, in a few minutes we will be making our final approach into Chicago's O'Hare airport. In preparation for landing, please fasten your seat belts, stow your tray tables, and bring your seats to their full upright position." The cabin grows quiet except for the sound of the engines.

I gaze at Rachel, asleep, her head on my shoulder. In my mind, I hear a song's refrain: "Nothin's gonna harm you, not while I'm around." Chanting the words in silent repetition, I hold on to them, hoping they might take on the protective power of a talisman. I long for angel wings—to spread over this young woman, my child—to shelter and bless her before she goes off into the world—where I *cannot* be around her and, someday, no longer shall.

In *Camera Lucida*, Roland Barthes speaks of a photograph's capacity to embody not only a specific moment but also, implicitly, an anterior future. As I look out at the vast landscape—water, sun, soaring skyscrapers, shoreline—there is an acceleration of images and of time. I wonder how this moment will be framed ten, twenty, fifty years from now. In the ineluctable series of attachments, separations, loves, and losses that characterizes the human life cycle, what will prove to have been the context of this moment in the story of our family? In the retelling of our family's lives, may someone be able one day to say that G–d seemed to have held us beneath His outstretched wings? My question becomes a plea. Softly, before the final descent, I murmur, "Amen."

ABOUT LAURA SIEGEL

Laura Mizel Siegel is a lifelong lover of language(s), with a passionate interest in the language acquisition process. She is currently a teacher of English as a second language. A graduate of the University of Chicago, Harvard, and Columbia, she resides with her husband, the concert pianist Jeffrey Siegel, in New York City, where they have raised two now-grown children.

Tom Evans

Love in a Fine Structure

Frances Itani

*I carry around a bundle in my arms. Because the bundle is
invisible, I'm the only one aware of its existence. I don't think about
it all the time, but neither do I set it down. It's just there, attached
to me, invisible and in my arms. Sometimes I open it to remove a
portion of its contents, but the bundle does not diminish in size.
For long periods, it stays closed. The bundle is love. Enduring love
for my only sister, Marilyn—known to me as "Mare"—who died of
a brain tumor, a glioblastoma, twenty-five years ago.*

Mare's illness struck quickly, in the spring. She and her husband and their two teenage children arrived at my home for
dinner one evening, and she was limping, using a cane.

"Is something pressing on a nerve?" I asked. "Have you seen a doctor? Is it your back? Don't trip on the step."

Within days, she was erroneously diagnosed as having multiple sclerosis. After tests, the diagnosis was changed and she was taken to the operating room for neurosurgery. By July, less than three months later, she was dead.

At Thanksgiving, a few months after her death, as we drove to my parents' home for dinner, I had to ask my husband to circle the block several times so that I could "get a grip" before we arrived at the door. My parents were upset enough without me heaping my grief on top of theirs. My children, eleven and thirteen at the time, were silent in the backseat. They'd become used to me breaking down suddenly and unexpectedly.

✦

Christmas morning two months later, I looked out my kitchen window and watched a crimson cardinal swoop to the feeder. A pale, velvety female followed and picked up a sunflower seed in her beak. It was cold and sunny outside, and I was reminded of the early summer day when two attendants and I had wheeled Mare out her front door on a stretcher. Before we reached the ambulance that would take her to hospital for treatment, she asked us to pause so that she could feel the sun on her face.

Thinking of this on Christmas morning, I pulled on my boots and, still wearing my bathrobe, I tromped through snow in my backyard and trimmed the lowest branch from a spruce. I carried it inside, bent it into a circle, tied it with ribbon, stuck in a few pine cones, and cried so hard I couldn't see my own creation. I dressed, set the wreath on the passenger seat of my car, and drove across town on roads slick with a layer of new snow. When I reached the cemetery, I crunched through a hard crust of ice into deeper snow that reached past the top of my boots. I set the wreath on my sister's grave and felt better for doing so. I drove home, stood under a hot shower, and used all of my tricks to compose myself. I restarted my day. I made a pot of tea and joined my family for breakfast. I listened to a dove hooting down the chimney like an owl, and I understood defeat.

◆

During the three-month period of Mare's illness, I helped care for her and developed a nursing plan that could be followed in her home. I alternated shifts with my mother and my sister's husband. I'd been a writer for fifteen years, but I became a nurse again and stopped writing for several months. Even so, I could not keep myself from looking on from outside. It's what a writer does. My head filled with words, songs, connections, portents. One morning, Mare told me that her head was full of obscenities. This was something I truly understood.

One of my friends, a radio producer, suggested that I keep a journal. "It will help," he said. "If not now, then later." He was wise, and he was right. By writing about day-to-day happenings and, most of all, by setting down my feelings, I was able to keep a space for me. Separate from the physical care and from the propping up of my parents and my sister's children. Separate from caring for my own two children. I protected this private space and articulated the overwhelming changes in my interactions with my living-dying sister. I knew, at the same time, that no matter what I would do to help her, it would not be enough.

◆

This is what I miss. This is what I had then that I don't have now.

I sit on the edge of the bed I have just made and pick up the bedside phone. I call Mare, who is drinking coffee at her kitchen table. We talk, go over ordinary events, share our work and the lives of our children. We hoot and complain, double over in laughter. We call up our past. Unafraid to enter the territory of childhood, we never tire of this. The emotional core is the same, but details vary. Endings match; middles don't. We are sisters, aren't we? Each has a version of events, and when these are placed side by side, it is like fitting mismatched scenes to a puzzle that has only one border. We roll old stories into new. We are descendants of a long line of storytelling women who know how to laugh at themselves and at adversity.

◆

But how does one laugh when one of us is dying?

Mare was three years older than I. She was the eldest and I was the middle of five children. We grew up in a tiny Quebec village on the banks of the Ottawa River, close to treacherous rapids. Most of the villagers spoke French. English children were bused out to rural one-room schools.

We shared a bedroom and a double bed. There were days when we did not speak, nights when we drew uncrossable lines down the middle of the bottom sheet. We looked after our younger brothers, did chores together, fought over the division of labor, took the bus to town for Sunday school and church, crossed the river by streetcar, and attended Saturday matinees at the Capitol Theatre, with its elegant balcony and grand chandelier. We sang together, learned to dance together, and practiced strutting across the kitchen linoleum in our "first pair of pumps." As teens, we coated our lips with deep, dark red and embellished ourselves with costume jewelry. To earn money, we babysat. And in winter we trudged side by side through snowy village streets, trying to sell boxed Christmas cards to families as poor as our own.

◆

Sometimes I dream about my sister. In the dreams she always has long black hair. This is the first detail I remember when I wake: *Mare has her hair.* Because in real life, radiation causes hers to fall out. She never gets to finish the series.

I stand in a large treatment room, beside my sister's stretcher. It is week four. We are both exhausted. Mare's pulse is thready and low. I am worried and afraid. Mare, whose speech center is now damaged, mutters in slurred speech and catches us both off guard. We find this enormously funny. We start to laugh and can't stop. We laugh and laugh, wheezing and choking. A technician enters the room, walks over, and pulls a curtain around the two of us. This sets us off even more.

After the treatment, the stretcher is pushed to the elevator. A stranger, a passerby, looks over, sees Mare's bald head, and pities us. "Your mother?" she asks. I do not respond. Mare closes her eyes. She is forty-four at the time, and I am forty-one.

We return by ambulance to my sister's home. A double bed has been set up in the living room because Mare cannot get up the stairs. When she is settled, I climb onto the bed and sit beside her. We are propped up by pillows, princesses ready to practice our royal wave. Her husband comes home from work, and we call out to him and place an order for pie.

When Mare becomes paralyzed on one side, when her speech center is more or less destroyed, when she can no longer be cared for at home, she is admitted to hospital, silenced and unable to communicate except with her eyes. The ward staff asks to meet with the family so that decisions can be made on her behalf.

Do you want resuscitation attempts made?

We have to put a note on the front of the chart.

No one has been expecting this. Being asked to make a decision to let her die. The surgeon explains that this means that the staff won't add new treatments. They'll decrease the IV drip to a minimum, keep her comfortable and free of pain.

No heroics, please.

The surgeon returns to his office at the end of the hall. Seconds later, I follow. I want to ask one more thing. Through the open doorway, I see him reclining in his chair, feet up on his desk. He's biting into an apple. I hate him at that moment. I hate his ability to disconnect, and his right.

◆

One afternoon, I arrive on the ward to see a minister standing beside the bars of Mare's bed. He is praying over her, reciting a prayer about death and decay. Mare looks so distraught, I want to pound him for frightening her.

What does one do with the anger, the hopeless yearning, the silence, the grief? Even knowing that everyone suffers loss, it becomes intensely personal when the "other" has helped to define you. What does a writer do?

I learned, over time, that Mare's death left me with a gift. The gift is my insight into what it is to have a sister. The gift is used in my work. I seldom make an overt plan to write about sisters, but, uninvited, in they come. That's not all I write about, but sisters are there, sometimes in the foreground, sometimes at the back. They enter stories, novels, essays, and poems. I have written about twins, artists, close sisters, arguing sisters, laughing sisters, sisters in families large and families small. Sometimes I am well into the creation of a novel when another sister sidles in, ready to be included. I frequently hear from readers who say, "You understand the relationship between sisters very well." My trusted publisher often tells me, "Don't fight it. This is an important part of who you are."

Of course, I still catch myself watching sisters, wondering who is older, who is younger, whether they shop together to buy clothes, what they share, what they say to each other in little asides. I admit to being jealous. And then I think, *strength.*

Did we give each other strength?

I hope so.

Validation.

Love. It is in the bundle I carry around.

◆

I receive a letter from a good friend. She is a visual artist, one of our country's best. She was a war artist during the Second World War and is now in her eighties. When we are together, we talk about art and hope, about writing and painting, about comparisons between the two. I have always admired her professionalism and her undaunted spirit.

On this day she speaks of the work each of us is doing now and she tells me, "It has so much to do with being able to contain the feeling—love—in a fine structure."

And I think, yes, that's exactly what we do. As artists, we draw not only on our defeats but on all experience. We draw on the past and use it as a kind of energy that will provide extra vision to balance loss. We add constantly to our bundles and take from them what we must. And then, with fierceness, we pour love into the finest structures we are able to create.

ABOUT FRANCES ITANI

Frances Itani, a Canadian novelist, short story writer, and essayist, was the middle child of five and grew up in a small village in rural Quebec. Educated as a nurse in Montreal before becoming a writer, she taught and practiced nursing for eight years in several Canadian provinces and at Duke University Hospital in North Carolina. She has a B.A. in psychology and English and an M.A. in English literature. She has traveled widely and has lived in many countries.

She has written eleven books, including her World War I novel, *Deafening,* which has been translated into seventeen languages, was optioned for film, won a 2004 Commonwealth Prize for Best Book and the Drummer General's Award, was shortlisted for the 2005 IMPAC Dublin International Literary Award, and won a number of other prizes. Her latest novel, *Remembering the Bones,* was shortlisted for the Commonwealth Prize and has been nominated for the 2009 IMPAC Dublin Award. She has been involved in humanitarian work all her life and at present volunteers with Habitat for Humanity. She is working on a new novel, and she reviews for *The Washington Post.* She has always enjoyed learning languages and studied American Sign Language while doing research for *Deafening.* She has two children and two grandchildren and lives in Ottawa.

Charles Simmons

Toothless

Martha Fay

In "Behind a Mask," one of several dozen stories Louisa May Alcott wrote pseudonymously or anonymously before *Little Women* made her rich, a mysterious young woman retreats to her room after meeting with the family that has hired her as a governess.

"When alone," Alcott wrote, "Miss Muir's conduct was decidedly peculiar." Kneeling on the floor, she pulls a flask from her trunk, knocks back a shot of cordial, and slowly reveals the hidden self behind the demure facade. She unwinds the false coiled braids that frame her face, scrubs off her rouge, and—my favorite part—removes "several pearly teeth" from her mouth, revealing "a haggard, worn and moody woman of 30 at least."

At least.

I can't remember how old I was when I lost my first baby tooth. I can barely remember how old my daughter was when she lost hers. I know exactly how old I was when I lost my first grown-up tooth: fifty-nine and a half.

For a while, like Miss Muir, I wore a removable substitute in public, awaiting the day I could finish paying off the implant that would restore me to respectability. In Italy, where I spend a lot of time, middle-class adults reveal checkerboard smiles with no sense of shame. In America, you might as well walk around with your skirt stuck in the waist of your panty hose. A few days after my upper left first bicuspid was yanked, my dentist gave me what he calls a flipper, a dead ringer for a real tooth, aged to match the rest of my flawed set. It was held in place by a pink retainer, just like the ones the A-student girls in algebra class always seemed to be sucking and clicking as they worked on their algorithms.

The first time I tried to insert the flipper, there in the dentist's office, it felt as if I were eating a toaster. You'll get used to it, my dentist said. And I did, but only sort of. In the beginning, it took me about ten minutes to find the angle needed to get the retainer in place, hugging my upper palate, while simultaneously maneuvering the tooth into its narrow berth. The general sense of mechanical misery this produced reminded me of having sex for the first time as a teenager in the back of a car.

I would occasionally think, the hell with it, I'll go toothless. But vanity invariably brought me to my senses.

Then suddenly my fingers knew just how to do it, and that part of the drama was over. What kicked in next was subtler. The gap in my mouth had called forth my inner old crone and with it the specter of decay that no amount of running in the park could stave off forever—although compared with a bad CAT scan or mammogram it ranked pretty low in the ominous-harbinger category. This was more along the lines of getting my first pair of reading glasses. I would say my vanity took the hardest hit of all, and I was uncharacteristically glad that the man I was seeing at the time was away indefinitely on business.

I took my tooth out when I was alone, because having it in was annoying and a little disgusting. Food didn't taste as good: it wasn't coming into contact with my real palate, only my plastic one. The flipper also made me lisp if I spoke too fast. And when I found myself stroking it with my tongue while thinking hard, I worried I might be innocently developing a troublesome thing for prostheses.

◆

My periodontist, Leslie, a sympathetic and funny woman exactly my age, had been preparing me for tooth loss for some time. She has been watching over my troubled gums since our daughters were in grade school, expertly scraping the plaque off my teeth four times a year while keeping the nitrous oxide on max and reassuring me that none of this was my fault (for this I have always been as grateful as for the nitrous). I was doing the best I could, considering the genetic tendency of some mouths to produce plaque more rapidly than others. I don't smoke, I floss, I gargle; but I also age, and so do my gums. After each cleaning, Leslie would pat me on the shoulder and say, "You're good for now."

"Now" was the crucial word. Sooner or later, she said, I would lose one of my two wobbly first bicuspids—and when that happened, she would recommend an implant, because my adjacent teeth were a bit wobbly as well and not the best candidates to hang a bridge on. I asked her how much an implant would cost. "About four thousand dollars," she said. "I guess that means I can forget about the Viking range," I answered, and we both thought this was pretty funny, though it really wasn't, since a Viking had never figured in my future calculations and an implant obviously was going to have to.

It turned out that her fee, for the removal of the dead tooth and the surgery to install the metal anchor on the implant, was only $2,500. The other $1,500 would go to my dentist, who provided me with the temporary flipper and, once the gum healed after surgery, would reopen, or uncover, the gum and screw in the new tooth. There's a three-month waiting period while the gum heals, which seemed like a reasonable length of time in which to come up with the cash. But add in my quarterly teeth cleanings ($240 a pop, paid on the spot), and it took me much longer than expected.

Roughly a year after I'd lost my old tooth, the end was in sight. I made an appointment for my "uncovering" and took off for Italy, where no one I know has ever mentioned a tooth implant but quite a few have been transformed beyond recognition by the installation of horse-size dentures. I arrived at my house (which I bought sixteen years ago for the current price of about ten implants and which I was readying for renters), took the flipper out while I did some gardening, and promptly lost track of it.

Late the next day, before I headed out to a concert with a friend, my tongue brushed the top of my mouth and I realized I didn't have my tooth. I couldn't locate it right away and gave up, assuming it would surface later. At the concert I ran into some English friends, another excellent category of people to consort with when you have a $4,000 gap in your smile. Afterward, we went for pizza, and with that initial heavenly bite— the first to burn the roof of my mouth in a year—I forgot all about my flipper. I never did find it.

When I got back to New York, I discovered I had misunderstood the timing with my new tooth. I was going to have my uncovering right away, but my gum would have to heal again for a couple of weeks before the dentist could measure me for my replacement, which, I learned, involves shoving a big blob of dental Play-Doh into my mouth, twice, to make a mold. The mold, my dentist explained, is then sent to a tooth-making company in New Jersey.

And how long will that take? I asked; I was going to my nephew's wedding in a few days. My dentist, who has spectacular teeth of his own, called the supplier to ask whether a tooth could be produced in two days' time. It could not, although he said he'd known some patients who had paid enormous sums to have a tooth made in twenty-four hours. Gee, I thought, how vain can you get? Later, I ran into the grown daughter of a friend in a store and discovered just how vain I could be as I mumbled my way through our catch-up chat.

About midway through my publicly toothless stretch, I picked up *The New Yorker* and read a fascinating piece titled "The Way We Age Now," by Atul Gawande. He began his explanation of the aging process with teeth, describing in detail how the enamel softens and the blood supply diminishes, the gums recede—it's not a pretty tale, but what floored me were the statistics this process added up to. By age sixty, he wrote, "Americans have lost, on average, a third of their teeth." I thought perhaps I'd stumbled on one of those freak typos that slip through *The New Yorker*'s famous fact-checking system every twenty years or so and went online to look for corroborating evidence. I found a chart that ranked the fifty states by percentage of residents age sixty-five and over who have had all their natural teeth extracted. The national leader was West Virginia, at 42.8 percent, compared with a national average of 22.1 percent and a national low, in Connecticut, of 12.4 percent. In New York, only 16.8 percent are toothless.

So I had to say things could be a lot worse. The longer I had a hole in my mouth, the less of a big deal it seemed. By the time I went to the wedding, I had already attended a book party, where I started out smiling with lips firmly pressed together only to forget myself—and the gap—anytime I heard something funny. There was no way I could pull off a pursed-lip look around my family, but if anyone snapped a picture of the hole in my mouth, I haven't seen it. And now it's too late.

A couple of weeks ago, I got my new tooth. It is made of porcelain and is indistinguishable from the one it replaced. It feels as though it will last forever. It had better—prices have gone way up at the tooth-fairy factory in New Jersey, not to mention the rent on doctors' offices with a view of Central Park. The bill from my dentist, which arrived a week before my final appointment, was not $1,500 but $4,000, for a grand total of $6,500.

It would not be quite true to say that I miss my flipper. But now that my "real" tooth has restored me to my former state of unself-consciousness, I do feel rather lucky to have had so gentle a preview of the greater indignities yet to come. Just last week a slightly older friend of mine, having dinner with his family in a crowded restaurant, removed his $2,500 earpiece because the amplified ambient noise was driving him crazy. A few minutes later, engrossed in conversation, he mistook the earpiece, no bigger than a cashew, for a crust of bread and popped it into his mouth. It took a bit of serious crunching—his teeth are just fine—but he managed to get half of it down before something told him to spit out the rest.

As intimations of mortality go, I'd say teeth are easier on the system.

ABOUT MARTHA FAY

Martha Fay is a freelance writer in New York. She is the author of two works of nonfiction and has written long and short essays on a wide range of subjects over the last twenty years. This is her first essay on teeth.

Sedat Pakay

Unmarked Trail

Laurie Stone

A desert is a place without expectation.
—NADINE GORDIMER

I wish myself to Arizona, having no idea where I'm headed. Cautious, I'm not. I am ten and standing on the second story of a house under construction in Long Beach, Long Island, and my best friend, Linda, dares me to jump out the window into a pile of sand below, and I want to impress her because we're in love in that best-friend way, and so I leap, and time splits into Polaroid snaps, and I see over a hedge into a backyard where swings beckon and further the ocean sparkles like the scales of a silvery fish, and I wonder about the best way to land when the sand reaches up to grab me and air punches out of my chest as I hit the mound. I sit, knees tucked under, gathering myself before I wobble up, smiling stupidly and thinking: I would do it again.

I come to Arizona for love, and if you ask me what love is, I will say it's the thing that makes you jump out a window. I have been in the desert for two years and only last week bought a car. In my dreams I'm still in New York, where you don't need to drive. Be careful what you wish for, or just wish away. What can it hurt?

I'm at Yaddo, the artist colony in Saratoga Springs. It's my sixtieth birthday, and Richard invites me for a walk. Usually after breakfast, he strides off by himself along the wooded paths that snake around the four small lakes dotting the gigantic rich people's estate where Yaddo is set. I'm happy he's asked, although I don't want to be. The day I arrive, I see him in a little parlor off the dining room, a slender man with salt-and-pepper hair who looks autumnal in brown and gray gear except for the fancy rectangular glasses he wears with flashes of orange and sapphire. He has a musical British voice and eyes that smile, although more often they sit catlike and watchful behind his specs. Human beings have an on/off switch that declares: you, yes; you, no. We smell each other, and mirror neurons fire. Richard is married. He doesn't say much about his wife, Suzanne, but he is married, and I am cutting down on opportunities for disliking myself.

Yet we are similar, we find, as we talk at meals: not depressed but not all that alive. He says that at seventeen he married a girl from his village, believing the baby she was carrying was his or simply feeling responsible—or wanting sex on a regular basis and to play at being adult. They weren't in love, and Marilyn wasn't faithful, and when the boy, Trevor, was three, Richard pulled himself out, and he and Trevor, now a man, do not speak. Richard is unguarded, and I see his sorrow, and the story attracts me because he has saved himself but not escaped the consequences. Trevor is owed an apology, Richard feels, although he hasn't offered one. "Isn't there still time?" I ask, and he shoots me a grumpy smile.

We walk into the cool morning air, and we're alone on the paths, strewn with wet leaves and fallen branches. It's just a walk. What can it hurt? Our jackets swish, nearly touching, and Richard is describing his early days in New York when he'd go to a diner on Columbus Avenue and order eggs over easy and every day get porridge or waffles because no one could understand his accent. He'd eat the meal anyway, and I can see him, too polite to send it back, and I like his forbearance and idiocy. "It's my birthday," I blurt out but don't say which one, although I think he can tell because a tear plops out. If you think there is a part of you that makes you unlovable, you will protect it like your child and show it to everyone.

When Richard recalls Yaddo, he says our way was smoothed after dinner one night when I cleared plates and silverware from the table—deftly, from the right, as I'd been trained to do as a cater-waiter. (Past fifty, I've started passing hors d'oeuvres at the kind of parties I used to go to as a writer.) He sees an act of service in the gesture, something soft and generous that hasn't surfaced before, and maybe he glimpses a French maid in my dipping at the waist.

We throw over everything to link up, although me, I don't have that much to throw over. My sister and I are caring for my mother, who at eighty-nine goes into cardiac arrest and in the course of open-heart surgery has a stroke. From then on Toby has to live with home aides and Ellen and I are on call. Love is somewhere in the mix between my mother and me, but we don't like each other, don't see eye to eye, don't get along. We fight about the way to pick a cantaloupe and whether a government is good because it backs the Jews. At the same time I'm tending my mother, jackhammering starts outside my apartment. Two thirty-five-story condos are going up, and I can't sleep or work. I steal into the hall to speak on the phone, not that it rings much.

At Yaddo, Richard and I don't make plans. He and Suzanne

have tender feelings for each other, but, as Richard puts it, they are roommates, and when he returns home they separate. Before I move to Arizona—where Richard teaches museum studies at the university—he says, "You'll miss New York, your friends, the streets, your life." I say, "Don't be ridiculous. I am a tumbleweed. I can work anywhere." When has anything you thought about the future turned out right?

✦

I am pushing my mother's wheelchair up the hill on Fifty-seventh Street. She is nearing ninety-two. Primrose walks beside her.

"Toothpaste, cotton swabs, witch hazel," Toby says.

"You told me twenty times." Prim's jaw is clenched, her eyebrows to the roof.

Toby waves her fists, bundled in a wool coat and fake fur hat that frames her pretty, hollowed face. I ask if she's happy to be out. "How can I be happy?" she says in a reedy voice, a question she might have posed at any stage of her life. "Don't give up your apartment," she says, jabbing the air, as we wait for a light on Columbus Circle. "Don't be stupid."

Cars whiz close to the curb. The glass of the Time Warner Center—New York City's first enclosed shopping mall with posh restaurants and shops—rises impassively over the empty fountain surrounding a statue of the Italian mariner. It's as if he's come all this way to be in the center of the world, the New York everyone noses to and feels shipwrecked from if they have to leave. Richard thrived here among people who are charmed by rather than snooty about his non-Oxbridge, Beatles-sounding vowels—*toof* for *tough* and *soofer* for *suffer.* Two mounted police patrol the gate of the park. Vendors sell souvenirs and framed photographs, including the famous shot of John Lennon with his round specs and shoulder-length mane, perched on a ledge on the Upper West Side. Richard and

I have talked about coming back. My place could be a base, although it's too small to stay in long and he needs the right job. It is a law of the universe—as firm as the principle that mass and energy are interchangeable—that you don't give up a rent-stabilized apartment in New York. You maintain your resident status, holding a chair against landlords who want your throat slashed so they can triple the rent.

I seem not to care. I am floating, blimplike, over my past, all of which—my early years in Washington Heights, my student days at Barnard and Columbia, my long tenure at *The Village Voice,* my love relationships and passionate friendships—has been tangled in the spaghetti streets of the city. It's so much my medium, I can't feel it. I mean, does a fish know it's swimming in water? In Arizona, when I call my mother, she asks if I talk to neighbors, if I've made friends, if I'm lonely—as if I am a bride without work come to live in her husband's world. She must have felt that way when we moved to Long Beach and she left the streets of the city that had given her a reason to get out of bed. I tell her I've met no one and don't care. When Richard leaves for work, I stay in our house and write. When I think about New York, I see my mother's body, her feet stretching down to the Lower East Side, her fingers up to Carnegie Hall.

At Columbus Circle, it doesn't cross my mind that when she speaks about my apartment she is thinking about *her* apartment, fearing that her aides will leave, worn out by her demands, and that she'll be consigned to a nursing home and exiled from the only existence that breathes life into her and that she contributes to with her huffing theatrics, my mother the character, my mother with a role in the only show she wants to attend. Even in her wheelchair, she buses to Fairway, searching for a nectarine that won't break her heart. I say her aides won't leave, but it makes no impression. I don't consider that she's worried about me. I can't hear her, can't hear my friends who say, "Don't lose your bearings. Don't lose yourself."

Me, a feminist, lose myself? I think they're saying, "You can't have love. You can't have happiness." They say: Look before you leap. But the horizon looks like Richard.

One morning at Yaddo I awake with an idea: consciousness and religion arrived together, the one mistaken for the other. I picture a gracile primate wandering across a savanna. Hearing hooves approach, she looks for escape in a tree and, finding none, registers the understanding in her head. She *hears* a thought, and it must feel like a voice originating from another source, a power greater than the animal and outside it. I want to share this notion, and the next thing I know *Richard* is in my head. We cross paths in a little parlor lined with books. There are throw pillows on the sofa and chairs, although they are straight-backed and uncomfortable. At first his hands rest on his thighs, and then he picks up a black stone with white stripes that someone has brought back from a walk. It's smooth as skin, and he rubs it absently as I unfold my theory. "Can you picture our ancestor?" I ask, and he says, "Picture her? I'm invaded by consciousness every day," and he talks about the numinous—moments that are terrifying and fascinating at the same time, like our awareness of death. And I think I could talk to this man for the rest of my life. I'm not being that rash. I mean, how much longer do I have?

"Laurie's not going to give up her apartment," Primrose says. She turns to me. "I tell her the same thing every day."

A light rain falls; Toby doesn't seem to notice. The sky is gray and pillowy, the air warmer than in recent days. A police horse walks close, and its wet hair scents the air. It snorts, and my mother jumps. "I'm afraid of horses. I'm afraid of everything. Laurie, don't let the horse get so close. It will step on me. It will bite me."

"More likely you'll bite the horse," Prim says, looking at Toby with the affection of their early days, her mouth swerving to the side.

"Me bite a horse? I don't even like horses."

"You don't like anything. You don't need anything, do you, Toby?" Prim says.

"That's right. I wish I could live by myself."

The light changes, and we cross. A pack of teenagers with a rainbow of skin colors lopes by; behind them ambles an elderly couple who navigate by themselves. Toby eyes them enviously. Two Wall Street types in long coats and leather boots bound up from the subway and jog to make the light, then disappear into the Time Warner Center. A bus wheezes to a halt and coughs out sundry denizens, some heading for the shops and others for Eighth Avenue. My mother could tell a story about each one. We, like strangers, like to lose ourselves in the common atmosphere. Across the street, I press down on her wheelchair, and she swings back like a patient in a dentist's chair. I hoist her up to the curb.

"Why are you going to Arizona?"

"To be with Richard."

"Do you pay for the plane tickets?"

"Yes."

"Why?"

"I want to."

"I wish I had your money." She turns. "Why are you giving up your apartment?"

"I'm not."

"You said you were giving up your apartment."

"I didn't."

"You don't know how things will turn out. Where will you go? Don't be a fool. No one gives up an apartment in New York. Why doesn't he come to you?"

"He has a job."

She turns her face to the side as we make our way through the glass doors, and I wheel her across the marble floor of the rotunda. Her profile is still beautiful. Her cheekbone juts glamorously. "He's a poor slob," she says in a dreamy, Mad Hatter voice, addressing the air more than me.

◆

I am turning into a Chekhov play, the one where the women stand at the window of their provincial outpost and pine for Moscow. Moscow, Moscow, Moscow is all you hear about in *The Three Sisters*. Moscow is society, surprise, strangeness—all the things a great city is supposed to be. In a city like that, the streets are your arteries and veins. "You have the look of the last Tasmanian," Richard says, "the only speaker of your language." We're on our white couch in our white living room that looks like the chamber where Keir Dullea is transported in *2001: A Space Odyssey*. We have the movie poster on our wall. On this bleached set, we are equally unmoored from our foundations.

Who even knew there was such a thing as a foundation? That you might not recognize yourself without the people you get used to passing, the smell of aggression and *luft* and theater that wafts up and down Broadway? Who knew you needed your stuff? My friend Alan lives in my apartment; technically it's still mine, but as I enter and see his belongings around, I become a restless, unhappy visitor. Richard speaks about two types of museums. The kind like Noah's Ark that aim to exhibit samples of everything that exists, such as the Museum of Natural History in New York. The other kind are cabinets of curiosity: idiosyncratic collections commemorating local history you find in any small town—or apartment. I have traveled frequently but never so far afield and never without believing I was coming back. Can you hear me, Major Tom? We are all the only speakers of our language.

We visit Kierland Common, an outdoor shopping mall designed to look like a village with a square and fountain in the center. The stores are the usual suspects: Barnes & Noble, Banana Republic, Eileen Fisher. Scattered about are a few expensive restaurants and a place you can get a sandwich and coffee, but this is not a neighborhood where people live; they arrive and depart by car. "It's based on Main Street, Disney," Richard says, "rather than an actual town square. It's an evocation of village centers that in reality have been abandoned." What a smarty-pants my boyfriend is, I think. He's wearing a carrot-colored T-shirt, and his silvery hair spikes up. These streets are a break from the Valley's dominant suburban sprawl, punctuated by strip malls and condo communities, and I'm trying not to live in my old patterns. But who am I kidding? Kierland is depressing and not all that different from other sections of the Valley with streets and shops; all have been constructed by developers and aren't attached to any sort of network. There's no urban area to get lost in.

Richard asks why I'm sighing, and I don't know that I am, and the air between us starts to get a blue-black, funnel cloud look, and I say this place, this place where we live is an indistinct fuzzball and in it I'm a fuzzball, too; even though I now have friends, it takes an hour each way to drive to see them, we are so spread out. I talk about the difference between an urban facsimile and a city that isn't planned—that grows as an emergent system, little bit by little bit, and is painted and shaped and governed by the language, clothes, art, and food of the people who live in its neighborhoods. Richard says that all cities are constructed around commercial interests and that western cities and eastern cities are based on different models. He says what eastern cities have is a patina of use and wear. My head goes on fire and I raise my voice a little that sounds to him like screaming and I say: Are you suggesting that the difference between a mall and a city is soot? And he says: You like to fight, you just like to fight.

You *need* to fight. It's something about you and your mother. And we are thinking: Why did I throw over whatever the hell I had for this hidebound flamethrower? But I am also thinking: I would be just as lost in New York without my love. But my love is pissing me off with his crack about fighting, even though he's right. And why is he protecting Arizona? I say: What's Arizona to you, huh? Every day when you write, you don't situate yourself here. You're in England, wandering down cobbled streets or trucking across windblown moors. Or you're in New York, riding the subway and looking out for muggers and listening to jazz. You have hardly any friends here, too! So what's this defense of Arizona? And he says: There's something to what you say, but I feel that bad-mouthing Arizona is snobbish and an easy target for outsiders, and I just hate snobbery. And I say: Well, I'm not a snob, and I want to comment on my experience without you thinking I'm attacking people who live here. And he shoots me a grumpy smile, and I see his even row of top teeth. It hurts him if I sound unhappy. I forget that. How do I forget that? And he says: What the hell am I defending? And it hits us both that we're defending ourselves against being swallowed up in the other.

At the start of a hike, I stand on the road while Richard studies trail maps. He explains where we are going, but I don't care. I know the trek will be arduous and hot and that I will not exactly enjoy it; rather, I want to go along and wait for moments of sudden beauty. We move through scrubby pines until we emerge onto a scene of blooming cacti, thorny ocotillo plants with licks of flame shooting from their tips, slithering lizards, and brown rabbits whose long ears have been adapted to circulate blood and keep them cool. Mountains in the distance look like giants around a feast, their backbones and rib cages jutting into the sky. The sun throws slabs of red and gold onto the hills, and shade, when it comes, paints startling, darker shades, cutting a knife edge against glaring light, bleeding across wide, vacant space. As we walk, dust gives way to red soil and everywhere are rocks burnished black with desert varnish—the effect of sunbaked bacteria, the oldest living things containing DNA. The desert isn't competing with anything to be itself.

Here, coyotes have drunken parties at night, celebrating a kill—someone's small dog or a cat they've captured. Their joy is contagious. The animals are yellow with burning eyes and extra spring in their steps. In some traditions, the coyote is a wolf howling to feel air cross its throat. In others, the coyote is a lazy schemer whose plans don't work out.

One day on a hike, we arrive at the top of a hill, and Richard sees a still higher point crowned by black, jutting rocks. As we scurry up, we realize we've come to the old wall of a fortified area. A small sign indicates an archaeological site, but it isn't marked to attract visitors. Surrounding us are petroglyphs: designs scraped out on desert varnish by people who lived in the region nine hundred years ago, all traces of them vanished except for this graffiti. I copy a stick design into my notebook that looks like a Giacometti figure—a pared-down twig thing— a remnant of ourselves we carry inside.

Inside Richard, the remnant is Suzanne. Before coming to Yaddo, he thought she was sick to death of him, so her grief shocked them both. These days they are talking about what couldn't be said before.

"How could you let him leave his wife?" asks a woman I slightly know, as we ride together on a train. She doesn't sound judgmental, more like a naturalist wondering where a scorpion stores its poison and how it feels to flex its pincers. "Richard decided," I say, but she knows I didn't put a gun to his head, and I know I didn't say, "Stop," fearing he might listen to me. The way we did it, leaping toward each other without a plan, is looking like a tendency: something leaning in your direction, a cat against your leg. Tendency is something that's almost irresistible but gives you an edge to play with, and it's the edge that gets you every time. Tendency is desire in the form of a question.

I am walking on streets I can't get to, a blur of color and action. The wind cuts my cheeks and messes my hair. My mother dreams of her legs running for a bus. "I'm not young anymore," she says to the tall man who guides her up the steps. "I wish I had your youth, darling, I wish you good health, you are so kind." I am sleeping in my city but awake to a sky that looks like the cloudless eye of a noir killer.

I'm best in a foreign country where I don't understand the language and customs, so everything is enigmatic and in my ignorance I attach a benign interpretation or no meaning at all. I have the sensation of hanging by a silk thread and feeling air move across my skin. I'm not afraid of falling, because nothing is stronger than spider silk.

ABOUT LAURIE STONE

Laurie Stone is the author of three fiction and nonfiction books. She has been a longtime writer for *The Village Voice,* a theater critic for *The Nation*, a critic at large on *Fresh Air,* a member of the Bat Theater Company, and a regular writer for *Ms., New York Woman,* and *Viva.* Her numerous memoir essays have appeared in such publications as *Threepenny Review, TriQuarterly, Stone Canoe, The Literary Review, Speakeasy,* and *Creative Nonfiction.* She has received grants from, among others, the New York Foundation for the Arts, the Kittredge Foundation, Yaddo, the MacDowell Colony, Djerassi, and Poets & Writers, and in 1996 she won the Nona Balakian Citation for Excellence in Reviewing from the National Book Critics Circle. She has served as writer in residence at Pratt Institute, Old Dominion University, Thurber House, and Muhlenberg College and taught at many universities and writing programs, including Sarah Lawrence, Ohio State, Fordham, Stonecoast Writers' Conference, the Paris Writers Workshop, and the Summer Literary Seminars in Saint Petersburg,

Russia. In 2005, she participated in "Novel: An Installation," living in a house designed by Salazar Davis Architects and working on a novel in Flux Factory's gallery space. She is currently at work on *My Life as an Animal: A Memoir in Stories* and *Unmarked Trail: A Romance in Stories and a Guide to Setting Up a Writing Partnership* in collaboration with Richard Toon.

Sedat Pakay

Bubble, Bubble, Toil and Trouble

Tina Howe

Put three postmenopausal women around a bubbling cauldron with a bunch of fresh reptile innards, and there's bound to be trouble! When men age, they just get cranky, but we cast spells and bring down tyrants. It's a female thing. Since life begins and passes through us, the membranes between what we should do and what we want to do get thinner and thinner as we age. As a result, there's no rage like old-lady rage, just as there's no tenderness like old-lady tenderness. Beware the aging saint, witch, or whore. One way or another, she'll bring you to your knees!

When we're young, we tend to think old people were born that way. That it's somehow a choice. Then suddenly we hit sixty-five, seventy-three, or eighty-two and wonder what's going on. That isn't us in there! It's someone else! Construction workers suddenly don't whistle at us anymore, and waiters call us "Ma'am" instead of "Legs" or "Sweet thing."

I was lucky. Because I inherited my mother's and grand-mother's alarming height, I was a curiosity from the get-go, the apex of every class photograph from kindergarten through middle school. My diminutive father was a mere five feet five. My mother delighted in towering over him, wearing her hair in an upsweep, donning a wiglet for extra height, and then topping it all off with a hat—not some discreet cloche or beret but a plumed number with feathers soaring six inches up into the air. When my parents walked down the street together, they stopped traffic. The message was clear: to be female was to indulge one's eccentricities.

WASPy women tend to be tall and uncomfortable in their bodies, so why try to hide it? Make an asset of your flaws. Wear feathered hats and high-heeled shoes. Affect an English accent. Carry a falcon on your wrist. One of my mother's favorite rings displayed a dead ant embalmed in a dome of orange plastic. She wore it next to her mother's Ceylon sapphire, emblazoned with the family crest. No "In God we trust" there. Their motto was "I trust in myself!" After I had fourteen pea-size gallstones re-moved in 1973, I had the largest one mounted in a ring for her. She wore it to all her dinner parties next to her embalmed ant and winking sapphire—which turned out to be made of glass.

If my mother was a character in her wig and hats, her mother was a show-stopper—over six feet tall, sailing around the house in floor-length velvet housedresses that smelled of lavender and dust. She too wore her hair piled in an upsweep, but her pièce de résistance was the locket she wore that hung down to her navel. There was no picture inside but a dark, disturbing mass.

"Mama's hair!" she'd trumpet, lifting the nasty thing up for me to admire.

My grandfather wore a gold pocket watch that played a pretty tune, but she wore human hair. It looked like something pilfered from a mummy—ancient, terrifying, and alive!

"One day this will be yours!" she'd hiss, sounding vaguely like the Wicked Witch of the West.

The other thing that would be mine was her baby grand Steinway piano, which she played with abandon and vigor—Chopin nocturnes—the aroma of lavender and dust becoming more intense as her dress slowly darkened with sweat.

Her other passion was guiding me through the family photograph album.

"This is your great-uncle, who was head of surgery at Mass General. . . . This is your great-grandfather, who was governor of Massachusetts. . . . This is your father's great-great-grand-father, who was one of the first presidents of Harvard."

Who cared about all those grim-faced geezers? I much preferred hanging out with the zippy Irish maids in the kitchen. Now that I'm her age, I'm more sympathetic. She was desperate to pass things down—Chopin, the locket, her family history—and I was her conduit. No wonder she leapt on me like a drowning woman. After I delivered my daughter, my first thought was of her twenty years hence, having her first daughter, and then that grandchild having her first daughter, ad infinitum. Girl babies are born with all their eggs, so the reproductive potential is there from the beginning.

Of course men have their role in the process, but if it is deliberately thwarted, the virgin is created, pure and incomplete, a figure that inspires both worship and sacrifice. Woman as mother, saint, or whore. Which one are we on any given day or decade? It's no wonder we strike fear in the hearts of men. They simply don't have our range of options. As we age, some of us turn to stargazing, prophecy, and other forms of mischief. We put Cinderella into bondage and lace Snow White's apple with poison. Their beauty drives us wild. It's not fair! We used to be the fairest in the land!

I live in the heart of New York City, whose streets are filled with the homeless and hungry, and it's always the abandoned women who are most poignant and frightening. One of the most harrowing things I ever saw occurred one bright spring day on the corner of Seventy-second Street and Broadway. I was waiting for the light to change when one of the bag ladies in the neighborhood suddenly stepped off the curb, raised her voluminous skirts, squatted down on her haunches, and peed! Right in front of the Korean vegetable stand, with people and buses rushing all around her. She just pulled down her tattered drawers and let loose. Everything came to a halt, it was such a shocking sight! Her smile of relief, the whiteness of her thighs against the dark pavement, the brilliance of her urine pooling in the gutter—and, most chilling of all, her utter lack of self-consciousness.

New Yorkers see men urinating against buildings every day, but a woman hiking up her skirts to relieve herself with such abandon? She violated every code of female comportment. We're supposed to use the "little girls' room" or "powder room," not the street! She might have been somebody's mother, for God's sake! What would her sons and husbands think?

Mercifully, there's another side to this coin, and that's Mother Earth—woman as protector, creator, and life force. Who do you picture when someone says, "Mother Earth"? A big-boned peasant woman in her fifties, who tips the scale at 175, gray hair pulled into a loose bun, rosy cheeks, ample breasts, and great laugh. She wears scuffed Birkenstocks and a flowered dress tied with a gingham apron. She and her husband, Father Time, have about ten kids. A set of twins, a boy with learning problems, and a couple of girls who want to be gymnasts. They're the most popular family on the block. All the kids want to play at their house because Mother Nature can do everything—sew, garden, cook, fix the boiler, write poetry, play the accordion, throw pots, weave serapes, and access the Internet. She's Creativity incarnate. Her progeny is just the tip of the iceberg.

And so we move to woman as artist, particularly older woman as artist: seventy-nine-year-old Georgia O'Keeffe squinting into the New Mexico sun through eyes that altered the way we look at the natural world; Martha Graham choreographing spine-tingling mating dances into her seventies; Louise Nevelson with her turbans and mink eyelashes building wooden cathedrals into old age; and Louise Bourgeois, the diminutive French sculptor, still going strong at ninety-two, filling every major art museum in the world with her astonishing creations. Bourgeois's subject, among other things, is the phallus, which she has re-created in bronze, marble, steel, and rubber in an astonishing array of shapes and sizes.

Of course we have our bearded old masters as well, Matisse and Monet, but the ladies tend to be friskier because of the abandon with which they celebrate their sexuality—O'Keeffe with her erotic flowers, Bourgeois with her penis costumes, Graham with her elegant mating dances.

And can we talk about Doris Lessing, who won the Nobel Prize in Literature in 2007 at the age of eighty-nine? As well as countless other grandmothers who've had a way with words— Toni Morrison, Grace Paley, Maya Angelou, Muriel Rukeyser, Iris Murdoch, Isak Dinesen—the list goes on and on. Yes, we may get frisky with reptile innards around an open fire, but look what we do with our chisels, paintbrushes, voices, and stories. We create life, nurture and decorate it—but ultimately, we transform it.

ABOUT TINA HOWE

Tina Howe lives in New York City, where she valiantly tries to cook edible meals for her husband of forty-nine years, bounces grand-children on her knee, swims, haunts flea markets, heads the new MFA program in playwriting at Hunter College, and writes plays.

Object Loss

Sharon Olds

The banjo clock, suspended in thirty-weight
dreaming marriedness, for thirty
years, doesn't come down easy from the wall,
rusted to the hook, then it lurches up,
its long throat glugs. Big-headed, murmurous,
in my arms it's like a diver's bell,
Davy-Jonesed. When I lean it by the back
door, it tocks, and ticks, it doesn't even
cross my mind I might wish to kick it.
Using his list, I remove his family
furnishings, the steeple clock,
the writing-arm chair, the tole and brass
drawing table—I had not known
how connected I'd felt, through him, to a world of
handed-down, signed, dated,
appraised things, pedigreed matter.
As I add to the stash which will go to him,

I feel as if I'm falling away
from family, as if each ponderous
object had been keeping me afloat. No, they were
the scenery of the play now closing,
lengthy run it had. My pitchfork
tilts against the wall in the dining room,
web thick in its tines, spider
dangling deep in one cul-de-sac . . .
What if loss can be without
dishonor. His harpoon—a Beothuc harpoon—
and its bone and sinew and tusk and salt-wood
creel, I add to the pile, I render
unto Caesar, and my shame is summer sunlight
on a pine floor, and it moves, it sways like an old dancer.

Merkin Ode

Sharon Olds

merkin, n. A pubic wig, worn by the elderly.

When I first heard the word *merkin,* I thought it had
something to do with mermaids and mermen, all
fresh fish below the waist.
And when I learned what a merkin was—
a little wig for the nether pate,
a fake beard for the nether face—
I wondered why anyone would want one. But now,
in the shower, when I look down, I see
the little dense riot of gleaming
coils is beginning to be quelled, my shrub
is in retreat, its wilderness
is slightly pushed back—my weeds are being,
by time, gently whacked. And in the order
in which they arrived, so are they, in reverse,
leaving, drawing back from their
heraldic border, withdrawing like ladies
to the withdrawing room, until someday they will be—
if I am lucky, and get to grow old—
like an adolescent boy's moustache
around the lips. When the first wisp
appeared, I would gaze down, as if it was a
thread of smoke from a fire at a great
distance, and when the second and third
arrived together, I thought of them as
party ribbons, as streamers for a maypole's

reverse space, down into the ground,
and in a dream they were whisker faerie
soldiers sprung up to guard an inward
candy mountain. And now the earth
provides, on my body, more and more signs;
No Fishing, No Eggs, Out of Milk. And as I am
heading, with a nice slowness, for the state of non-
being—instead of mourning loss,
or pasting, on Venus, a hirsute mask, I would
praise the waning alphabet
of nests and crescents and springs and spirals,
the pelf of having had, at both ends,
curly hair, like matter hugging itself.

SHARON OLDS

Sharon Olds's books of poems, published by Knopf, include *One Secret Thing; Strike Sparks, Selected Poems 1980–2002; The Unswept Room; Blood, Tin, Straw; The Wellspring; The Father; The Gold Cell;* and *The Dead and the Living.*

Her first book, *Satan Says,* was published by the University of Pittsburgh Press. Her books have been nominated for National Book Awards and have received the National Book Critics Circle Award, the Lamont Selection of the Academy of American Poets, and the Harriet Monroe Prize. She has served as New York State's poet laureate and helped found a writing workshop (now continuous for twenty-four years) at the Goldwater Hospital in New York City. She teaches in the Graduate Writing Program at New York University and is a member of the American Academy of Arts and Science and a chancellor of the Academy of American Poets.

Loving Mr. Bones

Erica Jong

Have you ever spent your days shuttling between one hospital and another? That was what my life became. My father was at Mount Sinai, my husband at New York Hospital—and I the flying shuttlecock between them, daring not to wish or dream.

When I wasn't at the hospital, I roamed the Internet, lonely as a cloud. I was amazed to live in a time in which both sex and death could be found online. What was next? Pets online? Offspring online? Plastic surgery online? Love online?

There was this tendency—I suffered from it myself in times of depression—to retreat from the world and reduce all human intercourse to virtual interaction. It was safer that way. And there were fewer smells, fewer doubts, fewer embarrassing noises, fewer pangs of despair. I had the feeling that if I were too upset I could just change the channel, visit a new site, erase my history by punching in "clear history." I could change my life by Googling myself and rewriting my story. I was supremely in control—as long as I never left the house.

At the hospital, it was different. My father was hanging on in the ICU. He seemed happy to see me, but he was intubated again, so he couldn't speak.

The nurse reported that he had pulled out all his tubes the night before. And had had to be reconnected by the morning shift. He'd even pulled out the feeding peg.

I sat by his bedside watching him doze and wake and cursed myself for what we were doing to him. We were not observing his living will. It was too hard to interpret. Nobody dared to play god. Nobody dared to make a decision. Perhaps my hysterical older sister was right. We should let him go.

Every night at Mount Sinai, my husband and I would watch the "coalition of the willing" bombing on TV. Little kids left legless after stumbling on cluster bombs, hospitals overflowing with people killed in marketplaces, in school, in cars just for turning the ignition key. This was the world we'd made under the aegis of Cheney-Bush. Yet letting go of a ninety-two-year-old father had not gotten any easier.

All my life there had been war on TV. And what had it accomplished? Inflated the price of oil and Halliburton stock and killed the brown-eyed children. The younger the children, the more they died. And the women died. And the youngest men.

When I thought about the legless children, I couldn't sleep. How could anyone sleep?

Well, my father could. At least if he was sufficiently drugged. He had been an athlete once, and now he was Mr. Bones. You could see his hips and pelvis through his coverlet. His legs were skeletal. He weighed less than one hundred pounds.

What can you wish for as you watch a beloved parent struggling in Ivan Ilyich's black sack? Should you wish for death or life? And how much do your wishes matter?

The lucky ones die in restaurants after a good dinner. Or die in their sleep in bed during an erotic dream about a lover long since passed to the other side. I hope to merit such a death.

The tall, skinny geriatrician from the palliative care team strides in.

"Mr. Mann," he says to my father, "I'm your doctor. How are you feeling?"

My father pulls out his tube with great élan and croaks, *"Malpractice!"*

"Dad, you really know how to get along with doctors!" I say.

"Let me out of here!" he scrumbles, trying to scream. He's undoing the tubes, detaching himself from the IVs and peg, and trying to stand up. He's very shaky, but he almost manages. The male nurse arrives.

"If you put that tube back in, I'll kill you!" says my father.

Standing there, I am proud and terrified at the same time. I take the geriatric doctor aside.

"Leave the tube out. If he dies, he dies," I whisper. "Don't torture him."

"Okay," the geriatrician agrees. But my father refuses to get back into bed. He doesn't want to be here. Who can blame him?

"If I promise not to put back the tube, will you settle down?" the geriatric internist asks.

"I don't know," my father croaks. But the nurse comforts him and somehow gets him back into bed without tubes and monitors.

"I want to go home! Home!"

So we start to make plans to bring him home.

It's not an easy proposition. We need to rent a hospital bed, hire a nurse, get morphine prescriptions filled. But, having gotten his way, my father seems to have made an astounding recovery. He is hoarsely yelling at everyone, ordering the palliative care team around, and they seem cowed.

"What is palliative care? It's how you turf the old out on the ice floe! You're the Angel of Death team, that's what you are."

In my heart I'm cheering him on.

"Take me back to Eleven West!" he shouts. That's the

swanky hotel floor of the hospital where they overcharge you to death.

My sisters return, and we accomplish the transfer out of the ICU and to the hotel floor. My father is triumphant. He's talking and breathing and screaming like a champ. His old strength seems to have returned. He is coasting on the propellant of anger.

"You know what Mark Twain said?"

"What?" I ask.

"Reports of my death have been greatly exaggerated!"

"You know what Art Buchwald said?" I ask.

"No," mumbles Daddy.

"I don't either, but he refused to die."

How this happened, I don't know, but even in his parlous condition, my father has made a special friend at the hospital. He's a geriatric psychiatrist named Dr. Cragswell, first name Fin, for Finnegan. He's got a long braid down his back and iron-rimmed glasses like an anarchist from the early twentieth century, and he thoroughly disapproves of the ministrations of the palliative care team. He has taken me aside several times to tell me that he thinks my father has "an acute but not fatal illness."

"He's playing to you," my younger sister says. "He's a star fucker."

"He's crazy," my crazy older sister says.

But he seems to be able to reach my father when no one else can. For this, I'm grateful.

"If you take your father home, I'll come see him," Dr. Cragswell says.

"Thanks," I say.

My sisters ignore him.

◆

They think he's playing to me. They tuck my father into bed and admonish him not to get up again. The sun is going down, and both the park and the sky have that neon blue color that tugs at the heart because it's so fleeting. *L'heure bleue.* I stay a little longer and then run to the other hospital to see my husband. I am so exhausted that I fall into a deep sleep on the chair in my husband's room.

Now it is midnight. The park has been snow-frosted all of January and February, and there are icy patches on the walkways and a crust of frozen snow over the hills. The snow seems blue in places, black in places. A gibbous moon lights the treetops. The streetlights leave puddles of blue on the snow. A procession of very old people in hospital gowns, some leaning on walkers, some on canes, some in wheelchairs rolling along by hand, appears. My father and a tall, thin doctor with a long braid down his back lead them. My father has a staff he has made from a fallen branch. Dr. Cragswell has a scythe. It looks like an Ingmar Bergman movie filmed in New York. My father is exhorting the old people to move along, not to give up, to disinherit their ungrateful children. His voice is scratchy, but he can be faintly heard from where I watch.

At first the procession consists of only a few people, but now my father has put down his staff and he is drumming on a snare drum he wears on a strap around his neck. *Mamapapa-mamapapa* it goes—as he used to say when he tried to teach me to play the drums. (My high school dates always loved coming to my house because of the full set of snare drums and cymbals.) And with his drumming, the procession gets longer and longer. He seems jubilant. He has triumphed. All the ancient people are following him over the snowy hills of the park. As they follow him, they get younger and younger. The bent straighten up and throw away their walkers. The wheelchair rollers sprint out of their wheelchairs. My father has become the Pied Piper of the Park.

"I never realized how much the old resent the young," I tell him.

"Of course we do!" he shouts. "If we could be young again, we'd know what to do! What did you *think*?"

"I thought you loved us!"

"That's secondary!" he shouts.

I start to shout at him but wake myself up.

"You certainly are a noisy sleeper," my husband says.

"I have a great deal to be noisy about. That was a crazy dream."

"Tell me."

"You know dreams—fascinating to the dreamer, boring to everybody else. I don't want to bore you."

"What do you remember?"

"My father in the park, leading a procession of dying people over the snow." But even as I told them, the images wafted away like smoke in the wind.

"We have no rituals for death," I said. "That's why it's so hard. We're supposed to disappear when we're no longer young. Our parents make us uncomfortable because they remind us of our fate. And we make them uncomfortable because we remind them of what they've lost. We need new rituals, new philosophies. If only we *believed*."

"In what?"

"That's the problem. How can you believe in God after the Holocaust, the Vietnam War, Iraq, Bush?"

The question lingered in the air like the smoke of my dream. My husband invited me to his hospital bed. He hugged me. Weakly.

"But why can't you enjoy what we have now and forget about the future? The future doesn't really exist. All we have is this."

"I know."

"If I die, I don't care if you wear mourning for the rest of your life like Queen Victoria. I want you to live. I want to *liberate* you to live. You liberated me."

"I know."

"For most of my life, I had no idea how to live. Now I do. I want to share that with you."

"I know," I said.

"You know, but you don't know at all."

"I know."

He hugged me very tight.

I tried to go back to sleep and reenter the dream. I wanted to hold on to the vision of my father stomping through the snow. But it was gone.

My husband was getting better as my father was getting worse. He still had not come home, but he was talking to his clients on the phone. He had shortened his condition to "a heart attack" for their sake. No point in going into long discussions of aneurysms and grafts. His clients were shook-up enough by his absence. They depended on him. And he depended on them. Talking to them on the phone made him feel useful again.

I wanted to feel useful, too. I started taking notes on what was going on. I thought I had sworn off writing for publication, but I began keeping notes on my father and my husband. That was when I started to realize how alike they were and how much I had depended on men to complete my life. Once I'd had an idea for a play in which a woman revisits all the old lovers in her life and they all turn out to be the same man. Was that my story? Was that every woman's story?

"What do you think of this all-female house?" my mother asked. That was the only reference she made to my father's hospitalization. She lay in bed, wearing diapers, waking and sleeping, attended by rotating nannies. When I looked for a vase for the flowers I'd brought her, I discovered that every container was veiled by greasy dust, something she never would have allowed when she was awake and aware. All the women in my family are mad housewives, compulsive cleaners. Veils of grease are not their style. This is the way the world ends, I thought, greasy dust covers all.

I gave her a big smooch and sat by her side in her wheelchair while she faded in and out of consciousness.

She woke up, saw the flowers by her bedside, and said, "I should paint them." But the truth was, she hadn't painted in years. She had forgotten how.

My mother tilts her head back and looks up at the ceiling with her mouth open as if she would swallow the sky. This is no life for the energetic person she once was. If she could see herself, she wouldn't be happy.

When babies spend their days waking and sleeping, we're not sad because we know their lives are going forward. But an old person's slipping in and out of sleep is only a warm-up for extinction. We know it. Do they know it? And if they know, do they care?

Yes!

What on earth are we going to do with our old, old, old, very old parents? If we have to choose between babies and old people, we know damn well what we ought to do. My mother always used to tell the story about the mother eagle that could save only one of her baby eaglets from a catastrophic storm that threatened to blow away their nest. So she asked each eaglet what he or she would do when she was old and utterly dependent on their care. The first eaglet answered, "Stay and take care of you, Mother, for the rest of your life." The second said, "Sacrifice everything for your welfare, Mother." The third said, "I will have eaglets of my own to care for, and they must come before you. If I can save them and save you, I will do it. But if I must choose, I will choose *them* when you are old." Of course the third eaglet was the one she saved.

Survival of the tribe is always more important than survival of the dying. Triage was my mother's lesson to us. It was far less ambiguous than a so-called living will. Yet how to follow it? We'd better harden our hearts as the earth becomes overrun with the dying. The old are rigid. They don't want to give up their power. Unless we replace them with flexible new people, we have no chance of changing the world. I assume that's why the immortals invented death. They must have known that immortality was no bargain. Remember Tithonus, the man who could not die.

Aldous Huxley, who was prophetic about so many things—from artificial insemination to euthanasia—envisioned the dying wafting to the next world on a cloud of music and "soma." Pain would be obsolete, drugs ubiquitous. We're almost there.

You don't really become aware of the body until its beautiful balance breaks down. My father couldn't eat, couldn't swallow, couldn't pee, yet wouldn't die.

If only I could get inside his head and know what he was thinking. But I couldn't even do that when he was well. He was always running away—to the airport, to the piano, to the drums, to the Metropolitan Opera, to the office, to Japan or Italy or China. He was an escape artist. And so, of course, was I. It took me years to find a marriage I didn't want to escape from, yet I kept having escape fantasies. Perhaps it was the escape fantasies that led me *not* to escape. Perhaps fantasy was the only way marriage endured, or life.

Now my dad could not escape except by dying. I wondered if he knew that. Of course, I didn't have the courage to put the question to him. All I could do was hold his bony hand, then go to the other hospital and dream of his escape through the park.

Of course, when he finally died, none of us was there. Even my mother was in the other room. We brought him home to a hospital bed, our pockets full of morphine and syringes that were never used. We settled him in bed, made him comfortable, and left him with one of his caretakers. He expired that very night, as if he had been waiting to come home. He died at one in the morning looking at the snowy hills of the park, still imagining his escape. I was not there.

"Is he in that box?" my mother asked at the funeral.

"No," I said, without lying. He was already far away.

When identifying his body, I kissed him on the cheek, leaving my lipstick print, but his expression was no longer his. How quickly the spirit flees!

"I love you, Dad," I said. I might as well have been speaking to a hollow doll. Without animation and warmth, without movement, the flesh is almost unrecognizable. What remains is inside us—memory, mirroring, our gestures, our words, our music.

Inevitably, as with all my nonobservant dead relatives, we had to rely on rent-a-rabbi. My father had never belonged to a synagogue. He refused to belong to any club that would have him (à la Groucho Marx). His mixture of insecurity and arrogance prevented him from being a joiner.

His will dictated that each of us should speak about him at his funeral. And we did. We would have done it without the will. Remarkably, for three such different daughters, we all stressed the same things. Music was in all our memories. He played the piano through our dreams. He dragged us to concerts and operas until we understood. He would not let us close our ears.

The bones clatter, but music covers all. His whole life was music to our ears—if not his own.

And the strangest thing is this: When he was alive, I thought all our conversations were partial, frustrating—unintelligible. But once he was dead, we really began to talk. We talked through all my dreams. We talked every night till the small hours of the morning. Alive, he was closed and careful. Dead, he told me everything. I think he may be dictating to me now.

ABOUT ERICA JONG

Erica Jong is a poet, novelist, and essayist best known for her eight best-selling novels, including *Fear of Flying,* with twenty million copies in print. Other best sellers are *How to Save Your Own Life, Fanny: Being the True History of the Adventures of Fanny Hackabout-Jones, Parachutes & Kisses, Shylock's Daughter* (formerly *Serenissima*), *Any Woman's Blues, Inventing Memory,* and *Sappho's Leap.*

Her midlife memoir *Fear of Fifty* also became a major international best seller. Ms. Jong is also the author of seven award-winning collections of poetry. Known for her commitment to women's rights, authors' rights, and free expression, Ms. Jong is a frequent lecturer in the United States and abroad. She has won many awards worldwide.

Erica Jong also regularly blogs for the Huffington Post.

Her twenty-first book and seventh book of poetry, *Love Comes First: A Collection of New Poems,* came out from Tarcher-Penguin in January 2009. She is immersed in a new novel and an anthology called "Best Sex I Ever (had, am having, will hopefully someday have)."

Rich Sandifer

Interview with
Dr. Christiane Northrup

CHRISTIANE NORTHRUP: I'd like to tell you my story so that you can understand where I'm coming from.

EMILY: *Please do.*

DR. NORTHRUP: I have nothing but excitement and optimism for my foreseeable future. I started life old. And now I feel younger in so many ways than when I was twelve. Back then, I was extraordinarily serious; I had classic migraine headaches. I was even hospitalized for a week at the Faulkner Hospital and had a complete headache workup. I had a perfectionist's approach to life back then.

My mother's pleasure in life came from activities that were absolutely the opposite of anything that brought me joy or pleasure. She hunted deer and game birds, skied, played tennis and golf, anything associated with vigorous outdoor activity which included swinging something at a ball or pitting her body against a mountain. Meanwhile, I liked to sit by the fire and read books. So we were an interesting mismatch.

I had a sister who died when she was six months old. She wouldn't eat. And the doctors never figured out why, though I suspect it had something to do with the large and continuous doses of antibiotics my mother was given for viral pneumonia during her pregnancy. And then my brother was born, and he wouldn't eat, either. I was eight years old. Having been told he would die, my parents signed him out of the hospital and tube-fed him at home, every hour on the hour. When he was a year old, they found a female doctor in Philadelphia who was a pioneer in pediatric gastroscopy. She discovered that his esophagus was about to erode through from the feeding tube, so she removed it and eventually he started eating.

Years later, when I applied to the University of Buffalo medical school, his first attending physician interviewed me and remembered this case. He was certain that my brother would be either dead or retarded, given that they had told my mother this would be the case if he lived. He now has a few little immune system problems, but he's a thriving guy at the age of fifty. Similarly, when I applied to med schools, my dad signed himself out of the hospital against medical advice. He had gone in with chest pain, and they thought he'd had a heart attack. But he did *not* have a heart attack; he had infectious pericarditis, an infection of the sac around the heart.

Because of all this, I grew up with an intense faith in the ability of the human body to heal and also a faith in the process of life, knowing that death is part of it. My aunt and uncle were both medical doctors, and Thanksgiving was like an American Medical Association meeting. My dad was a dentist who said you could tell the state of a person's health by looking at his/her mouth, and I went into the job of looking at the lower lips.

I had the same approach as a practitioner as he had, which was to look at a person's entire life and realize that the medical system looks at only one piece. They look at a germ, and then they look at a way to kill the germ. They don't look at the environment that makes a germ grow and the fact that the diseases that are killing people prematurely now are not infectious. Chronic degenerative diseases such as arthritis, diabetes, heart disease, high blood pressure, cardiovascular disease, and cancer are the leading causes of death. And they are seventy to ninety percent preventable!

I started life with a different indoctrination, as it were, than most people do. Most people believe that when you're sick, you go to a doctor and the doctor will make you well, and that your health is shored up in someplace called a hospital or a clinic. And I knew from the beginning that this was not true. Modern medicine can pull you back from the brink of death, but it does little to prevent chronic disease.

When I was about twelve, I came across a book called *Natives of Eternity*. I actually opened a package at a home where I was babysitting, 'cause the title on the box said *Natives of Eternity,* and although I was the quintessential good girl, that was a very intriguing title, and I couldn't resist ripping open the box. This book was about angels, and it was written by Flower Newhouse, a Christian mystic. I read that Flower Newhouse saw the angels of birth and death, the spirits of fire and flowers and air and wind, and it was as though everything I'd always hoped was true about the universe. And that others believed it too. There are unseen energies and forces to help us. Reading about this marked one of the most exciting moments of my life. It confirmed for me that we are not alone in a meaningless, linear universe and that there isn't any death of our essence, our souls.

These were things I already knew deep within. Remember, I was young—twelve, a time when what's known as the kundalini life force energy just starts to rise. This is right around the time of puberty, when you get your first period, and the change in hormones, combined with the desire to fit into society, tends to shut down a lot of your innate childhood knowing. After reading the book I began to have a series of breakfasts with Gretchen, the woman who had ordered the book and who, I soon learned, had studied in person with Flower Newhouse. We talked about spirituality and angels and past lives and Edgar Cayce. During my teenage years I sought out Gretchen regularly and she became an early mentor of mine. She was my mother's friend and would be ninety-six years old now.

I was always fascinated by the natural world, biology, and all of that stuff, so I majored in that field. But I never planned to become a doctor. When I finished college, I had won a lot of scholarships for graduate school. I was burned out after college, having attended Case Western Reserve during the turbulent sixties and early seventies. The Kent State shootings happened a mere thirty miles away. The world seemed as though it was falling apart. In fact, when I had my first astrologic reading, the person who did it said, "I have never seen anyone born in 1949 who actually went through college, med school, and residency and finished up without a big gap in between. Most dropped out for a while. You didn't."

When I went home after college, I didn't know what to do. So I worked as a clerk-typist at my boyfriend's father's firm for a while. I remember thinking "Oh, God, is this it? Is this all there is?" Because I knew I could run my department in a month. So I was feeling a sense of "Uh-oh! Uh-oh!" Then I decided to try med school because my college adviser, whose wife later went back to medical school and became a urologist, which was unheard of at the time, said to me, "Chris, why don't you go to medical school?" Now, remember, I'd seen my aunt and uncle, I didn't like the way they lived, I didn't like the way they thought, but I thought, "Okay, why not? An M.D. is a better degree." Besides, my father said, "At the end of four years you've got to be something. Might as well have an M.D. after your name." Made sense.

So I go to medical school. And you know, in the early seventies, when women were entering all these male professions in droves, we were so lit up, we were so excited by the possibility that for the first time, at least in written human history, we had a place at the table. We abandoned our mothers, so to speak. We wanted to be Not Mom.

I found it all very exciting. Med school was the first education that I really enjoyed. I also, by the way, had always wanted to play the harp since I could remember, even before I had seen one. I don't know where that came from. Maybe I associated it with angels. In any case, I studied the harp throughout high school. I'd come up to Maine and do summer harp study, and then I went to Case Western Reserve because my harp teacher was there. Her name was Alice Chalifoux, and she played with the Cleveland Orchestra and had been all over the world. Case Western also just happened to have a really good biology department, too, but I was never premed.

All through med school I played my harp in the Dartmouth symphony, and I remember that my adviser, who played the bass behind me and was head of the Arthritis Foundation, said to me, "This is the time for study, this is not the time for you to be playing music." I knew how wrong that was, and I thought, "If I just study, I'm going to be a disintegrated human being later on." I know it was very important to have this aspect of my life going on at the same time.

The reason I felt this way was because I had grown up with a father who knew the importance of balance. We had an organic garden. He played the violin. He didn't play particularly well, but still, he took his fiddle everywhere, because he believed it was his job to create a party, to be entertaining. And so the impact of uplifting others and the pleasure and joy of the natural, organic world were part of my upbringing.

When I went to med school, I met my husband, who was my surgical intern at the time. He was a tall, handsome, third-generation Harvard grad and an orthopedic surgeon. Very blue blood. And so I was married for twenty-four years to the man who I thought was the man of my dreams. I went through my ob/gyn residency . . . The rest is in my books. I had my kids and my career, and what everyone, all the baby boomers, did—with no road map whatsoever. We were making it all up as we went along. Our mothers couldn't provide any guidance for how to balance career and family. Most had never done it!

I took a fairly orthodox life path in an unorthodox way. At the end of my residency in Boston, my cousin called and told me how she was using a macrobiotic diet to shrink her fibroids. She introduced me to Michio Kushi, who was the founder of Erewhon Natural Foods and a pioneer in using diet and lifestyle to address physical ailments and also to maintain health. Michio came to the United States from Japan in 1949 and made a major contribution to the natural foods movement, along with Robert Rodale, the founder of *Prevention* magazine. While practicing medicine in Boston, I used to go over to the East West Foundation in Brookline. I'd sit with Michio when he did patient consultations, using what is known as Oriental medicine. As they changed their diets, I'd see how, every time, people's faces would change. I also watched many recover from many different conditions, including heart disease and cancer. Now, many of them did not recover, but believe me, every one of them had been given up for dead by the profession that I was getting board-certified in. They had nothing to lose. I reviewed their medical records and saw that the cancer patients had already had chemo and radiation. They'd all been through the Western medical wringer. And I watched many get better with dietary and lifestyle changes.

So when I started my private practice in Maine, I pushed the envelope and used a lot of dietary approaches in the treatment of my patients. At that time, I had to close the door in my office before talking to women with breast cancer about diet and lifestyle. It was considered so heretical, I was afraid I'd lose my license. At the very least, I'd have to endure the derision of my colleagues.

At the same time that I was practicing nutritional and lifestyle medicine, I was sitting on the board of the American Holistic Medical Association. During those early years, I also developed a large breast abscess while trying to nurse my first daughter and also work eighty hours per week. I know this was related to a lifestyle that was unbalanced. Because of my interest and belief in the laws of manifestation (how thought creates reality), I soon realized that I needed to change my life and create a workplace where it was safe and healthy for me to be a holistically minded mother, doctor, and woman.

Looking back now, I see that my entire life has been a hero's journey. For example, I lost the function in my right breast by trying so hard to prove my worth in a male-dominated world that didn't acknowledge the work of nurturing oneself or others. Hence, I developed the breast abscess while trying to nurse a baby (feminine) and also work eighty hours a week (masculine). When I gave birth to my second daughter, I realized that I had so totally scarred the duct system of the right breast from the abscess that no milk came out. My masculine mode of being had compromised my ability to fully nourish my baby. I had to nurse her exclusively on my left side, which worked fine as long as I nursed her often enough.

Soon thereafter, realizing that if I continued to work in this way, I was destined to get sick, I, along with three other female colleagues, started a health care center run by women for women. It was called Women to Women. From the beginning, we acknowledged the seamless relationship between a woman's biography and her biology. This experience led to my first book, *Women's Bodies, Women's Wisdom*. The six-year process of writing this book was like taking a pickax to concrete, because every part of a woman's body had, up until that time, been seen through a male lens. Even the anatomy of a woman's body is described using male researchers' names. Hence we have Montgomery's tubercles around our nipples, Gabriele Falloppio in our tubes, Bartholin in the glands around the vulva. It's as though the female body has been explored and conquered by males.

As I was deconstructing the field of women's medicine, I was also deeply engrossed in metaphysics and the science of the mind. Starting in 1983, I got my first astrological reading. I have also done work with numerologists and those who understand the kabbalah. And so, for years, I have been well aware that my soul has a specific journey and task in this life. And that there are no mistakes. And that I'm not a hapless victim. I've always had a sense of an unfolding destiny with particular challenges designed to help me along the path of my life. And I've known that my thoughts and how I choose to do things create the circumstances of my life. I've always believed this.

Because of my unorthodox approach to medicine, I eventually lost my connection with my former colleagues, all of whom I really loved but who couldn't get on board with the path I was taking. Initially I stayed in the fold of my profession, however, by having a sense of humor. So once when I asked one of them to cover my practice for a weekend, he said, "Well, I'll do it, but what do I do if someone calls in with sprout poisoning?" I was okay with the jokes, because I knew that as long as I was included in them, I was safe.

There have been three major losses in my life. The first was the death of my sister when I was about twenty-eight years old. The second was the death of my father. And years later, the end of my twenty-four-year marriage. My sister was killed in a car accident when she was twenty-three. I was twenty-eight and newly married. I was in the second year of my residency, and all my patients were young women dying of cancer. I learned how to relate up close and personal. This was around my first Saturn return. This is an astrological term that refers to the point in our lives, at about age twenty-nine, when we have to truly take on adult responsibilities. Saturn comes around to its natal position again between ages fifty-six and sixty. At this point, we are at a developmental stage that urges us to thrive, not simply survive. Saturn teaches us through limitations and restrictions. It forces us to question the bigger meaning of life and truly take responsibility for ourselves and for the quality of our lives. The first Saturn return is when so many rock stars have died of overdoses. My sister, Cindy, who was killed in the car accident, was four years younger than I. We had traveled through Europe together before I entered medical school. She was as free-spirited and fun as I was serious and studious. Her death, which occurred in the middle of my residency training, was like having a lightning bolt strike my heart and my family. And I remember thinking "Oh my gosh, at any moment, our lives can change so inexorably." There was a big blizzard in Buffalo, New York, at the time of her funeral, and so I couldn't get out of there to go back to Boston. It was just such a wrenching time. Luckily, my husband had known my sister, so we could share the loss. And one of his good friends was in love with her. So after her death, the two of us got together, reminisced about her, and grieved. I remember both of us going to see the movie *Heaven Can Wait,* which had a reincarnation theme. It was very helpful—and hopeful—for both of us. I knew that the only way through this loss was grieving and feeling the loss. There were no shortcuts. Nine months after my sister was killed, my dad dropped dead on the tennis court, playing tennis with my mom. He was sixty-eight and perfectly healthy. I'm certain he died of a ruptured cerebral aneurysm that might have been present for years. These are the experiences that forced me to grow up and learn about the inevitable losses associated with life.

I believe that we are immortal. We don't die. Our souls come here, and we have a piece of work that we're meant to do. The more joyfully and pleasurably we do the work we've come to do, the healthier we will be. Consequently, my teaching and message to people can be summed up in the words "Happy, healthy, dead."

An enormous amount of scientific research supports the fact that the immune, endocrine, and nervous systems work much better in a state of peace, forgiveness, joy, and acceptance. Examples include the work of Herbert Benson from Harvard, Walter B. Cannon, Norm Shealy, and Hans Selye. These people have been my heroes since day one.

Forgiveness and letting go—a process, not an event—is absolutely key for true health and happiness. The person we always need to forgive first is ourselves. The big lie in our culture is that you suffer because you're bad or have done something wrong. When I had my breast abscess, I really suffered and had tremendous pain. The surgeon said that it was the worst breast abscess he'd seen in thirty years and that it was dissecting into my chest wall. When I couldn't nurse my second child out of that breast, it was a big loss.

The fact that I couldn't feed my child fully and naturally, ultimately because of my own overwork, was so painful. I had to find compassion for myself, had to say to myself, "How could I have known? How could I have known that you can't work eighty hours a week, a hundred hours a week, nurse a baby full-time, do six C-sections in a row?" No one ever told me. Or supported me as a mother or as a woman.

One of the biggest turning points in my life came during a ten-day intensive with Anne Wilson Schaef in the eighties. All of us from Women to Women went. When we had left standard medical settings to start our center, we'd brought with us the deeply ingrained male model of working ourselves to death! We found that, within two years, we were as burned out, broke, and tired as we had ever been when the men were running the system. But there was no one to blame; we had met the enemy, and she was us! I thought to myself, "Okay, if it's true that we have some control over our lives and that our thoughts and emotions can influence our reality, then I'd better actually apply this philosophy to my own life." It's so much easier to blame the system rather than look at the way in which you're perpetuating it! I wasn't willing to do that.

At that time, we had to do an intervention with one of my partners, who we suspected was alcoholic. I thought, "Okay, we're going to do the intervention, and then we'll all go home, and she'll get into recovery, and blah, blah, blah." Well, that isn't the way it happened, because our bodies have a process. Labor is a process.

One thing I know about the body: it heals through a process. Wounds need to be acknowledged. You never get well unless someone acknowledges your wound. There are three parts to an intervention: one, tell the person how much they mean to you, how much you love them. The second part is to say what their addiction is doing to you. And in the third, you state the bottom line, like if the drinking continues, this is what will happen. In our case, the bottom line was that she couldn't be in the practice anymore because this is way too much of a liability.

So we were at the retreat center doing the intervention, and I started to tell this woman how much I appreciated her when she parked my car when I was in labor with my second child. Now, you have to understand, in the culture that we grew up in, you didn't trust other women; you were trying to be Not Mom. Our greatest resource for healing and wholeness is other women, but we've been taught that they're the enemy, because we're all arguing over the same guy or the same job or getting the boss's favor. Anyway, she parked my car. And as I started to say that, I began to weep, so Anne Wilson Schaef said, "Why don't you lie down and see what comes up?" That was part of the purpose of the retreat. Whatever your process was, you went there, and if you started to cry, going into it would be like the grappling hook that would help you deal with your pain. So I got down on the mat and I quickly pushed down the tears, which I was good at because you don't get through a surgical residency without being pretty stalwart. Then she said, "You're so tired." Having a woman give me permission to be tired was about the sweetest thing that had ever happened to me in my life. Because my mom's motto was "Don't ask for a lighter pack, ask for a stronger back." Better, bigger, more was what she was teaching. So I got down on that mat, and I started to wail. I mean wail like the Wailing Wall women dressed in black that you see in photographs. Sounds came out of me, I didn't even know where they came from, and then I went through all my own pain. What you do in Anne's process is, you see it as *the* pain. It's not personal, it's *the* pain. And then, when I was done with *my* pain, all the times I didn't rest, all the times I didn't whatever, then I went back through my mother, and her mother and her mother and her mother. And so I entered a trapdoor in the universe, down into what I call the pain of all women. And I knew that my work was sourced from those thousands and thousands and thousands of years of women suffering, and I also knew that's what I came to do. I came to address that suffering and transform it into joy.

E: *Are you fearful of the future?*

CN: I am fearless as I go into this next phase of my life. I believe that pain is inevitable but suffering and misery are optional. Misery is intellectual. It's the story you tell yourself about the pain, about everything. I have been with people who are dying, and I've seen the light that comes from them. It's the most moving thing you can imagine. I had one case, a thirty-seven-year-old woman dying of cervical cancer, and her body had been ravaged by the cancer. She'd done everything she could do to fight, and then she fell into a coma after some renal shutdown, and then she woke up out of that deep sleep. Everyone thought she was going to die but she didn't; she woke up out of this deep sleep and it was as though there was this light coming from within her body, and she started to laugh. Her room in the hospital was irresistible. The nurses couldn't stay away. She talked about her two cats being in the room with her, she could see them. They weren't there, but many times we have companion animals, and their spirit will be with us, in the shaman realm of life. You know, no one gets to be a real shaman until they have confronted death and gone through their own death in a way. So she had done that, she'd faced death, and she'd come back for a while. And she laughed, and she said, "All that stuff you've been saying, it's all true about nutrition." She was joyful. I remember my mom telling me that when she was with a dying friend, his last words, with a huge smile on his face, were "Oh. My. God."

Here's what I believe: we're all going to God, or we all are little bits of God.

E: *What is God for you?*

CN: What is God for me? God is the universal intelligence that is life force. That's all it is. Let me tell you what God is not. It is not a man in a white beard sitting up on a cloud. If I had to pick God as a deity, it would be the Divine Mother. I actually really relate to Mother Mary. My mother was excommunicated from the church when she was thirteen for allegedly painting the Blessed Mother's toenails on the altar. She didn't do it, but her excommunication is something I will always be grateful for. If it weren't for that, I would have had to recover from Catholic indoctrination about original sin, the evils of the body, and other ideas that don't support life or health fully.

There is a place where there is no suffering. It is described time and time again in all the near-death experience literature.

Melvin Morse, for instance, is a pediatrician who wrote a book called *Transformed by the Light,* about near-death experiences in children. He has done some studies on this in a hospital in Seattle with all these kids who've had near-death experiences. They see the light at the end of the tunnel, and oftentimes they meet loved ones or whoever they believe in. And they are transformed by this. Many of them never talk about it because they're afraid they'll be ridiculed. But their electromagnetic fields have changed—they've been rewired. Proof of this change in their electromagnetic field is the fact that more than twenty-five percent of them can no longer wear watches. The watches simply stop working when they wear them. Of course, you don't need to have a near-death experience to have experienced this. My youngest daughter is one of them. She's never had a near-death experience, but she's just incredibly sensitive and psychic. There are electrical phenomena around people who are intuitively tuned in. They often shut down their computers, especially when they are hurried or upset. There's a book called *Extraordinary Knowing* by Elizabeth Mayer, Ph.D. She took on the whole area of psychic phenomena. Her daughter's harp was stolen in Oakland, California, and the police couldn't find it. It was a very valuable instrument, and after months and months of dead ends, a friend said to her, "Why don't we ask a dowser to find it?" She called the head of the American Society of Dowsers in Arkansas (this was before the Internet), and he said, "Just send me a map of Oakland." She did, and he said, "It's in one of these two houses." He gave her the addresses, and she drove over there. She was afraid because it was a dodgy neighborhood, so instead of knocking on any doors, she put a flyer up with a picture of the harp on it. It said, "A reward for the return of my daughter's harp." And three days later she got a call from a guy who said, "Meet me in the parking lot of Safeway, I have the harp." She was so blown away. Her scientific worldview was very challenged by the fact that a man in Arkansas was able to pinpoint a harp halfway across the country simply by reading energy through dowsing. This sort of thing flies in the face of what we've been led to believe about reality.

A couple of years ago, I received a fax from a German doctor, saying that the Bruno Groening Circle of Friends was sending some doctors to the U.S. to present the work of the late German healer Bruno Groening, whom I'd never heard of. So I went to the lecture. The German doctors presented case histories of healing that cannot be explained. For example, people deaf from a forceps delivery at birth, people deaf for thirty years, got their hearing back after beginning to practice *einstellen,* which means "tuning in" in German. In the *einstellen* practice, you simply receive the healing stream. And people get better from this practice. This group has hundreds and hundreds and hundreds of well-documented case histories that medically document spiritual healing. One of my patients, who had terrible foot pain such that she couldn't walk anywhere, had a complete healing of her pain from this practice of tuning in to spiritual energy. We had another woman with food allergies. She was allergic to just about everything and was down to basically eating just broccoli and rice. Now she can eat everything and is very excited. I have read the case histories and I have met people who have had extraordinary healings, including a doctor who had a big inguinal hernia with an entrapped loop of bowel down into his scrotum. This was completely healed through spiritual healing. The list goes on and on. The healings are all documented, often with before-and-after MRIs. Robert Fritchie, an engineer, started the World Service Institute, a global group that also teaches people how to connect with the energy of Divine Love. Fritchie also has helped thousands of people heal through tuning in to the loving energy of the universe. It doesn't matter what you call it. The main thing is to know it's there and that we can open our hearts to it for healing of ourselves, others, and the planet (including water, trees, food, etc.). I believe in miracles, and I have seen my life transformed. I was divorced at forty-nine, which was the last thing I wanted, a huge loss in my life at the time. It happened right after I appeared on *Oprah* for the first time, and everything sort of came to a head. The truth is that the bigger I got in the world, the less my husband could tolerate me. And he was never proud of my work. But when it became clear that the marriage couldn't tolerate my becoming who I really was, I had faith in the fact that, painful as it was, it was all happening for a reason. And that I had to practice what I was preaching. You can't go around the world and teach women about true partnership while remaining in a hierarchical marriage that is not based on love. I had to make the best of it, and I had to see that this was orchestrated by my soul toward a higher purpose than I could possibly know. I remember thinking "Oh, boy, my life has disintegrated into a midlife soap opera where he gets married fifteen minutes later and has another kid with a younger woman. Hello!" I suffered. I felt pain. It took me nearly ten years to truly fully recover. But I was never miserable, because I knew it was a chance for me to reinvent myself. I also knew that we have these myths that we all buy, like after the age of fifty, no woman is ever going to remarry, no one wants you, they all want women twenty years younger. I knew that these were just beliefs, based on thoughts. If I could change my thoughts and beliefs in this area, I could change my reality, and by God, I have. This is one of my most exciting discoveries. This stuff works! Even for a fiftysomething-year-old single woman. I've never been happier in my life.

It boils down to having faith in something beyond what one can see, the belief that our lives have meaning and that there is a divine purpose and that what is happening to us is not simply God playing dice with the universe. You know, the famous Albert Einstein quote "No, God does not play dice with the universe." You start by getting very clear about your limiting beliefs and also what you really would love to see. Here's an example: "Okay, I'm not sure I believe that it's possible for me to be healthy and happy as a single middle-aged woman without a man. But I'm willing to look for evidence that this can be true. Let me start by making note of all the women of a similar age who are enjoying their lives—and who have met great men." That's how you do it. You use the power of your attention and thoughts to attract to you what you really desire. And the universe does the rest, as long as it's in line with what your soul really wants for you. Sometimes that's different from what your ego wants.

All of us, we're very old souls. There's a section in my book *Women's Bodies, Women's Wisdom* in which I recount the story of Martha, who actually was my mother. It was her story. She was starting to get abdominal pain—really bad abdominal pain—and, typical of my family, she decided she needed to drive across the country to visit my sister in New Mexico. (Going to a doctor would have been the last thing she'd have done.) As she drove across the Great Plains, the pain got worse and worse and then she was tasting blood, but there wasn't any blood there. And she was going past the stockyards and seeing cows up to their bellies in manure, and she was just getting an increasingly awful feeling as she drove and saw this out her window. And she got to a certain place, and then, she said, it hit her, she had suddenly become a Viking with a sword, and it was as real as anything she'd ever experienced. She took the sword and she put it in the belly of a pregnant woman and killed her, and the sword went into the belly right at the place where my mother was having that pain. She said she was the Viking and the woman at the same time and that she knew that she had done this thing and it was the worst thing she could ever imagine. And so when she got to Taos, she rested for a couple of days and she and my sister did a ritual to help heal this. My mother told me that she knows if she had not brought up this memory, she would have gotten gastric cancer and died. She's certain of it. I'm certain of it, too. I know that if I hadn't gotten out of my marriage, I would have developed inflammatory breast cancer in both breasts, the kind where you're gone in three months. I know it. Can I prove it? No, but I know it.

E: *Given your belief that our thoughts create our reality, how do you explain tsunamis, concentration camps, the Rwandan genocide, or 9/11, for instance?*

CN: None of us can take on the tsunamis or Auschwitz or 9/11, but I know there is a meaning our intellects can't possibly grasp and that the only area in which we hold true dominion is in our own lives, our own thoughts, and our willingness to attend to our own pain, our own suffering. It is our job to heal ourselves and transform our personal pain into joy. Doing this uplifts the entire world. That I know for sure.

ABOUT CHRISTIANE NORTHRUP

Christiane Northrup, M.D., a board-certified ob/gyn, is a visionary pioneer, a beloved authority in women's health and wellness, and the author of the *New York Times* best sellers *Women's Bodies, Women's Wisdom* and *The Wisdom of Menopause*. Her third book, *Mother-Daughter Wisdom*, was voted Amazon's number one book of the year in both Parenting and Mind/Body Health in 2005. *The Secret Pleasures of Menopause* was published in October 2008, and *The Secret Pleasures of Menopause Playbook* was published in March 2009. Following a twenty-five-year career in both academic medicine and private practice, Dr. Northrup now devotes her time to helping women truly flourish on all levels through tapping into their inner wisdom. For more information about Dr. Northrup and her work, please visit her Web site, www.drnorthrup.com.

Divining Love

Helena María Viramontes

We were a family as large as a small church congregation. We were raised in urban East Los Angeles poverty, and our survival depended on the ability to be responsible and accountable for one another's well-being, and although we had very limited material resources—which could have made us stingy and embittered at heart—our lives blossomed into a practiced generosity. Our mother loomed over us, radiating an abiding, generous love that never dulled and never waned. The kind of love so constant, so dependable, we could have easily taken it for granted.

My mother loved us deeply, profoundly, *in spite of* the brutal world of servility she was cast into. Her life provided little room for sentimentality. Though her father had studied to be a priest in the seminary at the turn of the century and her mother had converted to the Mormon Church, and though my mother married a man who was a patriarchal Catholic, she had no romantic notion of the afterlife as she had no romantic notion of her own on earth. For the sake of my father, she kept tidy a perfunctory altar of Jesus, Mary, and Joseph and grew accustomed to slipping important documents like our birth certificates under the feet of the statue of Jesus, clearly designating the sacredness of the altar's function beyond any religious belief.

Her body had created fifteen pregnancies, delivered eleven live births, and suffered two infant deaths, leaving a total of nine children. For years she cherished a newspaper clipping dated 12/04/58 from the *East Los Angeles Tribune* announcing, "Couple Has 11th Child at Beverly," accompanied by a photo of herself cradling my youngest sister, Barbara. Having to physically care for her brood must have played a distraction from the trauma of unplanned pregnancies (the math is remarkable—from age twenty-one to thirty-eight she was in a constant condition of pregnancy, taxing miscarriages, and anguish about children's deaths), for she complained little, and laughed a great deal. Only in much later years did the veneer of tolerance splinter, reminding us of the great sacrifices she had made, the pieces of flesh she had cut away to nourish us until she grew sallow and diminished. Ironically, Beverly Hospital was where she lay dying forty-one years after the published article.

Loss enlarges the vocabulary of the divine but reduces the vocabulary of speech; it is an unexplainable revelation and yet bonded to words. As the family-anointed scribe since 1999, I have written seven eulogies, approaching each with the same trepidation of crossing borders without proper documentation, with the same fear of being indeterminately detained in a no-man's-land. But whatever challenges remain in the writing of eulogies, nothing compares to the challenge of creating a metaphor for another crossing. One could research religious tomes on immortality or explore treatises about the afterlife, but witnessing my mother in the state of dying in 1999 helped bring revelatory understanding to the unforeseen deaths of my sister Frances in 2006 and my heroic brother, Serafin Jr., a few months later.

As we came together to assist in my mother's dying, our goal was to maintain her dignity in the face of medical indifference and to ensure that she would not succumb to absolute terror at the thought of losing us. However, in her Beverly Hospital room, it was my brothers and sisters, my nieces and nephews, and I who gave in to the depth of sorrow at the thought of losing her; we purged ourselves, weeping unabashedly. In these exhaustive, trancelike states, we rarely ate, slept in half-hour intervals, and divorced ourselves from the outside world until little else mattered except for the communal, mesmerizing hum of intercessory rosary prayers and the continuous playing of Gene Autry songs that my mother had loved so much as a young woman.

The netherworld of the dying invites a mystic union. It is the mediation between realities that one enters with total emotional investment, imbrications of *existences* between the living and those about to die. Just hours prior to his heart stopping for no apparent reason, my brother Serafin told me he was dying while his wife, Terry, adamantly objected. He had been hospitalized, recovering from a pulmonary infection, and was expected to go home in a day or two. When I asked him about his premonition, he replied in short breaths that my mother and sister Frances were in the room with him. A few weeks prior he had told me that he wished to speak to me of his death. He had struggled with Parkinson's disease since the age of thirty but refused to let the disease dominate his life. Though the illness would rob him of his independence, Serafin never allowed the humiliation of the disease to remove the dignity by which he chose to live. He painted intense self-portraits, then turned around and painted garden benches, learned calligraphy, nourished beautiful gardens, painted delicate Chinese symbols. He stumbled and bruised and broke bones but became a collector of baseball cards, coins, and stamps. He clenched with pain but was the chronicler, archivist, and organizer of photographs and a recorder of birthdays for the Viramontes clan. He trembled continuously but molded ceramic bowls, created ceramic flowers, designed wooden angels, and sewed buttoned dolls, and through it all, his sense of humor remained intact. Serafin defied his body constantly by becoming constantly busy. There was no space for self-pity. Right before being hospitalized, he took a French and biology course, receiving an A, and informed me, "The biology professor said I had the best collection of flies." He kept extremely active around the house, because for Serafin there always seemed so much to be done. And time, he knew, was limited.

And though it was the hardest thing for me to do, I had the presence of mind to listen, something I had not done for my dear sister. And so when he told me over the phone, I believed him and asked him if he was scared. And my sweet brother, always rising to the occasion, forever my hero, responded, "No."

As the dying body unshackles the soul from flesh and muscle, liberating a person's essence, one feels the antigravitational force of love shrinking the space between the life we know and the *presence* of another existence. We felt this presence as the family surrounded Serafin's bed to unplug the ventilator, just as we had felt it with our mother and Frances. And there is nothing more rapturous, beautiful, and terrifying than being given permission to enter such divine presence when a beloved is about to die.

My mother's dying gave us permission to contemplate the web of all relationships. First to her, for she was a different mother to her different children; to one another, for the deaths of our parents sever our roles as daughters and sons and enhance our roles as sisters and brothers; and then to the jazzed apathetic everyday improvised beautiful world. Outside the hospital room for a small reprieve—a drive home for a shower or running out for coffee—the boulevards and storefront buildings took on the aura of a Hollywood setting, another world of make-believe, complete with props and staging and extras walking the streets in ridiculously harsh sunlight. To be in the here and now of that everyday world was sacrilege, an act of infidelity. City block after block was animated, a cement-and-steel deception, and it was unfeasible not to be acutely aware of the juxtaposition of, say, a cluster of laughing children in a McDonald's Playland and the reverberating silence of my mother dying in her hospital room. When I returned there, I held my mother's hand, feeling extremely fortunate to be alive in my world, yet inconsolable that I could not accompany her into another.

In a suspension of hours, we had spent two days and three nights in the hospital room with our mother. Clocks became inaccurate measurements of time, and we grew familiar with the temporal stages of the day by the change of shift of the nurses. Buried in the uncanny mood of hours, we desired little. Some of us went home for a quick shower, while others refused to leave. At the request of my sister Becky, her husband, Phil, brought her a change of clothes. Upon opening the bag he had packed, Becky discovered a pair of underwear she could not recognize as her own, a pair of exercise jogs, and a pair of sexy high-heeled pumps, the sight of which set us off into such an incredible round of laughter we were scolded by the charge nurse.

When my sister Frances was hospitalized, a pastor arrived to "heal" her terminal cancer. Human will intercepted, and the divine presence intervened in astonishing ways as we all rallied to fight for her life. She was placed on a raw-food diet, my oldest brother, Gilbert, preparing the three daily meals, along with extracted wheatgrass juice that I mixed for her enema cleansings. I found a shaman to come and release Frances's energy so she could swallow a regimen of vitamins and feel the curative effects of acupuncture. I was willing to do anything, including believe in the pastor's powers to heal, and stood near him in prayer, his hands hovering over her body. Then he brought out a vial filled with healing oil. As he tried to open the vial, the cap refused to budge. Trying his teeth, then a cloth, then again grimacing as he tried to twist the cap off, it threatened to become a sick joke. Frances looked at me then and I looked at her, and clearly we were sharing a telepathic thought by the exchange of suppressed smiles. Man, we told each other, we're really fucked.

On my mother's last night, my courageous oldest sister, Mary Ann, took to pressing her palm on my mother's chest periodically to count her erratic heartbeats. Surrounding her bed, close to 3 A.M., Mary Ann whispered, "She's gone." I was chosen to deliver the news to my father, and Phil drove me there. I had only to look out at the dreary, forsaken shadows of the eucalyptus trees against the windshield, the gloomy streets absent of noise, to feel the gnawed sense of 3 A.M. fierce loneliness. Though I shook so hard my teeth clattered, I managed to cup my father's face to say "She belongs to the angels now."

By the time we wailed the release of our mother, our barbed wire clenching, the type of hold children clamp onto the hands of their mothers in mortal fear of getting lost, she had passed to us an extraordinary gift. On the occasion of her dying she began our apprenticeship into our own mortality. Her dying provided a barometer with which to measure our remaining years. After witnessing the divine so powerfully rendered in the temporality of our lives, we felt miraculously alive.

Mary Ann elected to wait for the mortician, her purse full of pending details nestled gingerly on her lap as if she were calmly waiting for a bus, while my sister Frances, who was a nurse employed at Beverly, sat guarding my mother to make sure no one, not one person, dared place her in a plastic bag and thus unwittingly allow for our mother to become "the body." Purged, humbled, exhausted, her other four daughters, who included me, met at the mall shortly after naps to get manicures in a state of giddy shell shock while my brothers were ordered by my sister Becky to get out their best suits, repair their shoes, make the calls, look after my father.

Getting manicures made perfect sense. From the time we were children we came to realize that doing things together seemed to lessen whatever misfortunes we experienced, especially in a female-heavy household and under the rule of patriarchal domination.

Such closeness made it impossible to separate from a beloved's presence. We remained in suspended mediation, teetering on a tightrope barely visible in the haze of my mother's funerary rituals. After we were driven home from the grave site by the morgue limo, my sister Barbara and I immediately jumped into my car and drove back to the grave site because we didn't want to leave our mother in her coffin alone. We had accepted her death; however, the thought of her being left alone overwhelmed us, and we zoomed down Whittier Boulevard to get to the cemetery. Barely twenty minutes had passed, but our mother was already interred, deep in the rich, moist earth, and we wept at our failure.

With the exception of dreams, where the dead visit routinely, we have to live with the fact that we will never see our dearly departed again. In the days following my mother's funeral, this thought filled us with great dread, and my sister Frances clung to my mother's empty bed, her shoulders quavering with sobs, burying her face in my mother's pillows. The memory of my mother, the nostalgia of seventy-eight years, was not enough to console Frances, and though she was two years older than I, when I tried to lift her off the bed in a fruitless attempt to lessen her sadness, her tears converged at the slope of her nose the way they had done when she was barely ten, and it was that sight, the childlike tears and quivering chin, that reduced me to the same childlike sobbing. Simone Weil reminds us, "the presence of the dead person is imaginary, but his absence is very real." This absence is why survivors rush to religions that promise a reunion.

Years after my mother's death, my sister Frances had a mastectomy, radiation, and chemotherapy treatment for breast cancer. Since she suffered from depression, Becky had arranged for all the family women to attend a one-day spa, where we soaked ourselves in a luxurious, dimly lit Roman-style hot pool. Stripped bare of our preoccupations, our memories of childhood bathing rituals, fistfights with our brothers, our adolescence of shared lipsticks, bras, and first menstruations, first kisses, naked in the face of first annihilating loves, first marriages, children and then *their* adolescences, we poked fun at our middle-aged bodies, pinched our menopausal bellies, held cellulite thigh contests to remind Frances that though she had had a breast removed, in the country of our own femaleness, she was still a full citizen, still our dearly beloved sister, and no surgical incision, no stitched scar, and no illness would ever change that.

My sister Frances's ashes are contained in an urn, which sits like a Japanese vase on top of my sister Ruthie's console. Here are the facts. She had a wry sense of humor. Her worldly possessions are piled in a U-Store-It unit in Ontario, California. The doors are unevenly hinged, and the monthly unit expense is one hundred dollars. I do not dream of her yet. Among the Viramontes women, hands down, Frances was the gorgeous one. Six months after her death, her husband remarried, with the stipulation that he wanted nothing to do with his former life. Their children now live with us in a communal parenting arrangement. We share the rewards and the emotional and financial burden of raising them because before Frances was a nurse, before she was a wife and mother, she was our sister. She was fifty-four years old.

How does one survive loss? My mother's death brought us all together, but the deaths of Frances and Serafin were unexpected and shocking, and years after, I find myself keeping at bay a deepening despair by shutting off memory to the point that I complain to those nearest me of a dulled emotional state. Now I slowly bring forth this incarnate memory of those who have traveled into the other world and I attempt to remain as strong as the hope I experience. This hope clings to the faces of Serafin's tall, beautiful sons and Frances's daughter and sons. My heart finally weeps at the sheer strength of otherworldly love, and I come to realize the irreconcilable: sometimes the divine is not holy.

ABOUT HELENA MARÍA VIRAMONTES

Helena María Viramontes is the author of two novels, *Their Dogs Came with Them* and *Under the Feet of Jesus*, and *The Moths and Other Stories*. Named a USA Ford Fellow in Literature for 2007 by United States Artists, she has also received the John Dos Passos Prize for Literature, a Sundance Institute Fellowship, a National Endowment for the Arts Fellowship, and the Luis Leal Award. Viramontes is currently a professor of creative writing in the Department of English at Cornell University.

Songs for Cricket

Beth Powning

I'm writing a novel whose working title is *Vanished Lives*. I'm obsessed with how all things fall away. I can't believe that people, with their laughter, their loving eyes, have disappeared. Or *will* disappear. I cling to the past, as if in my recollection of its sensual truth I can keep it from thinning, paling, like last summer's leaves—rain-drummed, snow-pressed.

Over my desk is a picture of my father. He's two years old, sitting on his mother's lap. His pudgy fingers hold a place on a picture book as he shies a glance at the photographer. His arms are taut with young flesh. His mother has carefully laced his tiny leather boots. He is meshed in the moment of his life.

Now he's eighty-seven.

My two granddaughters, four and seven, live just over the meadow, in the old schoolhouse across from the church. As their lives stretch ahead, unknowable, details yet to be sketched, I have a new vision of my own life. I see it from start to finish, just a few minutes long. I could write it down, a spare list: *birth, growth, pain, love, grief, death.*

Yet.

Something is beginning. Last week, I saw the spruce trees sharp and light-sparked as sun broke from scudding black clouds, the fields soft and taupe as deer hide. I might, at that moment, have been a blind person granted sight. Other moments shock me into stillness, out of time. Seven fox cubs sitting in a row, red fur blowing in spring wind. Or the fat silkiness of a granddaughter's braid. Or rain-jeweled moss.

There's an unfolding of time, during which I do nothing, make nothing, expect nothing—and then the sensory blossoms, explodes.

✦

I'm reading books on horse whispering, since I have a pony I'm trying to tame. She's coppery russet, black mane and tail burning in the winter sun with strands of henna red, eyes peering through sheepdog forelock with wondering intelligence.

I'm predator, I realize, and Cricket is prey. She is the vulnerable one. Her eyes are widely spaced, on the side of her head, so that she can see all around her, whereas mine are close-set, sharply focused, forward-looking. She lives in the moment of her wild instincts, sensing danger in every quivering branch or new shadow. My arms reaching toward her face are threatening; my fingers are like claws.

I can't pat her. In the pasture, she either runs from my outstretched hand or circles, presenting her rump in demented repetition, like a polar bear in a zoo.

I study horse language. It is expressed by half-cocked, flattened, or swiveling ears; flared or pinched nostrils; a toss of the head; a thrust of the nose; a presentation of rump. I must not only understand this language but learn to speak it. She reads my hands, the slant of my shoulders, the unambiguity of my approach.

I have to live in her wild moment. When she turns her rump to me or lifts a hoof, I must stand firm. I can't be afraid, else she will never learn not to fear me. She wants order in her life. Safety.

Control, I learn, is something entirely different from how I have always thought of it. It is not something I *do*. It's clarity, calmness, the result of attention. Of listening.

◆

Our farm is at the end of a valley, at the dead end of a long lane. Fields sweep up to forested hills. Foxes trot across the pastures trailing light-dusted tails. Ravens fly low with their swishing wing creak, their oilcan cry. At night there is no sound but the rushing of waters or the trilling of peepers. Sometimes, on misty mornings, we see moose drifting long-legged across the upper fields.

The wild, coming close.

Old age, now, coming close.

"Hands are good," I say to Cricket, placing my hands on the edge of her stall. I long to repair damage, to fold this frightened creature into my heart. "Hands are good."

The barn is quiet, shadowy, smells of sun-dried timothy. I listen to the moan of winter wind.

The pony turns her back to me, stands looking away as if she's listening for someone else, not me.

I feel a flood of grief. I remember the stillbirth of our first child. And how, afterward, the joy of creation, with its burning energy, became edged with the need to control. Never again to be so wounded. Twenty-eight years old, I sat in the cellar stoking the wood furnace, face in my hands, heartbroken. The child who had been born, and was not alive, had rejected me. Had returned to the mystery.

To the place of creation, life's heart.
Stillborn. Born still.

◆

For weeks I try everything I can think of: cajoling, offering treats, standing tall and commanding. Still she resists. Or whirls, lifting a hoof. Or bites me.

I am heartsick. Finally, I give up. I simply go into the barn and sit by her stall.

One day, I begin to sing quietly to myself. Her eyes go to my face. Her jaws stop their steady grind. She listens, wide-eyed.

So I begin to sing to her. If I'm singing, she lets me feed her pieces of apple. I sing, and she lets me clip her to the cross ties, lets me brush her mane, her tail. One day, she submits to the soft brush traveling gently over her sides, her belly. I'm singing as I run my hand down her foreleg. I sing as I lead her back into the stall and lean against her furry warmth.

On a sunny morning in late February, I'm sitting in the barn, looking up into the cobwebbed timbers, thinking about the swallows—how they arrive, astonishingly, like all blossomings. One June morning, I'll enter the barn to find it ringing with their busy chirping as they reclaim their nests. All summer, they streak through the barn door, their wings a golden blur in the mote-hazy light as they feed the babies who clamor shoulder to shoulder in the mud-walled nests. And then they vanish, just as mysteriously, in early September. There's a familiar moment when I'm shocked to realize they have left.

And when the birds have gone, I stand in the door, looking down the valley toward the south. They're like the Canadian summer, its beauty a piercing ache, amplified by brevity.

I begin to sing.

She's like a swallow, that flies so high . . .

Cricket picks up her head, pricks her ears. I watch her and sing the next verse.

She's like a river that never runs dry . . .

I reach over, still singing, and ease a wisp of hay from the corner of her mouth.

Something new is spinning between us. Music gathers our attention.

I sit back, bundled in coat, hat, and scarf. And I sing, arms crossed, not looking at her or trying to touch her. Not, even, thinking about her.

Just. Listening. My voice sliding up, resting on sound.

◆

It's late March, and I'm standing next to Cricket in the barn aisle. The air is filled with the sound of running water as the snow evaporates.

I slide my arm over her neck.

She turns her head and slowly lays it on my breast.

I am shocked to stillness. I put a hand to her cheek and we stand, together.

She's like a swallow . . .

My hand slides to her nose. Her lips make a shuffling motion.

. . . who flies so high . . .

◆

Ever after that moment, she is changed. Her eyes are steady, calm. She no longer tries to bite. She no longer turns her back to me, circling. She never offers to kick.

She follows me when I walk in the pasture. She doesn't know where I'm going or if there will be a treat at the end or even something unpleasant or frightening. She simply comes with me.

Sometimes I take her on a lead line, and we walk down the dirt lane, watching as winter yields to spring, a slow dissolution beneath pressure: pussy willows bursting from their packets, ice borne away on the brook's fish-gray waters.

If I call her, no matter how far away she is—up on the ridge by the pines or grazing in the meadow—she throws up her head.

Interrupts her grazing to listen.

✦

A storm brews in the south. There's a mutter of thunder. Clouds are coming up from the sea.

Out in the pasture, I see Cricket turn her rump toward the dark sky. She'll stand outside, even though the barn door is open. She will feel the rain trickle through her winter fur, loosening it. She lowers her head, waits.

Doing nothing.

I lean on the barway. It's April, and the warm air smells of soil.

Always now, inside me, are the ones who have gone before. The child who was born and died. The beloved grandparents, aunts, uncles, friends who have passed away.

My own approaching old age.

I think of how I yield as I grow older. It's not passivity or defeat. I have enormous energy. I love the erotic quiver of possibility.

But there's a new language to be learned. It's wordless and springs from the root of trust. It's trust that the swallows are in the right place when they vanish. It's trust that the storm will free Cricket of her winter coat. It's trust that my own life has its place within the speechless order.

I think about the ones who have not yet left. My father, my mother.

I feel the warm drops strike.

Trust that within stillness is stirring.

ABOUT BETH POWNING

Beth Powning was born in 1949 and grew up in Hampton, Connecticut. She graduated from Sarah Lawrence College and studied creative writing with E. L. Doctorow. Since 1972, she and her artist husband, Peter, have lived on a farm in New Brunswick, Canada. They have one son, Jake Powning, a swordsmith, who lives nearby with his wife, Sara, and daughters, Maeve and Bridget. Beth Powning is the author of *Home: Chronicle of a North Country Life* (writing and photography), *Shadow Child: An Apprenticeship in Love and Loss* (nonfiction), *The Hatbox Letters* (novel), and *Edge Seasons* (nonfiction). *The Hatbox Letters* was long-listed for the IMPAC Dublin Literary Award. Her new novel, *The Sea Captain's Wife,* was published by Knopf Canada in January 2010. Her newsletters and photography can be seen at www.powning.com/beth.

Barbara Lief

Dancing in the Kitchen

Joan Nicholson

1

In my youth, my passion was for dancing. From age ten through college
and beyond, ballet and modern dance bewitched and transported me.
The fantasy of dancing in New York City sustained me. Fantasies
of adopting children kept me somewhat earthbound. Being the child
of a single parent may have been an influence. My father never made

any attempts to visit me. Did I identify just a bit with orphans?
I danced with children in hospitals. Directed children's theater.
Created art classes for nieces, nephews, neighbors. Yet, I wanted my own
children who would come home with me. Children to cook for and dance
with in the kitchen. I would teach them my favorite trees and clouds.

Take them to Paris, even Barcelona. Inheritance from the family
movie business allows me, at age sixty-one, to adopt an eight-year-old girl
from India. I am thrilled. I am mesmerized. And flabbergasted.
Oh! to have a real child in my life! Sara is quick and endearing.
A natural dancer, natural athlete, and comedienne. And she loves school.

2

Daily, Sara gives my heart back to me. We drive to the market.
"Mommy, I love you." She is talking to me and smiling. I did this.
Chose her from all the photos. An old soul pleading from a two-inch
frame. Once a tiny girl age seven on a video. Playing barefoot in the dirt
with a stick. Now eight and a half. And ready for her American school.

I did this. Did the paperwork. Paid the money. Caught the airplane.
Found Bal Asha Dhom—Home of Hope—in the middle of Mumbai.
Sara came into the office on a September afternoon. Stood beside me.
Took my hand. Showed me through each building. Around dozens of
babies in the first ward. Introduced some twenty children in her room.

"This is my mom." Showed me her little iron bed in the center row.
I met her favorite caretaker, Mary, and Farida, the cook. One woman
divorced. One widowed. Their own children in another orphanage.
Now Sara takes my hand after stories. Holds it close to her chest
before sleep. "Mommy, why didn't you come sooner to get me?"

3

Sara's early years in India were marked by abuse. She came with rivers
of rage. I was given no warning. The first tantrums were small.
She thrashed around in her own circle. Stress of adoption, I said.
Everything was new. Wearing socks was new. I was very new.
Gradually, however, she became defiant and mean. During her third

year in America, outbursts are fierce. One Sunday, I find her asleep on
the living room couch at 2:00 A.M. after watching a Hindi movie, full
of music and dancing and her Hindi language. I turn off the movie and
move toward my bedroom. Silence awakens her. Sara comes after me.
Hits me in my chest. Pushes me to the floor. Did she imagine that

I might take her culture away? Medications and special schools
follow this upset. I can create songs and games for her. I cannot cope
with such explosions. She needs greater supervision. She requires
regimented structure. She begins therapeutic schools in Oregon and Utah.
We consult psychologists and psychiatrists in California and New York.

Shocking diagnoses are suggested: Retardation? Borderline personality?
Bipolar tendencies? She longs to be at home. Periodically we try home.
With unhappy results. Just after celebrating Sara's fifth year in America,
I am diagnosed with a heart condition. No longer can I endure
a life of stress with my daughter.

4

My niece volunteers assistance. Sara makes an attempt to be part
of a new family. Until her wild episodes overwhelm my niece.
Sara comes home to me again. With teenage years, new frictions emerge.

After more physical assaults, I come to feel some distance from this
girl whom I adore. Again, consultants recommend special schools.

Therapists tell me that someday, if Sara can overcome post-traumatic
stress issues, set in motion before and during her orphanage years,
with medication, she may have a life. She has an aptitude for
photography. She speaks of becoming a chef. Perhaps one day
we can find an appropriate vocational school or arts program.

Still—in a flash she can be vicious, even frightening.
We do not know if Sara's difficulties stem from fetal alcohol
syndrome, malnutrition, childhood trauma, or a "bad seed."
I do know that a level of melancholy I could not have imagined
often overwhelms me.

5

For eight years I stumble and rebound. With no respite from anguish.
Or doubt. Is this the best school? The right medication?
Is this enough structure? Is he really the best doctor?
Fatigue beyond measure moves into body : mind : psyche.
I begin to disappear. I must become less available to Sara's needs.

There is a new school on a farm in Montana. Now, at age seventy,
placing my trust in equine therapy, farm chores, possible friendships
with other students adopted from foreign lands, I relinquish Sara.
To a new landscape. To guidance from a new band of therapists.
Already I miss her laughter. And dancing in the kitchen.

JOAN NICHOLSON

Joan Nicholson's poems have appeared in *Heresies: A Feminist Journal of Art and Politics, Dominion Review, Edible Ojai, Tamarind Press,* and *Rivertalk.* She studied with the poets Toi Derricotte, David St. John, and Robert Creeley. She taught modern dance, choreographed, and directed theater at Oregon State University, Mount St. Mary's College–Doheny, University of Delaware, and University of Wisconsin. She produced The Very Special Arts Festival (for handicapped students in Los Angeles), 1978–1982. She lives in Ojai, California, and creates workshops in the area. Her chapbook *Therefore* was published in 1998. TreeHouse Press published her collection *My Coat Is a House* in spring 2008.

Gail Tirana

Not Yet

Jane O'Reilly

I am not old. Not *old* old. Not yet.

I am *young* old, part of the "seventy is the new fifty" crowd. I am a long way from being part of the "one hundred is the new eighty" group.

My hair hasn't turned gray. Not entirely.

My teeth haven't fallen out. Not completely.

Women do sometimes offer me their seats on crowded buses, but men sit tight beneath signs urging them to give up their place to the elderly. I would be astonished if one of them considered me sufficiently an elderly to qualify.

Actually, men have been ignoring me for decades now. Quite a long time ago I realized that construction guys were no longer whistling. After years of hissing feminist curses in their direction, I had gotten what I wanted and I didn't want it. By now I find myself almost completely invisible to the entire general population, male, female, or indeterminate. This ability to pass unnoticed would be convenient if I should want to take a new life turn as a burglar or a terrorist. Oddly, while one somewhat older woman is as evanescently noticeable as a wisp of exhaust, two somewhat older women together are solid enough to be greeted with "bless your hearts" followed by "dearie." It is enough to make an adorable two-year-old spit, much less a decidedly unadorable seventy-three-year-old.

THE VOICE OF EXPERIENCE (offstage):

No one but an intimate friend or relative may be allowed to address us, at our age, by our first names. Doctors, nurses, caregivers, garage mechanics, bank tellers, and such should use the stately "Ma'am." We are Duchesses, not feeble teddy bears.

At least I no longer have the absorbing burden of worrying about the way I look. When I think of the time I wasted worrying about panty lines and imaginary fat I tend to make firm remarks about wasting time to my granddaughters, whose capacity for gloom over lip gloss would, I now feel, be better directed toward striving for world peace. My breath is wasted: they have managed to combine lip gloss with a concern for world peace. I am lost in admiration. Still, they look fine no matter what they do. I looked fine at their age. Better than fine. Show me a woman of my age who does not look at an old photograph and discover a much better-looking person than she ever remembered being. Despite the pin curls. If only we had known. We all looked fine. That is nature's plan. Attract. Reproduce. Etc. Of course I never thought I (*moi?*) would wrinkle and fold, and as it occurred I grieved for the youth I had never appreciated. But that was also a long time ago. Now I have let myself go and I don't really give a damn. Or not much of a damn. More sunblock would have been a good idea, but the evidence around me suggests that surgical enhancement would not. Nature's plan nowadays is: wash, brush, button up, and forget about the high heels.

My lifelong compulsion to make an impression, usually along the lines of imitating a human pinwheel, remains. I wish it didn't. I know now that being fascinated is more attractive in the long run than being fascinating. I wish I had taken advantage of a lesson I learned when I was twenty-two: almost no one really notices what is going on in other people's lives. They may notice clothes or obnoxious behavior, but they actually prefer, by and large, to remain oblivious to what others are doing and thinking. I was pregnant my entire senior year in college. Unwed and pregnant. It was 1958, when sex meant subterfuge, suppression, and shame. No chance of marriage. No abortion. If the authorities had found me out I would have been expelled. I cannot imagine now how I thought I would pull it off. But I did, with the help of some friends. I took my last exams wearing an enormous raincoat. Only one friend noticed anything odd about me, and she accepted a denial. A week later I gave birth to a seven-and-a-half-pound baby girl in the hospital wing of a Salvation Army Home for Unwed Mothers. A week later I said goodbye to the baby and signed the papers giving her up for adoption. It was the worst afternoon of my life up to that point, and all the way to this point.

As human tragedies go, it wasn't much. But it was as much tragedy as I could bear. I was never the same. On the other hand, I wouldn't have wanted to go on being who I had been. I will never know who I could have been. But I do know that the moment I saw my daughter I understood, completely by surprise, love as an unconditional river of acceptance and connection. And I understood that I had passed a test. It was my first real experience of the skein of life, the twist of triumph and tragedy, of loss and change, which I have never reconciled. Not yet. I have begun to learn to deal with the twists, but I imagine the final reconciliation comes somewhat beyond the point of usefulness.

THE VOICE OF EXPERIENCE (offstage):

Meanwhile, don't forget to brush and floss. It is no fun to outlive your teeth. I would also suggest cutting back sharply on the use of bodily ailments as conversational topics. Let me also point out the importance of striving to be a glass half-full instead of a glass half-empty person. You know who you are.

The thing about the skein of life, I find, is that it doesn't just unwind up into the air like the string on a rising balloon. It winds up into something, perhaps a rather gnarly sweater or, in my case, into a rather lumpy ball of flat cheap ribbon such as I was given for my birthday when I was very small. The lumps then were presents, little dolls and charms and rhinestone rings that emerged as the ball was rolled out. By now, the lumps in my life ball could be rolled out in a similarly totemic way: little children raised, tiny dogs, small books written, love affairs regretted and love affairs smugly remembered, tiny Taj Mahals and submarines and Provençal meals, feminism, a scuba mask, a few awards, flowers and vegetables and a chairwoman's gavel. Lots and lots of things. Even husbands. And mentors. Parents and siblings. Houses and bedrooms and hotel rooms. Friends lost, abandoned, gone wrong, cherished, and dead. I carry all those things with me, tightly wound, memories becoming ever more tangible as time goes on.

I absolutely hate it when I meet someone new and they don't recognize me as an amazing repository of wisdom, experience, adventure, and relevance to today's world. It is so irritating to feel my context dissolving, things becoming irrelevant that were once taken for granted, such as the infallibility of the pope, the supremacy of Detroit and automobiles, the practice of calling all members of an infinitely extended family "cousin," the importance of sterling silver flatware, the reasons why a young woman of twenty-two felt she had to give up her baby for adoption. All are now mere flickers of history. I myself am not a flicker of history. Not yet. My friends, the most precious being those who know who I was before I became who I am, keep me current, living in the now, with due respect to the then. We have always sustained each other, but we imagined ourselves doing it in a communal house by this time. We still talk about the theoretical house even as we add new husbands, faraway grandchildren, houses in Maine, and new jobs. But we always end the conversation with "not yet." We are not old enough. Yet. I wonder if we ever will be? Or will it, someday soon, be too late? I just hope I am not the last one to die. Some of us have already died. Their brave example is comforting. I miss them very much but they are vividly alive to me still.

THE VOICE OF EXPERIENCE (offstage):

Time goes faster when one is going downhill. Don't waste it. If the next ten years go as quickly as the last ten, there won't be time to go to the grocery store.

My parents used to warn us that old age was not for sissies. My father lived to be ninety-four. He had a pacemaker, a hearing aid, and a very bad knee. He also had a girlfriend, a generous heart, and an insatiable curiosity about what made things work. When the knee became too painful, he decided to take a chance on death and had an operation to fix it. The surgery was a success; the staph infection killed him. My mother, not as fortunate, had died ten years before, of Parkinson's disease. I became close to my father, and indeed to my family, after Mother died. She and I did not get along. I miss her now. I like to think we could have become conversational, even friends. But she wouldn't have been pleased when I became the matriarch of the family, the oldest, the first little toy penguin advancing up the incline and standing first at the leap of the precipice. Being and becoming suddenly become became.

As matriarch, I try to remember what I learned from the earlier incumbents, that it makes everyone feel better if I do not express disapproval, offer unsought advice, take sides, or forget birthdays. It is very hard. Now that the children are grown up to be competent adults (more or less our age) we (my sister, my brother, and I) try not to feel that we are like furniture, comfortable but not supposed to talk. I wonder, often, what my children think of me. They think it is very odd that I should wonder. I wonder if I have as incomplete an understanding of them as I think they do of me. At what point will we ever discover the truth? What is the truth? And so on.

THE VOICE OF EXPERIENCE (offstage):

Much depends on luck. For example, why are so many dogs running starving through the streets of the subcontinent, while other dogs are curled up on a soft cushion at my feet? Luck. The task is to try to improve the odds for everyone and everything. Some of the truth rests in the word "try." Becoming reliably helpful is a good start.

I have developed a rather bombastic way of opening conversations with my younger friends and family members. "At my age . . ." and "In my experience . . ." and "When I was young . . ." A while ago I heard myself say to my daughter, "Oh, are you beginning menopause? I don't remember having any trouble with it." I remembered wrong. It was a terrible time. One minute I was skating along, writing gallant little pensées about turning fifty and being grown up at last, my career excellent, figure intact, falling in love, son at college. I was writing wonderful things, changing the world for women. (Weren't we all? Aren't we proud? I am.) To comfort myself after the defeat of the Equal Rights Amendment, I went to Key West and worked as a treasure diver. I was, in the current parlance, hot!

THE VOICE OF EXPERIENCE (offstage):

Do something new. It almost doesn't matter what it is, as long as it is new and takes a little effort. Being afraid is especially effective.

And then everything crashed. Not really due to menopause but to an accumulation of unexamined bad habits. I emerged eighty pounds heavier, suffering from a suicidal depression, unable to write, unwilling ever to approach any moment that might lead to sex (eighty pounds extra made avoiding it a lot easier). I didn't take hormones because—luckily, as it turned out—they gave me migraine headaches.

Skein of life wise, it turned out quite well, eventually. Prozac was invented and I was one of the fortunate people it helped. So did therapy, finally. I had never been very good at finding a helpful therapist, but as I got older my instincts improved, or perhaps the therapists improved. I wasn't much good at love affairs, either, although I was way too good at sex, and without either I discovered that men could be friends. Better late than never. (By now sex itself seems rather an improbable idea.) Not being able to write was the second worst thing that ever happened to me. Writer's block is real, sort of like trying to use a trash masher to form a sentence while sitting inside the trash masher. It was like losing myself. If I couldn't write and my son was grown up, who was I?

THE VOICE OF EXPERIENCE (offstage):

It is important that my point be understood here. It is actually true that doors open when other doors shut. Not a cliché of choice when the hem is still stuck in the slammed door, but true nonetheless. Clichés usually are.

If I couldn't work I couldn't afford to live in New York, so I moved to a little house in a little town in Vermont, which is what I had dreamed of doing for twenty years. I learned to garden and was elected to office and made new friends and for ten years taught an infinitely satisfying workshop on writing memoir. Grudgingly, while still in Key West, I had come to believe I was an alcoholic and my life was unmanageable. I recommend highly the Twelve Steps for anyone seeking manageability. I can even recommend a slogan I first heard in AA meetings and, naturally, dismissed as too sickeningly sweet to be true: Miracles Will Happen. A miracle did happen. My daughter found me. Same daughter. Only daughter. The long-lost daughter. Thirty-two years after I gave her up. She has three children. Grandchildren!

My son now has a wonderful wife and a baby daughter. I have had a chance to take care of her and to practice wisdom learned late in life, such as remembering that babies mean doing one thing at a time, rejoicing and focusing on the moment, and becoming aware that if I am unable to do anything else, such as read the newspaper, then I am already doing what I am supposed to be doing. All these beautiful interesting nice people are my family. My descendents. I am so grateful. I think gratitude can be felt properly only late in life, when it is a sustaining emotion. Gratitude and also love, the quiet sort of love that is merely an absence of malice.

THE VOICE OF EXPERIENCE (offstage):

One of the most useful things I have learned is to be willing to apologize, even when I am right. If I can get in a quick mea culpa, a grovel if necessary, it saves so much time and energy. It's all part of the Great Cliché: Do unto others as you would have them do unto you. In modern parlance, what goes around comes around. The eight beatitudes also offer wise counsel in the management of life. See any Google site for tips.

I turned out to be a nice person.

I am now a nice person who sold the little house and moved to Boston to live in a loft and take painting lessons. It seemed a good way to turn seventy. My Buddhist friends advise me that their spiritual goal is to rid themselves of the idea of self, but that is too deep for me, although it might be a good preparation for what is to come.

Meanwhile, anything is possible. Some things can get better. The United States turned again toward the light at the last election. Of less cosmic importance, except to me, is the fact that I no longer hobble. It turned out that the pain was due not to unavoidable age but to years of wrong shoes and bad posture and is now much improved by exercise and orthotics. A revelation! Transformative! Perhaps now it would be worth thinking about a diet!

THE VOICE OF EXPERIENCE (offstage):

It is not yet too late. Not yet. Restoring and reversing are still possible. Such small blessings may make life worth living.

On my forty-fifth birthday, I interviewed a woman named Muriel Gardiner about her experiences trying to rescue people from the Nazis. She was the real Julia, if you remember Lillian Hellman's story about a similar woman. As it happened, Muriel Gardiner never actually met Lillian Hellman, but she was as admirable as Ms. Hellman had described. During lunch, I told Ms. Gardiner that all my life I had been afraid that if the Nazis had taken over my country, I might have turned in my friends in exchange for chewing gum or nylon stockings, or because I was frightened for myself. I asked her how I could develop courage.

And she said to me, "You never know. You never know until it happens."

I have decided that in a lot of ways, most ways, "you never know" applies to life. I don't know if I will cling to life when or if it becomes unbearable. Not yet. I do know that death in the young is an insult to hope and to faith. But for me, well, I am getting used to the idea. Not yet, but I can see a time when it will seem only part, although the deciding part, of life. In the meantime, I take as my guide three friends of my grandmother's, who had been bridesmaids at her wedding and came to my own first wedding. It was the day of their fiftieth college reunion, and this year it will be fifty years after that. My grandmother was dead, but her friends Florence, Edith, and Eleanor sat on the lawn and wished me well. Before I threw the bouquet, they rose to leave. "We are so sorry to go now, dear," they said, "but we are flying to Istanbul tomorrow and must finish packing. Eleanor wants to swim the Bosporus one more time."

Onward, to the end.

ABOUT JANE O'REILLY

Born in Saint Louis, Missouri, Jane O'Reilly graduated from Rad-cliffe College in 1958. During the early sixties she worked for the nascent public television in Washington, D.C., reporting on urban and rural poverty, the Johnson administration, and the resistance to the war in Vietnam. In 1967, she moved to New York City, where a new friend named Gloria Steinem introduced her to the life of a freelance writer and to the women's movement. She was one of the group of women who founded *Ms.* magazine. Her cover story in the first issue, "Click! The Housewife's Moment of Truth," has by now inspired three generations. She is an award-winning essayist, jour-nalist, political reporter, book critic, and travel writer whose books include *The Girl I Left Behind: The Housewife's Moment of Truth and Other Feminist Ravings* and *No Turning Back: Two Nuns' Battle with the Vatican over Women's Right to Choose,* written with Barbara Fer-raro and Patricia Hussey. Her work has allowed her an adventurous, wide-ranging, and useful life, but if she had it to do over she would prefer to be born Jon Stewart.

Interview with Marta Casals Istomin

EMILY: *Over the years, despite the loss of your two husbands, you have maintained an extraordinarily active, accomplished public life. I'm eager to know how you coped privately with these losses and what if anything helped you to get through them.*

MARTA CASALS ISTOMIN: Well, loss, as you know, is always a very difficult thing to go through. When I was with Casals, I knew in a sense that we were living on borrowed time because he was so old, but he was so young in his spirit and in his mind that I didn't feel that he was old. Thank God, he lived until the last minute totally coherent and bright, and his last heart attack occurred while he was playing dominoes in Puerto Rico with some friends. He was ninety-six plus. After he died, I started to expect that emptiness—but I had the whole world around me. I was surrounded by love for him. I received thousands and thousands of letters and telegrams, articles about him, and it took me a full year to answer all of these things. It was very hard, but on the other hand, it was like a continuation. He wasn't there, but he was there. I never had the time to feel, in a sense, that he wasn't really there. I'm dealing with his things right now. I'm putting order in his papers. Still, to this day, I receive three or four letters every week that have to do with his foundation, his trusts, a competition—with a Casals Puerto Rico Festival or a Casals Kronberg Academy, with a Casals this or a Casals that. So there has been a sort of gradual transition, but one day you do finally know that he's really not there.

E: *It seems that there was a tidal wave of activity around you.*

MCI: A tidal wave which never stopped. That was perhaps my husband's greatest legacy, to be so active. But that was also ingrained in me from my parents, because they're the same way. So I was always busy, and one thing led to another. Eugene [Istomin], as you know, was a great friend of Casals and was very special to Casals. After the death of Casals he was trying to help me, and that brought us together. So one thing led to another and I was asked, with my experience, to take over the Kennedy Center. And I had already taken over the Casals Festival Organization because I had done it with Casals for years. I worked hard.

E: *So really the investment in work and activity forced you forward, as it always does.*

MCI: Exactly. And then eventually I married Eugene and he was very encouraging of my taking the position of artistic director of the Kennedy Center, which I did for eleven years.

While I was with Eugene, we had promised each other to never be separated for more than a week, so we were always flying here and flying there. It was a whirlwind of a life.

I was still also working on Casals' things—his presence was always with us—and then I was asked to be president of the Manhattan School of Music. I didn't want all of this responsibility, but Eugene encouraged me and I accepted.

So that's what I did, and I was still at the Manhattan School when Eugene suddenly got sick with cancer. He lived for an-

other year and a half. He was another strong one—he continued his activities and only for the last six months stayed at
home. He was a fighter and remained active. Even when he
was very sick he got up every day, even the day he died. For
the last six months I took a leave of absence so that I could be
with him. We never talked about death.

E: *Were you frightened?*

MCI: I am frightened sometimes of something I could have
done and haven't done, but while things are happening I am
strong, strong, strong. That strength was given to me, it doesn't
have to do with me.

E: *You never thought "What will become of me?" or felt despair
or aloneness?*

MCI: No, that never came to my mind. I was busy holding
the fort.

E: *And later on, once you've begun to miss these people, once
you've begun to feel the absence . . .*

MCI: Yes. And the second time was worse because you're
older. And you know, when you lose someone in later life, you
feel that your life is sort of fulfilled. There it is. I'm not young,
I am now seventy-one, and Eugene passed away already four
years ago.

And you have to think about how you want to use the time
remaining to you. A year and a half after Eugene died, I quit
the Manhattan School of Music because I had an apartment full
of stuff that had to be dealt with. Eugene had a six-thousand-
volume library of rare books, first editions in English literature,
American literature, art, history, I mean, really an important
library. So I sent six thousand volumes to the University of
Maryland. Eugene's biography is now being written, so I'm or-
ganizing all his papers. While my brain is in its place I have to
make sure that everything is done!

E: *So really, your husbands have remained totally in your life.*

MCI: Yes, but it's not the same as having the person next

to you discussing things. With Eugene, and with Casals also, we'd be about to say something and we'd just look at each other and know what the other person was going to say. I often feel I need the support that I don't now have, and that I miss very, very much, because even though I have many friends, I am basically alone. My family, who are very, very dear to me, don't understand my way of life or my responsibilities. If something happened to me today, they wouldn't know what to do with all I am responsible for.

E: *Yes. And like many women of my generation, you did not have children. Many in my generation are missing the traditional supports that children and grandchildren can bring.*

MCI: Yes, I miss that, because I see how loving and caring people's children can be. That's my only regret, but it has hit me only now. Not before.

E: *You were too busy and too fulfilled.*

MCI: Exactly. And I wouldn't have changed any of that.

E: *So if I were your daughter, you would say to me, "Look, it's terrible to lose these people, but there's nothing we can do about it and you go on and you involve yourself in your work and surround yourself with friends, and that's life."*

MCI: Well, it's not as simple as that. You are in a constant battle with yourself, a battle not to let yourself be sad, because you know, for me, especially, if I listen to music I dissolve.

E: *I understand. Of course. Of course.*

MCI: Being a musician, you would. It's not easy—you're always at the brink of letting yourself go and really feeling sorry for yourself and feeling that horrible emptiness.

E: *So you do wrestle with that.*

MCI: I do, but if I feel very, very sad, I just get up and I say, "I have to do this." Whatever it is. Usually things that don't make me think too much or that take my mind totally away from whatever I am thinking. That's my remedy. I usually go "Zoom!" I have a list I go to. If I get too depressed from reading some of the letters or from memories, I leave that and I do something totally different.

E: *Having had these two extraordinary relationships, are you able to convert the sadness sometimes into gratitude?*

MCI: I have been the most fortunate woman in the world, and what a privilege, what a joy. Some people have never had half an hour of the joy that I have had, and that wonderful feeling of participating in those wonderful worlds.

E: *So you would say you've had extraordinary fulfillment, even if you never love again.*

MCI: Oh, I am sure. You can never say never, but I am sure I will never not only not look but not even consider anything else.

E: *I admire you for having had the courage to marry Casals when you were twenty.*

MCI: I don't know where I got the stuff for that. I was the product of a very traditional Catholic education, but I was very liberal in my own way. You have to try and do the best that you can. Sometimes it's not what the book says, but you try anyway. But I held on to those very basic principles that I grew up with and still have. They now really nourish me and sustain me, as they did during the months of grief before and after Eugene's death.

My only regrets in the dark hours of the night are about when I think that I might have done something better, and if I find myself getting upset about something that happened fifteen, thirty years ago, I just say to myself, "You know, you really did the best you could," and then I pray and I fall asleep.

E: *You do pray?*

MCI: Yes, I do.

E: *And that's helpful?*

MCI: Oh, very.

E: *Have you maintained a traditional religious belief?*

MCI: Yes and no. I continue to go to church. It gives me

strength, but I'm quite liberal with it. I don't follow it all the way, but it does give me strength. Both my religion and my faith give me a lot of strength.

E: *Do you believe in an afterlife?*

MCI: Yes, I do.

E: *And do you believe it is based on how we perform in this life?*

MCI: I think so. But I also think that God is so good. I don't believe that people will go to Hell. But I do believe that your purpose in life, your good deeds, are very important. Not only for the reward but just because you feel better. Because people do know when they're doing wrong things and good things. You want to be a good person, to give a good example, and you want people to emulate your good deeds.

E: *It's not just for the after reward, it's for . . .*

MCI: The now reward. You'll feel better.

E: *A sense of integrity as we go through this life.*

MCI: Oh, yes, my husbands had a lot of that. I worry about the world we live in. It's so polluted, you know?

E: *Terrible. And how do you understand that, given your belief in a good God?*

MCI: Well, that's a very difficult question, but you know, we are given a free will, and people can choose to be good or bad.

E: *And you believe that this struggle is ongoing.*

MCI: Exactly; the same struggle that I have inside me, not to get into a—

E: *A funk.*

MCI: Right, or in the depths of my sadness. I think that life is a struggle, but if you live it with determination and faith and belief that what you're doing is the right thing, then it's not as impossible.

E: *And does your belief in an afterlife make you fear death less or even not at all?*

MCI: We all kind of fear, not death but God. But the fear in my case now is just that I hope that I live to do the things that I want to do, that I feel I need to do. But is death the end? No.

E: *Do you believe in an afterlife with wings and harps?*

MCI: I don't know if there are wings, I don't know what it is, but I know that it is a place where we find God, which means goodness and peace and justice and well-being.

ABOUT MARTA CASALS ISTOMIN

Marta Casals Istomin was born in 1937 in Puerto Rico to a family of amateur musicians and became an outstanding cellist. She is a former president of the Manhattan School of Music and artistic director of the Kennedy Center for the Performing Arts in Washington, D.C. She was appointed by President George H. W. Bush to be a member of the Council on the Arts, and she has been the chairwoman of many prestigious international music festivals. She has been honored with six honorary doctoral degrees and has been decorated with the highest cultural honors by the governments of Puerto Rico, Spain, France, and Germany. Casals Istomin is currently a member of the Manhattan School of Music's board of directors. She is the widow of Pablo Casals and of Eugene Istomin, both giant figures in the world of classical music.

Sedat Pakay

Googling Home

Andrea Marcusa

With several easy clicks in Google Earth, entire cityscapes and mountain ranges come into my private focus, or I can rest the small white cursor's hand on lands as far away as the Pyramids, the Eiffel Tower, or Greenland's icy shores. A slight tug of the mouse, and I can spin the whole earth on its axis like a god.

In one click I am there, hovering high above the routes of jets and migrating birds, somewhere between New York City and Hartford. Another click to the southern corner of Long Island Sound, and, like a plane descending, the terrain draws closer, to a place until recently I called home. I trace the familiar boot-shaped peninsula on the screen with my finger and examine the tiny yellow lines and street names: Shore Road, East Way, West Way. I follow the route as I have so many times, first by foot, then by bicycle, and finally by car to home, an out-of-focus blur, the yellow exterior and the black-and-white-speckled roof.

I know that the image was filmed months earlier via satellite camera, then stored on one of Google's giant servers, where gigabytes of data are available to anyone with a computer and an Internet connection. Will I find my mother there, kneeling along the front pathway, digging up weeds, or my father, walking along the beach? There was a time when I believed that my mother and father would be in that house until their end.

My parents, at the ages of eighty-two and eighty-five, packed up their home of fifty years and moved cross-country to live nearby my three oldest siblings, who'd settled thirty-five years ago in Northern California. It seems so natural for my parents to still be there, as I train my eyes on the screen in search of a trace of my mother, a speck of my dad, or even the sight of their navy sedan in the driveway. But the yard, road, and drive are as empty as the hollow that formed in my stomach when they left.

To some close friends, the sadness and shock that overtook me during their leave-taking were incomprehensible. How could I, a middle-aged woman with my own family, become so undone by elderly parents leaving their homestead for the comfort of a milder climate and slower pace?

When my parents entered their seventies, my mother walked me around the house, paused at the den, and said, "When I can't get up the stairs anymore, I'll turn it into a bedroom." Then she looked at me and said, with a tone that only a mother who had commanded a horde of five kids could summon, "I don't want to die in a hospital. Just get me a nurse and let me stay in this room, where I can see the cove, my flowers, and the birds." My mother was a woman who hiked several miles every day and delighted in hours of raking, weeding, and snow shoveling. It was impossible to think of her impaired, even immobile.

A few weeks later, she sent her and my father's notarized end-of-life wishes, providing me with uncomfortable evidence that it was I, her youngest child, to whom they entrusted such weighty decisions.

I settled into a comfortable routine with them. Regular weekend visits, Thanksgiving at my apartment, unless they were taking a biannual trip to California to spend time with their West Coast children. Christmas and Easter were celebrated at their home, where we carried on Mom's traditions of Christmas crackers, Easter egg hunts, and annual flag raisings, where my son Daniel and his cousin David would mark the end of winter by raising the American flag as my son Mike played reveille on his trumpet. As our kids grew older, they looked forward to walks along the beach with their grandparents, sharing stories of soccer triumphs or hearing their grandfather describe life during the Great Depression. After spending a day with my parents, absorbing the warmth of their attention (an intimacy rarely felt when the five siblings were gathered), we would pull out of their driveway, and while the boys chatted in the backseat, I would squeeze my husband's hand and feel filled up with a joy I'd never known before.

◆

News of their plan came to me as it often does in a large family, through a sibling. I was finishing up lunch with my middle sister, Gabrielle, who'd come east for a visit. "I think Mom and Dad are moving to California," she said quietly.

No way, I thought, as Gabrielle waited for my response. "They'll never leave Old Greenwich," I said.

Later that day, my mother said, "She shouldn't have told you. Nothing's been decided."

"So you're thinking about it?" I asked. "You said you were going to die in that house." The shrill tone of my voice felt foreign and forbidden. My heart pounded loudly and felt sickeningly hollow.

"We've always talked about living in California," she said.

"No, you haven't," I said.

"Your kids are getting older, they won't want to visit me."

"They love you."

"I just know," she said.

While I spent the time between Christmas and Easter trying to persuade the two of them to stay, my mother, a woman of vision and energy, created mental lists and developed plans for selling her home and convincing my father that the move was inevitable.

The more I pressed my mother, the more she withdrew. It was an emotional dance we'd practiced before. During past conversations, I had always tried to preserve the bond between us and was resigned to making excuses for her. It was safer than being direct, an approach that always resulted in clipped sentences and a chilly tone that signaled a period of emotional exile from her. I had come to accept her nature, her need to avoid conflict, at the cost of a kind of intimacy I always longed for. Now the stakes felt much higher. I didn't back down the way I often had in the past and pressed her for answers. "How are you going to drive down that winding mountain road to an emergency room?"

"Don't worry, we'll manage," she'd say and quickly bring our phone call to an end.

Gumption, pluckiness, and impassiveness were the qualities that helped my parents, part of the generation who lived through World War II, prevail. I don't think either of them knew how to deal with my emotion-charged pleas to reconsider their plans.

My father tried several times, listening with great empathy until my mother entered the room and we both knew to drop the subject. He would try to explain his position, which always made me teary. "You know your mother has been very good to me all these years," he said. "I'm doing this for her," he said unconditionally.

"Won't you miss your Retired Men's Society and your volunteer work at church?"

He'd smile ruefully. This was a fight he wasn't willing to make with my mother. His quiet resolution made me feel protective, something I could never have imagined even a few years earlier when he, at eighty, had delighted in outmaneuvering me on the tennis court.

My West Coast siblings were compassionately neutral in taking sides. My sister Liz and I were losing our parents; the West Coast group was about to inherit parents who hadn't been part of their day-to-day lives for thirty-five years. While Liz and I had celebrated most of the holidays in our parents' home, my older siblings made annual cameo appearances. We knew these brief encounters were not even a slim version of the adult relationships we had with our parents.

Liz, always my "big" sister by a mere eighteen months, showed her typical strength. "Look, we've had them during the best part of their lives."

"Yeah, but I wanted to see it to the end. Christmas just won't be the same without them."

"And it'll be a drag in California," she said. "No snow—just a bunch of rain."

"Too many happy people. No grit." We were easterners through and through.

◆

Some of my friends focused on how wonderful it was for my parents to be fit enough to make such a move. Often their own parents had died years before or the task of caring for elderly parents was going to be theirs. They thought I was fortunate to have gotten a "pass" on the caretaking while having had a chance to enjoy them in their "golden years."

Other friends reacted as I had, with a gulp and an "I would fall apart if my parents did this." They were sympathetic and always confided in me how close they felt to their parents and how important this intimacy was to them. Then they'd offer an optimistic remedy: "You'll just have to fly out to see them every other month."

At Easter, the last time my sister and I celebrated in their home, I photographed every room. In looking at the photos now, though, I see my mother's stoic expression, her fists slightly clenched, while she poses with her grandsons. My sister's smile is as forced as the day felt.

I don't know if I will ever really understand how my mother could leave. I am someone who puts down deep roots. Perhaps I will have to wait until I reach my eighties before I can appreciate her need. Or maybe it is as simple as her dislike for the encroaching urban sprawl that she always spoke about, a complaint that I didn't really ever hear. "This used to be a sleepy town," she said fairly regularly. "Now there's too much traffic, too much attitude."

When I visited them in California for the first time, their new world reflected nothing of our shared past. How could my father suddenly sport denim when khaki had been fine for fifty years? While I missed the maple trees and privet hedges and the bilgy smell of low tide, they enthusiastically showed me around. "It's a solid house," said my father as we sat across from each other. He listened carefully to my description of the six-hour flight and two-hour drive it had taken to get there in a way I didn't recall him doing when we enjoyed the easy exchange of shared lives and time zones. He put another log on the fire and settled back onto the couch. Despite his obvious enthusiasm for this new home, I found it hard to accept his sudden fondness for mountains, grazing pastures, and vegetation hearty enough to last the area's punishing high summer temperatures and cloudless dry skies. Only our graduation photos and old paintings on freshly painted walls and a few pieces of furniture—the family dining table, an old chest of drawers—were mildly comforting in this foreign house.

We hiked nearby, my mother leading the way, as she always has, through scrubby, rocky paths and birch trees. I wanted to like it as much as she did, to appreciate what she saw. "It's so quiet," she said, "especially at night. Out on the patio, you can see all the stars." I thought of the times we had walked together, after dinner, searching for the Big Dipper or Orion's belt. I could still feel the cold on my face and hear the wonderment in my mother's voice, so infectious that I eagerly learned from her how to locate all the constellations.

We paused beside a man-made lake. The ducks were black, not the shimmering green-blue or brown of the ones back home. Did she miss them or her garden the way I did? I could still feel the hurt sitting there in the back of my throat and didn't want it to ruin our few days together. This is a way to create something new, I told myself, a bridge.

For a long time I was quiet. "It's been a mild winter back east," I said finally.

We walked up the drive toward the new house. "I have daffodils in January," she said. There were still months of winter yet to endure back east before spring would burst forth and hundreds of daffodils would bloom unattended in her garden. We entered through the garage. "I want to show you my potting shed."

I gazed out its window to the wide valley below and wondered if there would be enough time for me to grow accustomed to this new home. How many seasons would have to pass before I understood what my mother meant when she said, "I just love it here." Would there be time for me, or the two of them, to put down even shallow roots?

"I went past the old house."

"The new owners were going to pull it down," she said, looking surprised.

"No, Mom, it's still there," I said, recalling a recent drive past it on a snowy December day. I needed to go by it one more time, after they had gone, the way I imagine people visit a gravestone. It was too cold to walk around, as it often was there, when the winter wind whipped up off the cove.

"You know they pulled down all the houses around us and built on every shred of land," my mother said.

I wanted to hear a hint of nostalgia, even apology, in her voice, but it wasn't there. I wanted to ask her how it was possible to turn her back on everything that had meant something for fifty years; and finally, to ask how she was able to leave *me* with barely a glance back? Such a demand would send her further away than any geographical distance. The door on this part of her life was shut tight.

I click the mouse again, zoom out, and shoot back across the county to the Connecticut shore where the house still stands, having survived hurricanes and high tides and where pink tulips bloomed every spring and white tea roses climbed along the split rail fence all summer long.

ABOUT ANDREA MARCUSA

Andrea Marcusa is a fiction and essay writer. Her work has appeared or is forthcoming in *Newsday, The New York Times, The Christian Science Monitor, The Ontario Review, Copper Nickel, Ghoti,* and other publications. She was a finalist in the Ontario Review's 2007 fiction competition and winner of the Tiny Lights Essay Competition and the Alabama Poets Society's 2003 writing competition. In the spring of 2008, she won first place in *The Antigonish Review* Sheldon Currie Fiction Contest. She divides her time between writing fiction and essays and working in the areas of health care and sustainable agriculture. She lives in New York City with her husband, two teenage sons, and pet cockatiel, Turko.

Sedat Pakay

The Ghostly Laughter of Old Sick People

Paula Fox

"Living well is the best revenge" is, I believe, a Spanish saying, rakish, triumphant, and somewhat fallacious. If one lives well, a need for revenge vanishes, at least in most of the people I know. One finally becomes indifferent to past betrayals or witless actions of malice. And even living well, as well as a radiant princess in a fairy tale, life still brings you as inevitably to old age as living ill.

Even in the relative poverty in which I lived—not well—as an adolescent, I had sudden, unexpected flashes of pure happiness for no apparent reason. Perhaps only because I was alive. I still have them.

One evening an old woman came into the Greek restaurant in Los Angeles where I worked as a waitress, sat down at a table, and began to beg for food in a loud, plaintive voice. I was carrying in a tray of shrimp cocktails from the kitchen and handed her one, clumsily. It dropped to the floor. She cackled and said, "One day you'll be old like me. Then we'll see." Like the fragments of glass fallen to the floor, her words fell into my mind and stuck there. I recall them especially this year, my eighty-third.

But I've had no flashes of happiness this last year about the deaths of four people I have loved.

Marjorie, my oldest friend, whom I first met when I was seventeen and she nineteen, was born in Santa Barbara, California. For many years she lived in the East. When she moved out west for keeps, we wrote and telephoned each other from time to time. Ten months ago, when I phoned, her companion, Sylvia, told me Marjorie had developed Alzheimer's disease. She carried the phone to where Marjorie, who was by then beyond speech, laughed. It was the sweet, now barely audible amused and compassionate sound I had heard and taken comfort from for five years.

I telephoned a few weeks later. Again Sylvia carried the phone to Marjorie and held it close to her mouth. I heard nothing but her breathing. I felt desperation and grief, knowing it would be the last human sound she would make. She died a few weeks later, unable to swallow.

Floriano, whom I had first known in Italy, was a close friend for more than thirty-five years. Last year he died of a heart attack. He lived alone in New York City in an apartment that in its size, its furnishings, and its atmosphere transported you to Italy, to Rome. He was a painter and a traditional artisan. Another painter said about him years earlier: Floriano is as lovely as new-fallen snow. He was also a splendid cook.

He had lived alone since the death of his lover in a car accident in Italy. When he became sick and old, he made arrangements for a friend and neighbor in the city to call him in the late evenings. If he didn't answer, the friend was to stop by in the morning.

The friend phoned on a Friday toward the end of last year. There was no answer. He stopped by in the morning and found Floriano dead of a heart attack.

For months after his death, I would not know I had been thinking about him but then discover tears on my cheeks.

I recall his laughter when I telephoned him; he would say my name, adding "*cara*" to it in his endearing Italian accent.

There was Bill, married to a close friend, who lived across the continent on an island off the coast of Washington. Now and then he and his wife would spend a few weeks in their Brooklyn home.

He had worked for Naval Intelligence. He was tall and rangy and good-looking. His voice was deep and had a quality of protectiveness in it even when he offered me a second helping of turkey at a Thanksgiving dinner we had together with our spouses.

At some of our evenings, Bill and my husband would talk war—they had both been soldiers in the Battle of the Bulge—with intense seriousness, touched at moments by a kind of gratification as though they were recalling pleasant schooldays. I thought to myself that it was their youth they were speaking about so eagerly, youth in a dark circumstance.

I had a sense when I was around Bill that he would know what to do in any situation. Even when he was so ill with the cancer that finally killed him this year, he was profoundly reassuring—I don't know about what, perhaps life itself. I imagine his tall frame, the grace with which he moved about a room as he carried a glass of bourbon in one hand, speaking in his humorous, affectionate voice, every so often erupting into deep, contagious laughter. He was eighty-two when he died.

The fourth friend, Fred, who died last year, was a novelist who lived with his family in upstate New York and taught at Colgate University until he retired about a decade ago.

Fred and I wrote to each other regularly. He and his wife,

Judy, came to Manhattan every so often to meet with an editor or give a reading from one of his many books. We would meet at some small restaurant in Greenwich Village to have drinks and supper.

His many letters, single-spaced, no longer arrive in the mail. I can't telephone him on a sudden impulse, or write, or see his bearded face grinning at me as he speaks ironically about publishing. But I can still hear his laughter, which puts me in mind of the hubbub of the children's playground outside my study window. I don't know why. True laughter is unique, like a fingerprint.

Gradually the sharpness of my anguish has been succeeded by a kind of dull sorrow. Memory brightens and fades, brightens and fades.

Sometimes I laugh aloud in an empty room as I remember a funny remark one of those friends made, or I listen intently as if to another's earnest observation.

I take a kind of remote comfort from Matthew Arnold's definition of divinity: the stream of tendency by which all living things seek to fulfill the law of their being.

The four of them, Marjorie, Floriano, Bill, and Fred, seem to me, in their individual fashion, to have fulfilled the poet critic's word, to have striven to fulfill the law of their being.

Perhaps I should have interpreted the Spanish saying less dourly. But the years weigh. I can't help but think the sentiment expressed in it is trivial when I compare it to real life and real death.

ABOUT PAULA FOX

Paula Fox was born in New York City in 1923. When she was eight, she moved to a Cuban plantation, where she stayed for two years.

Before and after Cuba, she seldom lived anyplace longer than a year or two.

She has written twenty-one books for children and a number of novels for adults. Ms. Fox has won a number of literary awards, including the Newbery Medal and the Hans Christian Andersen Award.

She has worked as a teacher of troubled children, which is when she started to write, at age thirty-nine. She also read books for Warner Bros.; was a salesgirl, a model, and a worker in a rivet-sorting shop; and was last a lathe operator at Bethlehem Steel during World War II.

Ms. Fox has two sons, Adam and Gabriel, and two grandchildren.

The Heart of Loss

Gretchen Haight

The first time I felt loss was when I was fifty-two years old and broke my arm in a fall from my bike on the way to the beach in L.A. Looking back now, seeing myself standing alone, holding a swollen arm bent out of shape, I see I was vulnerable as I had never been before. You'd think by that age I would have experienced any number of losses, and I had, including one we consider major: separation and divorce from my husband, the father of my three children. But I'm ashamed to say that when we divorced, I didn't call it loss. In 1974, at age thirty-three, married for twelve years, I defended myself by saying I'd married too young and that marriage was an old-fashioned institution anyway. I knew my children's sadness, and unfortunately my fear of their pain scared me so much I looked away. That's the thing about loss: if you're not on speaking terms with it, you'll go to extremes to avoid it.

I was moving ahead, trying desperately not to look back. If

I had felt loss, I might have changed my mind. I didn't want that to happen; I'd fallen in love with another man. Which, I might add here, is an excellent camouflage for feelings of loss: move on to the next person or event before you've finished with the last. He was the right man for me, it turned out, but the ungrieved loss of the previous marriage sat there in the form of a low-grade depression I couldn't overcome until my children were grown and on their own and I could take a deep breath and cry.

In addition to loss not felt, I had a pile of losses I had prevented from even happening, by acting in advance to avoid them. Perhaps that was also the case with my marriage: he might have divorced me if I'd stayed, so I got out first. I ran from possible rejection as though it were a burning building.

I left college for the same reason, afraid that in the end I wouldn't do well enough to graduate. In truth there was little possibility of this; one semester I'd even made the dean's list. I left anyway, to get married, but mainly to ensure that I wouldn't fail. Same with a job I might have been fired from. Feeling on unsure ground, I resigned with the excuse that I was separating from my husband and wanted more time with my children.

So when I went to a psychiatrist at the time of the marriage breakup, my past was strewn with unacknowledged losses of various sizes as though a suitcase on a car roof rack had blown open, littering the highway with my personal belongings as I sped along oblivious to the fallout. Scattered among the debris were gains, because I hadn't claimed them, either. And oftentimes it wasn't clear which were gains and which losses, or the extent to which one of life's remnants was both.

Gathering up the pieces and mending the fabric of the past didn't happen neatly with a few years of therapy; it is taking a lifetime. And still my whole body can seize up in a flash at the threat of even the smallest loss—car keys misplaced or a computer file not found—as though my life were threatened.

Loss wasn't part of the emotional economics I grew up with in corporate America during the postwar heyday of the 1950s. In Bethlehem, Pennsylvania, life was about social standing and competition, and you had to be a winner. So long as you were a winner, you'd have a good life. Loss was for losers. We lived behind the proverbial white picket fence with roses, and if such an idyll wasn't the truth of your life, you pretended it was. We believed in a kind of American Christian promise having to do with God's favor and manifest destiny. An easy life was what we deserved because we were good people.

My fall from the bike stopped me in my tracks. At the foot of a hill, water glazing the surface of the street, the bike's front tire lost traction on the slickness; the bike fell, I fell, and the handlebars cracked the bones in my arm. Awareness of loss didn't come with the fall itself. Weeks later, after two surgeries, I was sitting out on the patio in the afternoon sun, my arm in its cast lying in my lap. For the moment I couldn't drive a car, I couldn't write my name, and it didn't matter. I surrendered the person I thought I was, and I felt even more myself.

Who was this self, if not the person who could take an action or be divorced or fired from a job? The "I" I newly identified with was beyond behavior. Perhaps this is what some people mean when they refer to one's soul.

It was only a few months later that my husband and I found ourselves at a Sunday-morning service in a nearby church. I say "found ourselves" because neither of us can explain why we'd gone. I made no connection to my patio experience. All I knew was that I hadn't gone to a church service in thirty years.

I loved church as a child—the quiet, dim light of the stained-glass windows, the reassuring lilt of the Episcopal liturgy. But an even stronger childhood memory—one closer to the comfort I felt on the patio—was of going off by myself after school, following the creek that ran past our house. I walked along its bank, then to my island, across a shallow stream with enough rocks sticking out of the water that I could carefully pick my way from one to another without getting my feet wet. The island was not much bigger than I was. I lay in the long soft grass wondering about the sky's vastness. I'd say the Twenty-third Psalm, which I'd memorized so I'd have those calming words with me always and not have to lug along a Bible.

Sitting on the patio with a broken arm, I'd rediscovered that island place inside myself where I was content. I didn't have to worry about looking good, measuring up, or winning. In the glory of the afternoon, I had all I needed—and nothing to lose. We have trouble holding on to serenity because the world constantly distracts us with things we then worry about losing. But we can at least know such peace is there and practice staying in touch with it in whatever way works for us. It is "the peace that passes all understanding," to use words from the Episcopal Church's Book of Common Prayer.

I found this inner quiet—rather, it found me—long before I could name it, and just in time, because it was only two years later that I learned that my son's life might be lost to drug addiction. He had lost his job, his car had been impounded, and he couldn't pay the rent on his apartment. He had lost weight, and his teeth had turned gray. He was addicted to heroin. When my daughter told me the horrifying truth, I froze. Yet almost immediately I allowed myself to be supported—by my husband, my daughters, my former husband and his wife, good friends, people at church who were recovering addicts in AA, and others who were in Al-Anon, for families of alcoholics and addicts.

I went to Al-Anon meetings, cried as I tried to speak, and was surrounded by people who knew the pain I felt. I didn't have to finish a sentence. I had never let myself show weakness, never let others hug me and help me. It wasn't entirely comfortable, but it also felt good. I was able to be in a group, which I never had been before. And it changed me.

My husband and I urged my son to go into a rehab center—we'd pay for it—but he wouldn't go. Not an unusual scenario, I learned. I thought he might die. What I learned at Al-Anon meetings was that I might not be able to prevent that from happening. I could help him as best I could, but the disease of addiction was out of my control.

The feeling of loss usually comes with something that's out of our control, which is why we have so much trouble accepting it. We can give our children the best, but we can't ensure their happiness or even survival. As for ourselves, we can eat healthfully and exercise, we can feel confident we'll live a long life, but there's no guarantee. We can drive carefully, but it didn't prevent friends of mine from being killed one New Year's Eve by an oncoming car driven by a drunk driver.

In the end, we were blessed that my son did go into a rehab center, has been clean and sober for fourteen years, and knows more than I do about having nothing to lose. I remember his once saying, when he was stressed out about a business deal possibly falling through, "But I'm not falling apart. That's the good thing about having hit bottom. I know I can survive anything."

Our culture teaches different lessons: that loss need not exist and that we're in control. So much of what we have is routinely thrown out and replaced. Big items are "covered" by insurance. And the biggest loss—death—usually happens offstage, in a hospital or an old-age home, so we don't have to bother with it. We can keep our living separate from dying.

Which is exactly what I did when my father died, back in the years when I was often emotionally numb, before my fall from the bike and before my experience with my son. When my mother called to tell me Dad had died, she said he had been rushed to the hospital, unable to breathe, that she had stayed in the waiting room until the doctor came out and told her Dad had died. "He was afraid," the doctor said, "but he was very brave." By the rules I grew up with, it was okay that he was alone; he was being taken care of by professionals, and that was what was important. My mother's not being with him was only playing by the rules.

Other rules had to do with not making a big deal out of his dying—that is, not being too emotional about it. He was eighty years old, after all. She told me that whenever I could get there was fine, that I shouldn't feel I had to take too much time off from work. And I responded with similar dry-eyed practicality, arranging for a flight back east and getting my work in order so I could be gone for those few days of bereavement leave. Within days of the memorial service, his personal things were gone from the apartment, and my mother was moving ahead, not out of rejection of my father but in the image of strength and decorum.

In the months and years that followed my son's time in rehab and his beginning a new life afterward, I began a new life too, one with more feeling for loss—and for everything else. It started with a woman in our church who was single, in her seventies, and dying of cancer. The cancer had made it difficult for her to read, so I read to her once a week and we had lunch together. She asked me if I would be one of the persons to accompany her through the death process. Feeling totally inept, I assured her I'd be with her.

Each week my ambivalence was enormous: I'd hesitate at the door, afraid to enter her small, dark apartment. Yet I was drawn by her desire to have me keep coming back. Marcia was generous in sharing her hopes, her fears, her questions about the meaning of life and death. Through a year of visits, sometimes taking her to one doctor or another, I grew more comfortable with such intimacy.

In the last few days, as she slid away from us, I was amazed and reassured by how natural and gradual her death was. Life and death were no longer opposites. I began to understand why people speak of a person "passing away." That's just how it felt, like a candle flickering, then going out. In an article about death and dying, some months after Marcia had passed away, I wrote, "It was a gift I had no idea I wanted or needed, but it surpasses most others I've ever received."

Through the experience with Marcia I met a hospital chaplain who offered to give me some training if I'd help her out as a volunteer at Santa Monica Hospital. I discovered that I loved visiting patients, hearing about their lives if they were feeling good, and being with them in whatever way I could if they were feeling bad. Eventually I took a formal six-month training course in hospital chaplaincy and have been a part-time hospital chaplain ever since.

Of course, I can't help but ask the question: How could a young woman so strongly defended against loss morph into an older woman who could sit with a patient in the middle of the night to ease his fear? Aging itself had softened my edges. And the island calm of my childhood had always been there to be reclaimed. But it was the fear of losing my son that shook me awake. For the first time I breathed the freshness of uncertainty and hope. I was lighter—and kinder. I had to give up sure ground as having been an illusion. I'd never stood on sure ground. I'd been lucky.

Loss is usually sad, to be sure, but it contains within it a spare beauty—quiet, slowness, and simplicity. Even the face of a person who has died is beautiful, different from the victorious vitality expressed in the face of an athlete as he breaks the finish line of a race but beautiful nonetheless. It's the human face of the tranquil beginning notes of Mozart's *Requiem*.

Having befriended loss and death, I was able to feel close to my own mother when she was dying six years ago. I went back east to stay with her for the last weeks of her life, and at the end both my sister and I were there supporting her as cancer took her away.

At the moment of death, we were not at her side, which is not unusual. She had encouraged us to leave the hospital, saying, "Why don't you girls go have a nice dinner together," which we did, toasting her with a glass of white wine, her favorite. Later, at Mom's apartment, we were wakened from sleep by a call from the nurse: "At midnight I went in to ask your mother if she'd like a glass of water, and she said no, that she was ready to go. I didn't realize what she meant until I returned ten minutes later and found that she'd passed away."

My sister and I dressed quickly and drove the short distance to the hospital in South Carolina's steamy summer heat, car windows open to the nighttime chorus of tree frogs. A hospital guard let us in a back door from the parking lot. Then we sat with our dear mom, held her hands, and said good-bye to her. She had surrendered—not in defeat to an enemy but to life's natural end.

In matters of loss, death is the elephant in the living room. But there are plenty of smaller losses to keep us occupied and complaining. As we round the bend toward seventy, a myriad little losses appear on a daily basis. We encounter a new emotional economics in which losses mount and gains can seem inadequate. Yet we drive ourselves by the same old expectations for performance and accomplishment.

Living in Los Angeles, denial capital of the country, I'm all too aware of aging women pathetically trying to hold on to their youthful looks. I see them shopping in the supermarket, so much cosmetic surgery done on their faces that their mouths are pulled taut like Howdy Doody's and their eyes are wide open like a doll's, in amazement and terror that they might age. Obsessed with being thin, they look skeletal as they rip open a bag of chips before getting to the checkout counter; they're starving to death.

I can't put all the blame on culture for our bumbling ways with loss. Human beings appear to be programmed for survival so crudely that the momentary deaths and rebirths that happen throughout our lives go unnoticed. We have eyes only for strength and progress. We lose baby teeth in order to get ones that are bigger and "permanent," we outgrow our clothes and get ones we think are more fashionable. We get stronger, we get smarter. So when the scale tips in the other direction, we're totally unprepared. It used to be that this was the point at which most people died, so it wasn't a problem. But now that we live to be older and older, it looks as though life is playing a trick on us: ". . . You are born to live and you die instead," says the elderly protagonist in Philip Roth's novel *Everyman*.

Resilience is what's required, according to my eighty-one-year-old friend Martha, a psychoanalyst. Through her own experience and the stories she has heard from patients over many years, she has become convinced that resilience is the most valuable attribute a person can have. Yet it isn't clear why one person is resilient and another one isn't, or why a person is resilient in one particular situation and not in another. It's individual, Martha says.

Her own experience is with losing her eyesight, which she did in her early seventies. She had always been physically active, skiing and hiking, and loves to travel. She is assertive and opinionated, and I would have expected her to be angry and impatient with all that she suddenly couldn't do. But I was wrong. She is better informed about current events than I am, listening to news on TV and to *Newsweek* on tape. She laughs about never having read so much as she has since she went blind. She has listened to tapes about American history and is now listening to the classics of American literature. "I really feel that I'm having a whole second life," she says.

She continues to supervise psychoanalytic residents, which is one of the things she's grateful for: that she had a career she could continue in without sight. She says she's also so glad she lives in an age with many technological advances to help her: she works at a special computer that speaks its commands and has a watch, Gloria Glockenspiel, that calls out each half hour, so she knows what time it is. She appreciates her partner, Nadia, whom she can rely on for help, and the fact that they live in a house she loves, in a quiet neighborhood.

Nadia loves to travel and goes on a trip every few months, and Martha says she has no desire to go. Even though she loved traveling in the past, now not being able to see well enough to enjoy it, she finds she's happy to stay at home. In other words, she has no yearning for what she can't have. How's that for resilience?

Martha believes in community. "I think independence is overvalued," she says. "Why do we admire independence so much? What's so great about the ninety-year-old still living in the big old house? I think it's crazy. The trick is to accept our dependence on others without feeling the guilt that can come along with it."

I agree with Martha that our culture overrates independence. I certainly have. As a young adult I idealized it, especially the solitary artist's life. I pretty much disdained any group because I made no distinction between community and conformity. It was all conformity as far as I was concerned. Age has given me the confidence to venture into a group and know I won't be swallowed up by it. But I'm an introvert, so I have to pay attention to finding the right balance between solitude and pushing myself out of the nest.

Community is crucial, even if it's only one other person. I've seen the pain of isolation. Visiting patients, I am stunned to discover how many people, especially the elderly, are, indeed, alone. I've never forgotten a visit I made early on in my chaplaincy career. The man I stopped in to see, in his eighties, was too weak to sit up in bed, so he lay flat, the starched white sheet covering his long thin frame. He turned his head toward me as I sat next to his bed, and we chatted about how he'd ended up in the hospital and how he was feeling. When I asked whether he had family nearby, he responded sadly, "Yes, I have a son who lives in Bel Air, but, you know, he's busy." The man's loneliness made him seem weaker still.

Another person stands out in my mind from those first impressionable days—a friendly, round woman who was sitting in her chair when I entered the room she shared with another patient. I sat across the tray table from her, and she talked eagerly about her life, mainly about her husband's having died five years before. As she told her story, she began to cry, then looked up in surprise, and said, "This is the first time I've cried since his death." When I expressed surprise in return and asked whether she had friends she could talk to, she said, "I see neighbors when I walk the dog, but they don't want to see someone crying."

In a *New York Times* interview not long after losing her father and her dear friend Susan Sontag, the photographer Annie Leibovitz, in her mid-fifties, said that losing both of them within weeks of each other had changed everything. Her startling conclusion: if only people experienced death earlier, they would know how important it is to show kindness to one another.

I used to admit that life was short, but I didn't really believe it. In my sixties I began to know it in my gut, and then life got rich. I'm more comfortable in my skin even though it doesn't fit as well as it used to. My marriage, my children and stepchildren, friendships, an art exhibit, a walk on the beach, a hospital visit are all precious. I can actually catch myself getting negative and stop it, not wanting to waste hours in a mean spirit. Negativity is a terrible loss and, finally, one I can control.

In the morning when I meditate, I try to let go of worries and details and drop for a few moments into a quiet that is reliable because it isn't the promise of sure ground. It is only stillness, which holds more weight than sure ground. It was this that I knew instinctively on my island when I was a child, before I got derailed looking for answers and certainty. The fact is that I don't know where I came from, nor where I'm going. All I do know is that I'm more peaceful when I allow myself to live into the mystery.

ABOUT GRETCHEN HAIGHT

Gretchen Haight lives in Los Angeles and is a writer, spiritual director, and part-time hospital chaplain. Her essay "Prayer in a Hospital" appeared in the anthology *In Times Like These: How People Pray*, edited by Malcolm Boyd and J. Jon Bruno.

After All

Emily W. Upham

I often stare at a painting by Chagall in which a damsel lies naked on the banks of the Seine, a book by her side, Notre Dame in the distance behind her. Hovering over her in a rosy sky is a man who, from the waist down, is a phantasmagoric creature. His fluffy tail seems to be wagging with the pleasure of his offering, and he is extending to the young woman a bouquet of flowers. There is also a *bateau-mouche,* there is a requisite chicken in an odd place, as well as a faint and upside-down figure who floats in the sky, but there is, above all else, a sense of the moment of connection between the man and woman.

This painting recalls for me my first meetings with S. A man renowned throughout the world of film and almost forty years my senior, he appeared in my life when I was a professional piano student of twenty and living in Paris. We fell in love, and our story tore a path through our lives for the next four decades.

Several years ago, when S. was ninety-three years old and I was fifty-five, I was gripped by terror at the prospect of living in a world without him. I feared that I would become untethered, unmoored, and that I would drift away, a faint, disembodied being. I imagined myself hovering eerily upside down, neutered and barely visible, like the Chagall person floating in the same sky as the man with the fluffy tail.

Now S. is gone. I remember walking gingerly into a field the day that he died and, as my foot touched the ground, thinking, I am taking a step in this grass, and for the first time in my life I am taking a step when you are not on this planet with me. To my surprise I did not turn upside down. My feet moved. The grass remained green.

Some months later, I talk, work, love. But I am askew and dislocated, as if the tectonic plates beneath my ground have heaved and shuddered. Yet there is a gratitude, an astonishment stirring for all that he gave me.

◆

Because S. and I were often separated by great distance and circumstances, the phone wires and the post were our constant messengers.

———

Dec 2004

S—

I loved hearing your voice. I think I had taken some time off from us, needing a rest from the intensity of it all. Meaning that most of all I find it excruciating that you must bear the punishments of your ninety-three years!— and I suffer with you. Often you are in my dreams and there is an E.T. feeling about them that is poignant. You are E.T. and I am the little boy attached to you, trying to infuse you with life, waxing and waning myself as you wax and wane. Hoping to bring you fully back to life, all the while knowing that you are bound for some distant planet and will leave me behind.

Jan 05

Dearest S

Okay, damn it, if you have to stay hooked up to that machine for a few more weeks, then we will bring the world to you. The doctors say that all is going well and that another month or so of torture and cortisone and you should be feeling much better. In the meantime, make no effort and let us try to distract you.

Here it is freezing cold and we are in the midst of a blizzard. Two feet of snow have fallen and more is coming down. This is when I start thinking about Indians in teepees in winter and about how tenuous is our existence. Easy to forget in cities.

I am happy in the country. In my little village, there is a post office, a liquor store, a funeral parlor, and most recently, a GRAND PIANO STORE. What that is doing here I will never know. It feels like what might happen if you took LSD in the middle of Main Street. You would hallucinate a grand piano store. And there it is, by god, with Bosendorfers in the window. Go figure.

The streets are not ploughed, nothing is moving, no one is about. The world has been blotted out by the snow, and it feels like a moment of permission given, almost, to forget the whole bloody thing and just hunker down.

I have promised to bring you the world and instead I am telling you how it feels to be cut off from it. Nevertheless, I can place this paper in a little machine called FAX, press a button, and you will have it, an ocean away. Amazing.

Hold on. You're tough. It's going to get better. I love you.

———————

March, 2006

S.

I am having my yearly "Ides of March" moment, bringing me back to our time together in Toronto, our luscious Toronto time, so many years ago. Every year it happens the same way, yet takes me by surprise.

I rarely know what date it is, nor what month, unless I think about it. But what happens is that suddenly the wind blows, carrying with it the heavy, wet, gentle smell of thaw that is particular to the northeast, and always to the month of March.

And I am immediately transported back to a moment of our wondrous Canadian sojourn when I was about to leave for the airport. I had gone out to buy flowers to put on your pillow. I can still see the street corner, the color of my coat, the wind blew, and I smelled the earth that was exhaling after the hard winter . . . it was the Ides of March that day, and every year when that same wind blows I am back there with you.

Now you are ninety-five and I am almost the age you were when we met. Incredible. At fifty-six, I often look at my twenty-year-old students and see them as you must have seen me, separated as we were by forty years of living.

You know that I am rambling on in the hopes of providing you with a few moments of distraction. I know how much you are suffering. I will be there in a few weeks. Wait for me.

October 06

Dearest S—

Funny—at about the time this morning that you left me a message (a crackly one with the sound from overseas) I was driving to school and talking to you.

As you know, I give a class on Saturday mornings, and drive the beautiful route I once described to you. Over hill and dale, wealthy horse country, riders in top hat about to fox hunt. Terraced cornfields, pastures and paddocks, October's leaves, blue skies, crisp air. Apple picking time. Robert Frost. Fences, birch trees, stone walls, New England.

And as I drove I was telling you about the stunning Iduna, a buckskin filly I have just purchased (against all reason, I know). I saw her standing in a pasture, and could not turn away. It is now or never, I thought, and here we are, embarked upon what I hope will be a thirty-year adventure.

"Name her Iduna" said a young student. Later I learned that Iduna was the Norse goddess married to the god of poetry, eloquence and music. She guarded the magic apples, which, when eaten, gave eternal youth.

As I was telling you this, onto the radio came Ravel's "Valses Nobles et Sentimentales." Although they are amongst my dearest compositions, I rarely listen to them because they tear me apart, leave me limp as a dishrag, flat as a pancake. They are so evocative that I cannot bear it. They always return me to our Paris, usually Montmartre, everything white with a special Paris light. The waltzes are so rousing, so yearning, so ineffable—and I was telling you how it made me see all of our beloved dead come back to life for a day, waltzing in the air à

la Chagall—in the air that hovers over Montmartre.
You rose from your sickbed in your bedroom and you
waltzed. You waltzed with your departed wife, you
bowed to your dead son, you danced with your mother.
We all waltzed and twirled in the Paris air with our
cherished ghosts—and I could hear from afar your dear
Lenny [Bernstein], singing, "And we flew . . . we were
great . . . we were airborne . . ."

January 07

S,

A short while ago on the phone, when I asked you
what I could do to help, you answered, "Don't forget me."

Knowing that illness and medications have taken a
toll on your memory, I know that you have forgotten
much about us. That is OK. I hold the memories of you
and me. But I hesitate to write because I don't want to
tire you. I hesitate to write because I don't know what
you remember about who I am to you or who you have
been to me. Is it best for you that I remain a presence in
your life, or that I disappear? It is hard to know, because I
know how tired you are, and that you are struggling.

Well, here I am. Emily. I am the girl who fell in love
with you when I was twenty and who has loved you
ever since. We were neighbors in Paris where we shared
an ancient and kingly staircase, and it was on those
steps that we began. For the past forty years we have
corresponded endlessly and been together whenever
possible. We have told each other everything. When you
were fifty-nine I ran my long hair down your bare back.
When you were ninety-two you made love to me.

I have not forgotten you. I take you with me all
the time. Here, in the countryside of New York State

where I now live, we take the most breathtaking rides together. You are often with me when I drive to school, the Goldberg Variations playing, Glenn Gould humming, piercing landscapes revealing themselves as we reach the top of every hill—horses running against a rising sun, a buffalo with horns! beside a fence, deer that leap like Nureyev as they cross the field.

But mostly I take you with me to New York City, because that is where your heart lies, and I love pushing you into the throb of it all, knowing I will find you fired-up and radiant at the end of the day. In fact when I next arrive I am going to bring New York City to you. Here is how. I am packing my suitcase, and have put all the avenues on the bottom. I have stuffed Broadway and Madison and Lexington in the corners. In the various pouches and pockets there are stored a few Manhattan traffic jams with guys yelling "Fuck you!" and "Up yours!" as they are wont to do. I've also packed the subway full of street musicians, and in my carry-on luggage I've put the smell of the boiling streets and their vendors selling hot dogs, pretzels, sauerkraut. Under my arm there will be a photography book of New York as you knew it when you were a child. Penn Station before they tore it down! The mansions along Fifth Avenue. The horses and carts bringing ice to the tenements. Another world, long gone.

Forget you? You are with me more than ever.

July 2007

My beloved S.

I am coming to be with you as soon as I possibly can. I will be arriving at the end of August, which is only weeks away. Please wait for me. I miss you and long to be holding you. Keep this fax by your bedside so you can know that I am arriving very soon.

———

After I parted from S., in a city halfway around the world, I was stumbling along the sidewalk, crying. I noticed a weed poking its head through the smothering concrete, and I smiled. Bravo, I thought.

"True love," I tell the many young people around me who are struggling in their love affairs, "is like a weed. Showing up, uninvited, in the strangest of places, it is fiercely persistent. It will not go away. Drench it in poisons, bury it in concrete, build cities on top of it . . . turn your back for a moment, and there it will be."

EMILY W. UPHAM

Emily W. Upham, a pianist, is a native of Connecticut and was a student of Donald Currier of the Yale School of Music. She began her performance career at an early age as a winner of the William Inglis Morse Prize for Music. After she graduated from Sarah Lawrence College, her subsequent training, in Paris with Reine Gianoli and Nadia Boulanger, and in New York at the Manhattan and Juilliard schools, led her to coach and accompany singers of classical music in concert both in the United States and abroad, and to found the vocal performance group ArtSong Nouveau.

Emily has been active as a French interpreter for the U.S. State Department. She has studied at the National Psychological Association for Psychoanalysis and practices as a certified coach to help people define and achieve their goals. She lives in the Hudson Valley with her husband and their many animals and can be reached at uplandvl@valstar.net. Visit her at www.emilyupham.com.

Lauri Bradway

Chorus of Cells

Margaret Howe Freydberg

The poet Margaret Freydberg is 101 years old and is still driving to do her errands in Chilmark on Martha's Vineyard. On the occasion of her friend Nina Schneider's death (Nina was a fellow writer), Margaret wrote for a local publication:

> If ever there was a visible expression of immortality, it is . . . in the splendor of this garden of Nina's she created so lovingly and attentively. She is, and will continue to be, eternally in the climbing roses, the espaliered apples, in the three trees that flower in the spring like pale pink clouds. . . . Few were ever given grace to stay on earth in such demonstrable beauty.

Chorus of Cells

Every morning,
even being very old,
(or perhaps because of it),
I like to make my bed.
In fact, the starting of each day
Unhelplessly,
is the biggest thing I ever do.
I smooth away the dreams disclosed by tangled sheets,
I smack the dented pillow's revelations to oblivion,
I finish with the pattern of the spread exactly centered.
The night is won.
And now the day can open.
All this I like to do,
mastering the making of my bed
with hands that trust beginnings.
All this I need to do,
directed by the silent message
of the luxury of my breathing.
And every night,
I like to fold the covers back,
and get in bed,
and live the ark, wise poetry of the night's dreaming,
dreading the extent of its improbabilities,
but surrendering to the truth it knows and I do not;
even though its technicolor cruelties,
or the music of its myths,
feels like someone else's experience,
not mine.
I know that I could no more cease
to want to make my bed each morning,
and fold the covers back at night,

than I could cease
to want to put one foot before the other.
Being very old and because of it,
all this I am compelled to do,
day after day,
night after night, directed by the silent message
of the constancy of my breathing,
telling me that I'm alive.

ABOUT MARGARET HOWE FREYDBERG

Margaret Howe Freydberg was born in Rochester, New York. Her first published writing, entitled "Paris Snapshots," was a weekly column for the *Rochester Democrat and Chronicle,* written when she was living in Paris in 1931. Subsequently she wrote six novels, a memoir (*Growing Up in Old Age*), short stories, and a book of poetry. She began to write poetry six years ago. She also worked as an editor in a New York publishing firm and as an instructor in New York University's Clinic for Professional Writers. For several years, she conducted a creative writing course for mentally ill teenagers at Linden Hill School in Hawthorne, New York.

Bruce Weber

Last Word

Edna O'Brien

The waiting, the wanting, the grieving, the hating, the hoping. Rudderless. The heart closed not only to the self but to others, fearing to reach out because the wounded being is the least likable. There is prayer, but not everyone prays. There is drink, but, as Keats wisely said, "Wine is only sweet to happy men." And there is literature. I say this not as a writer but as a reader. For me, the link between literature and spirituality is irrefutable. It is not a fashionable theory, but I know it to be true. In loss, loneliness, thwartedom, and many adversities, great writing can be a consolation. Not long ago I was in a hospital in Ireland, first in intensive care and then in a public ward that seemed like Bedlam, what with teams of visitors, giant television blaring, children wretched at being parted from their sick mothers, consultants, doctors, nurses, students, cleaners, and, more than once, watching some unfortunate woman being given the last rites. I was kept sane by one book, Rachel Carson's *The Sea Around Us,* which I had in my handbag on that blithe day before illness struck. Reading her wise and prophetic words about the universe and how we are destroying it was not only salutary but made my circumstances more bearable. Had I had *King Lear,* I would have read that, perhaps the scene when the broken king wants to believe that Cordelia is alive, or I might have read the piquant scene in *Henry IV* among Falstaff, Mistress Quickly, and Mistress Doll Tearsheet in the Boar's Head Tavern in London or jaunty Mrs. Dalloway buying flowers in *Bond Street,* or Sylvia Plath's profound poem "Poppies in July." So when we hit rock bottom we can read the words that exactly mirror our emotional state. Therefore, I say, God, stand up for literature. There is the thrill of reading, and there is the wisdom within it. Great writing allows us to share the physical and psychic intensity of the author, thereby vitiating our own woes. Goethe said, "All my works were fragments of a great confession." In times of tribulation we need to be reminded of the great confession, a motto not just for an hour or a day, but for all the days and all the nights as we slouch toward eternity.

ABOUT EDNA O'BRIEN

Edna O'Brien is one of Ireland's leading authors. She has published more than twenty works of fiction, including *Down by the River, Wild Decembers, In the Forest,* and, most recently, *The Light of Evening.* She has written a biography of James Joyce, and her *Byron in Love* was published in June 2009. Awards include the Irish PEN Lifetime Award, the European Prize for Literature, the Ulysses Medal from University College Dublin in 2006, and the American National Arts

Gold Medal. She is an honorary member of the American Academy of Letters.

After James Joyce, O'Brien is the best-known banned Irish writer of the twentieth century. She was born in Tuamgraney, County Clare, in the west of Ireland. She left Ireland in the late 1950s, when she eloped to London with the Irish-Czech novelist Ernest Gebler. She began her writing career in 1960 with *The Country Girls*. The novel's immediate success and notoriety quickly propelled her into a new world. The Irish censors banned the book, objecting to the sexual awakening portrayed, and further condemnation followed from the Irish hierarchy and the then minister for culture, who deemed it "a smear on Irish womanhood." In her native village there was anger about the book, abetted by a few copies being burned in the grounds of the parish chapel.

When asked why so many writers leave Ireland, she responds, "I cannot speak for my great forebears James Joyce and Samuel Beckett, but as for myself I felt constrained and unnerved by that particular censorious climate of the late 1950s. It is nowadays much more tolerant and unshockable, but I hope that the interest in and appreciation of literature have not waned under the auspices of Celtic Tiger. Anyhow, County Clare remains the physical and emotional landscape for all my fictions." O'Brien credits the genesis of her writing career to Joyce, whose work she describes as "my first and definitive literary education."

Her plays include *Virginia* (on the life and writings of Virginia Woolf), and *Triptych,* which premiered at the Magic Theatre in San Francisco in 2004. Her new play, *Haunted,* premiered at the Royal Exchange Theatre in Manchester, England, in 2009.

She divides her time between London and the west coast of Ireland.

Acknowledgments

With deepest gratitude, we thank our agent, Susan Ginsburg of Writers House, who, with so much skill and thoughtfulness, has guided us to the realization of this book. Malaika Adero, our editor at Atria, has been passionate and supportive; her enthusiasm sustained us as we brought together the many original pieces for this collection.

Bethany Strout, assistant to Susan, and Todd Hunter, assistant editor at Atria, have both been ever helpful and patient! Many thanks as well to designer Kyoko Watanabe; to Lynn Anderson for her sensitive copyediting; to Sybil Pincus, senior production editor at Atria, for her expertise; and to Bilal Mashhood for his steadfast, gracious technical help.

We are grateful to our intrepid, generous contributors whose spirited participation enlivened the entire process and whose new friendships are unexpected gifts!

—Emily W. Upham and Linda Gravenson

✦

I thank with profound admiration J. Gerald Young; Thomas Grubb; Jeffrey Siegel and his family; my remarkable and devoted friends around the globe; my siblings—Martha, Lauren, and Daniel—and their families as well as my second family—Murray, Martha, and Andrei Zimiles—and my most beloved husband, George, for all that you have given me time and time again.

I owe much to Victoria Skurnick as well as to Marisa Harris, Joy Kane, Deirdre English, Fanita English, Jacob Brackman,

Peg Wright, and Amy Boggs for their participation. Thank you, thank you.

My new friends who are the contributors to this book have enriched my life and kept me afloat in the most trying of times. David Blackburn provided me with the necessary blue booties along the way. Special thanks to Sedat Pakay, renowned portrait photographer, whose work is represented in collections around the world, and whose remarkable photographs of James Baldwin are in the collection of the Smithsonian. I am pleased that he could photograph, when possible, a number of the women in this book, and so appreciate the love and enthusiasm he brings to his work. We've traveled many a mile and shared countless adventures in pursuit of the revealing photo.

And to S, who supported me fully in this endeavor, as he did in so many others. Know that we triumphed.

—E.W.U

The writers' group in Rhinebeck, New York, has always asked the crucial questions. Many thanks to its early members Jillen Lowe, Rachel Pollack, and Carla S. Reuben. I am indebted to Carla S. Reuben and Gail Tirana, whose inspired, generous participation in this project has been so helpful.

Lifelong friendships with Sybil Baldwin, Wendy Gittler, Ann Jaffe, and Gail Tirana are a constant reminder that kith can become kin.

I thank my son, Nick Guthe, and daughter-in-law, Heidi Ferrer, screenwriters *extraordinaires,* for their support and for lively discussions on storytelling. And for my grandson, Bexon Lightning, who has brought such joy.

—L.G.